Influence of Social Media
on
India's Foreign Policy Making

Influence of Social Media on India's Foreign Policy Making

Prof. (Dr.) Vijay S. Khare

Foreword by

Prof. (Dr.) Sukhadeo Thorat
Former Chairman: University Grants Commission &
Indian Council for Social Science Research
Professor Emeritus, Jawaharlal Nehru University, New Delhi

PENTAGON PRESS LLP

Influence of Social Media on India's Foreign Policy Making
Prof. (Dr.) Vijay Khare

First Published in 2021

ISBN 978-93-90095-20-9

Published by
PENTAGON PRESS LLP
206, Peacock Lane, Shahpur Jat
New Delhi-110049
Phones: 011-64706243, 26491568
Telefax: 011-26490600
email: rajan@pentagonpress.in
website: www.pentagonpress.in

Printed at Aegean Offset Printers, Greater Noida, U.P.

Dedicated to

Chief Architect of Indian Constitution

Dr. Babasaheb Ambedkar

Contents

Foreword *xi*
Preface *xv*
List of Abbreviations *xix*
List of Tables, Charts and Figures *xxi*

CHAPTER I
Introduction

1.1 Social Media 7
1.2 What's the Difference Between Social Media and Social Networking? 8
1.3 Are Traditional Media Also Social Media? 8
1.4 History of Social media 9
1.5 What is Social Media? 9
1.6 Characteristics of Social Media 11
1.7 Role of Social Media 13
1.8 Negative Role of Social Media 15
1.9 Importance of Social Media 17
1.10 Importance of the Research Topic 18
1.11 Importance of Social Media 18
1.12 Definitions Related Terms & Definitions of Social Media by Different Authors 19
1.13 Social Media Terms 20
1.14 Definitions of Foreign Policy by Different Authors 20
1.15 Definition of National Security by Different Authors 21
1.16 Objectives of the Research 22
1.17 Limitations of the Study 24
1.18 Scope of the Study 24
1.19 Research Methodology 24
1.20 Pilot Study Conducted 25
1.21 Technical Tools of Social Media 31
1.22 Social Media Consists of a variety of Tools and Technologies 32

CHAPTER II

Review of Literature

2.1	Introduction	36
2.20	Summary	47

CHAPTER III

An Overview of India's Foreign Policy 1947-2019

3.1	India's Foreign Policy are discussed into four Phases	51
3.2	1947-1962: Primary Stage of Indian Foreign Policy	51
3.3	1962-1990: Idealism to Realism?	53
3.4	1990s and Beyond: Constructional Changes	55
3.5	A Paradigm Shift	58
3.6	Conclusion	60

CHAPTER IV

Foreign Policy Decision Making in India

4.1	Introduction	63
4.2	Actors of Foreign Policy	64
4.3	Institutions Involved in Foreign Policy in India	65
4.4	Ministry of External Affairs	66
4.5	The Cabinet and Cabinet Committees	66
4.6	Role of Cabinet in Foreign Policy Decision Making	67
4.7	Role of the Cabinet Committees on Foreign Policy	68
4.8	The Prime Minister's Office	69
4.9	Role of Prime Minister in Foreign Policy Decision Making	69
4.10	The National Security Council	70
4.11	The Strategic Policy Group	70
4.12	The National Security Advisory Board	70
4.13	Joint Intelligence Commerce and Industry	70
4.14	Ministry of Defense	70
4.15	The Parliament	71
4.16	Role of the Parliament on Foreign Policy Making	71
4.17	Pressure Groups and Media	71
4.18	Procedures of Making Foreign Policy in India	72
4.19	Conclusion	72

CHAPTER V

Comparative Study: Indian Foreign Policy and P5 Countries: (China, France, USA, UK, Russia) in the Context of Social Media Use and its Effect on Foreign Policy

5.1	Chinese Foreign Policy and Social Media	74
5.2	France Foreign Policy and Social Media	89
5.3	The United States of America and Social Media	110
5.4	UK Foreign Policy and Social Media	124

5.5 Russian Foreign Policy and Social Media 143
5.6 Importance of P5 Countries 158

CHAPTER VI
Influence of Social Media on Foreign Policy: Case Studies Indo-US Nuclear Deal and Media

6.1 India-China Border Disputes 165
6.2 Indo-Pakistan Relations: Post Mumbai Attack 167
6.3 Impact of Social Media on Global Politics 171

CHAPTER VII
Data Analysis, Data Interpretation and Presentation

7.1 Data Analysis of the Pilot Study Conducted 175
7.2 Data Analysis of the Entire Respondent Group 175
7.3 What are the Challenges? 217

CHAPTER VIII
Twitter Data Analysis

8.1. What is Twitter Data? 225
8.2 Twitter Analytics 225
8.3 Tools for Twitter 225
8.4 Klear 226
8.5 Buffer 226
8.6 Klout 226
8.7 ManageFlitter 226
8.8 Methodology adopted for Twitter Data Searching 226

CHAPTER IX
Conclusion

9.1 Introduction 268
9.2 Conclusion and Findings 269
9.3 Social Networking Sites: Examples of Banning 270
9.4 What exactly is the 'Social Media Communication Hub'? 272
9.5 Keeping a Check on Happenings Abroad 274
9.6 The Tool Should Be Able to Identify 'Fake News' 275
9.7 Social Media and its Impact on Foreign Relations 279
9.8 Recommendations 283

Appendix I: Questionnaires 285

Bibliography 293

Index 301

Foreword

I am glad to write a forward to this book which deals with an unexplored theme namely "Influence of Social Media on India's Foreign Policy Making" by Professor Vijay Khare. Increasingly the Social media has been occupying a position of an intermediation between the government and public. Among many other spheres the role of social media has become equally important in sphere of foreign policy, the field which remained unexplored. The social media not only serve as avenue of information on foreign policy to the public, but it also acts as platform where the government receive feedback from the public priorities and often the foreign policy formulation. Thus, social media serve as platform of interaction between the governments and public, rather it serves as factor of an interrelation between social media and foreign policy. The discussion is divided into eight chapters.

The Introductory Chapter makes the readers acquainted with the social media, its types and tools. It embarks with the quote of Malcolm, emphasizing the entity of media and its effect on the human mind. Apparently, the media power is deep-rooted in society and prevailed in the personal, professional, educational and financial lives of humankind. While pointing out the media, the researchers have focused the light on the wide use of digital social media in society. Apart from LinkedIn, Skype, the digital platforms like Twitter, Facebook have become an Online Movement and Voice of everyone. In the same chapter, Dr. Khare has gradually dealt with the journey of social media and its encroachment/expansion in the Military territory and in foreign policy. Earlier, the media policy of government was in threshold. Dr. Khare has appropriately pointed out how during First Gulf war and Kargil War, the social media in the form of ground reporting method invaded invisibly and empowered gradually which could not be controlled. Similarly, Dr. Khare has done genuine attempt to ponder over the impact of social media on foreign policy. We can find social media and foreign policy work in different fields like public diplomacy, in the political communication literature, in working papers and articles generated by foreign policy Think Tanks such as academic journals dedicated to area studies of foreign policy. Dr. Khare is aware of pros and cons of social media that could do the development and heightens the risks of India's vulnerabilities. While dealing with this, the present study sincerely shares how the social media has become the platform for justice stimulus by reaching at massive level and they have handled it as platform to open threat to community by various terrorist groups.

Dr. Khare has rightly pointed out the disparity between Social media and social networking. While doing this, the journey of social media from traditional media to present advanced technology of social media has been highlighted conspicuously stating its role, types and features and its quick spread in the globe as a most influential participatory forum. Dr. Khare has shown that the social media would be stronger and more persuasive than television in influencing people. Here, the present study illustrates the positive and negative role of social media by citing appropriate examples. Similarly, it explains how the social media is used by the public for India's Foreign Policy. As it prevails almost in the social media in all the sectors of the globe, can it be a platform for contributing public's views to India's foreign policy? The present study is an appreciative task in the light of above raised question. The first chapter is the foundation for the study.

In Chapter II undertake a Review of Literature and noted the insights for the present study and also the gaps. The chapter III undertake an overview of India's Foreign Policy-1947-2019. It examine the goal of the country's foreign policy, with a primary focus on policy on international relations, the strategies chosen by the state to safeguard its national interests. Dr. Khare has traced the journey of evolution of foreign policy from Jawaharlal Nehru to Narendra Modi by highlighting the objectives and the basic concern of the foreign policy. It stresses the cultivation of foreign policy right from the Nehruvian. It also examine changes in the global scenario change in four phases. It brought out a shift in Indian foreign policy in the tenure of each prime minister at micro and macro-level with the implications of international affairs on it. It conspicuously highlights many changes at the international level such as the breakdown of USSR and many others and its repercussions on emergence of constructional changes of Indian foreign policy. It accounts how political party is manifested a fundamental change in construction of Indian foreign policy and disseminated the global Indian face.

In the chapter IV namely "Foreign Policy Decision Making in India", Dr. Khare has discussed an intricate and multi-staged procedure of foreign policy. Many factors played a vital role in shaping the foreign policy decision making process. The discussion systematically captures exertive and perspective process of shaping the foreign policy. Similarly, it discusses how actors, agencies and institutions play a critical and creative role to develop nations' foreign policy. As we know the instrumental role of the Ministry of External Affairs in India's external relation but apart from it; there are various other agencies such as The Cabinet and Cabinet committee, The Prime Minister's Office, The National Security Council, The Strategic Policy Group, The National Security Advisory Board, Joint Intelligence Committee, Ministry of Commerce and Industry, Parliament and Pressure Groups and Media contribute to shape the Indian foreign policy. Beside various institutions, NGOs and think tanks have also contributed indirectly in the process of foreign policy; the author has analysis the process step by step.

The chapter V examined the 'Comparative Study of Indian Foreign Policy with respect to P5 countries: (China, France, USA, UK, Russia). It discusses the Social Media; its use and repercussions on Foreign Policy. In this discussion author undertake an analytical elucidation of P5 Countries' foreign policy outlook where social media has proved one of the interactive tools. It construes the foreign policies of above countries studiously. Similarly, comparative study of India and P5 countries in social media (in the sphere of political, social, cultural and economic background) confers on the exact anatomy of social media and its role in the making of foreign policy.

The chapter VI in order to bring the insight on the Influence of Social

Media on foreign Policy, it take example of Indo-US Nuclear deal, India-China Border Disputes, Indo-Pakistan Relations: Post Mumbai Attack, Impact of Social Media on Global Politics. It emerged that social media has transformed the dimensions of modern political communication in which the politicians interact with voters and with each other via digital platform. It also provides evidence on the use or at time manipulation of global media for the political agendas or national crises.

In chapter VII on Data Analysis, Data interpretation and presentation displays author examine the use of social media by various stakeholders. It undertakes the segregated data analysis of each question in pie chart in such a way that the readers can have a glance at the worldwide countries' data. The chapter VIII entitled Twitter Data analysis focuses on the information and tools of twitter account by citing many worldwide personalities who handle their twitter account. In this present chapter, Dr. Khare exhibit and analyze the tweets by several global strategic players. The data shows how government maintains inter relations with other countries through twitter account, especially regarding foreign policy. This data reflects the role of social media in defining the foreign policy. The concluding summarizes the findings and makes recommendations. Dr. Khare has pointed out the risk associated the way social media is often used as a tool of threat to national security and potential for communal conflict. The study has useful lesson, as this 'predictive analysis' could be used in analyzing the worldwide comprehensive data and its global application. It also imply that since ban on social media is not possible, it certainly can be regulated. This is particularly so when social media in the form of Facebook and Twitter accounts are the most influential tool in constructing the nature of Indian foreign policy.

This book will be of great help to research scholars, political analysts, government officials, strategic think tank, foreign policy makers and so on.

Professor Sukhadeo Thorat
Former Chairman: University Grants Commission
Indian Council for Social Science Research
Professor Emeritus, Jawaharlal Nehru University, New Delhi

Preface

In today's global scenario many advanced technologies have occupied every field of the world. So, it has become not only entertainment tool but serves as a forum for the exchange of opinions, thoughts and ideas. Amongst it, the social media has become part and parcel of social structure. Its entity has been accepted and appreciated in the entire world. Social media has become equally important in sphere of foreign policy field; yet few areas are completely unexplored. The present book states how the social media does not only serve as an information provider but also proves to be a platform of interaction between the government and public where government receives the feedback.

I have genuinely attempted to contemplate over the influence of social media in the process of making India's foreign policy. It meticulously discusses the pros and cons of social media which directly and indirectly affects the foreign policy of the country. The present book systematically construes an unavoidable gradual growth of the social media and its more persuasive impact on people than any other media in the world. Similarly, it asserts how the social media has prevailed in personal and social lives of human- beings. This book consists of useful information with predictive analysis which will be instrumental in analyzing the worldwide comprehensive data and its global application.

Initially, the present work is a result of research project submitted to the Indian Council for Social Science New Delhi. I would like to thank the Indian Council of Social Science Research for its constant support and financial assistance to complete the project. I pay my sincere thanks to my joint collaborators who shared their valuable suggestions and recommendation for completing this book. I am thankful to Prof. (Dr)

N. Sukumar, Delhi University, Late Prof. (Dr) Sanjeev Bhaduria Central University Allahabad , Prof. (Dr) Bharthi Das, Central University Allahabad (Dr.) Sushama Bhosale; Principal Waghire College Saswad, and Dr. Surendra Kamble S.P.D.M. College Shirpur for their untiring support and noteworthy suggestions and without them this book would not possible.

I extend my sincere gratitude to Prof. (Dr.) Nitin R. Karmalkar, Hon'ble Vice Chancellor, Savitribai Phule Pune University for his constant encouragement and kind support for completing this book. I am grateful to everyone who are the part of the Departments of Defence and Strategic Studies from Universities in Maharashtra State and other Universities, such as Savitribai Phule Pune University, Pune; KBC North Maharashtra University, Jalgaon; Goa University, Panjim; Jawaharlal Nehru University, Delhi; Institute of Chinese Studies, Delhi; Chandigarh University, Chandigarh; Gorakhpur University, Gorakhpur (UP) and Central University Gujarat, Ahmedabad and so many others. During this research journey, I have had an opportunity to interact with the students and faculty members of various University departments through the questionnaire designed for inculcating their views for this purpose and I was elated to have such a huge excellent response from all of them. So, I express my sense of gratitude especially to the Heads of the Department of these Universities and faculty members and students who participated in this intellectual marathon and provided us the thought- provoking opinions on various questions asked in the questionnaire.

I am thankful to Prof.(Dr.) S.K. Patil Former Librarian and Head, Department of Library and Information Science Savitribai Phule Pune University, Dr. Dimple Chaudhari, Dr. AnkurYadhav, Dr. Savita Patil, Mr. Khache, Gaurav Kokil, Mr. Onkar Sonwane, Mr. Omkar Sonwane , Balaji Kamble , Ms. Shivani S. Singh, Sagar Gaikawad, Ms. Sheetal Jagtap, Dnyaneshwar Gaikawad, Satish Gaddare, Bharthi Kokil, Raisa Choudhary, Vijay Mohad, Ganesh Shinde, B. Munnuswami and my faculty members of DDSS, and all serving officers who are students and Residence Scholars in the department, and research scholars in the department for their untiring and unconditional help in completing this book. I am also equally thankful to the students and research scholars from the Department of Defense and Strategic Studies, Political Science of other Universities for contributing their valuable opinions through the provided questionnaire. Amid my research, I organized an International Conference on 'Impact of Social Media on Peace and Security' in collaboration with University of Applied Science, Nysa Poland, University Galati, Romania and Indo-European Education Foundation, Poland wherein I invited eight (08) international experts from various countries to share their views on Social media and its impact on foreign policy making mechanism. I take this opportunity to express my sincere gratitude to all those speakers who enlightened us in this sphere.

I am indebted to Mr. Rajan Arya and his entire crew from PENTAGON PRESS LLP for bringing out the book within the short span of time. I hope the readers will find out my efforts worthy and the book will serve their expected needs.

Finally, I express my deep sense of gratitude to my parents, my all-time inspiration my wife late Dr Lalita Khare and my son Dr. Abhishek who is always with me to understand my academic tasks.

I record my thanks to everyone who helped directly or indirectly to fulfill my research.

Prof. (Dr.) Vijay S. Khare

List of Abbreviations

AP	Associated Press
ASEAN	Association of South-East Asian Nations
AU	African Union
BBC	British Broadcasting Corporation
BJP's	Bharatiya Janata Party's
CIS	Commonwealth of Independent States
CoN	Commonwealth of Nations
CSTO	Collective Security Treaty Organisation
DCCC	Democratic Congressional Campaign Committee
DNC	Democratic National Committee
DOAJ	Directory of Open Access Journals
EEU	Eurasion Economic Union
EU	European Union
FAIR	Fairness and Accuracy in Reporting
FCO	Foreign and Commonwealth Office
FPDM	Foreign Policy Decision-Making
GCBD	Guizhou on the Cloud Big Data
GST	Goods and Services Tax
IAEA	International Atomic Energy Agency
ICWA	Indian Council of World Affairs
IGOs	International Governmental Organisations
IMF	International Monetary Fund
INGOs	International Non-Governmental Organisations

IPSO	Independent Press Standards Organisation
ISIS	Islamic State of Iraq and the Levant
LAC	Line of Actual Control
LAS	League of Arab States
MACV	Military Assistance Command, Vietnam
MEA	Ministry of External Affairs
MoD	Ministry of Defense
NAM	Non-Alignment Movement
NATO	North Atlantic Treaty Organisation
NSC	National Security Council
OAS	Organisation of American States
OECD	Organisation for Economic Cooperation and Development
OIC	Organization of the Islamic Conference
OSCE	Organisation for Security and Cooperation in Europe
PLO	Palestine Liberation Organisation
PMO	Prime Minister's Office
RAS	Receive-Accept-Sample
RDF	Revolutionary Democratic Front
SCD	Standing Committee on Defense
SCEA	Standing Committee of the External Affairs
SCO	Shanghai Cooperation Organisation
SMISC	Social Media in Strategic Communication
SNEP	Subterranean Nuclear explosions Project
VPNs	Virtual Private Networks
WB	World Bank
WTO	World Trade Organisation

List of Tables, Charts and Figures

TABLES

Table 1:	Showing distribution of questionnaires and its percentage	176
Table 2:	Use of social media networking	176
Table 3:	Showing use of social media tools	177
Table 4:	Shows frequency of visit to the Website of Ministry of External Affairs to know updates on India's foreign policy	182
Table 5:	Showing views when central govt. changes, it change their policies	184
Table 6:	In United Kingdom, following table showing the active users of social media in January 2018	193
Table 7:	Preferences of social media tools and its percentage	220
Table 8:	Narendra Modi's Twitter Data Report	228
Table 9:	Nirmala Sitaraman Twitter Data report	232
Table 10:	Raksha Mantri Twitter Data Report	234
Table 11:	Sushama Swaraj Twitter Data Report	236
Table 12:	MikePompeo Twitter Data Report	240
Table 13:	Theresa May Twitter Data Report	245
Table 14:	Gavin Williamson Twitter Data Report	246
Table 15:	Jeremy Hunt Twitter Data Report	249
Table 16:	Emmanuel Macron Twitter Data Report	254
Table 17:	Florence Parly Twitter Data Report	259
Table 18:	Russian MOD (SergeyShoygu) Twitter data report	263

CHARTS

Chart 1:	Use of Social media by various stakeholders	176
Chart 2:	Use of Social media tools	178

Chart 3: Showing purpose of using social media tools 179

Chart 4: Opinions of the stakeholders when Central Government changes, it change their policies 184

Chart 5 Frequency of the use of social media tools to understand Indian Foreign Policy 212

Chart 6: Showing percentage of using social media tools of various medias 220

Chart 7: Showing awareness for India Pakistan conflict during Kargil war 223

FIGURES

Figure 1: Social Media 7

Figure 2: History of Social Media 9

Figure 3: What is Social Media? 10

Figure 4: Characteristics of Social Media 12

Figure 5: Positive Role of Social Media 14

Figure 6: Negative Role of Social Media 16

Figure 7: Technical Tools of Social Media 31

CHAPTER I

Introduction

"The media is the most powerful entity on earth. They have the power to make the innocent guilty and to make the guilty innocent, and that's power. Because they control the minds of the masses."

— Malcolm X

The social media has a strong impact on every aspect of human being in today's scenario. People and society are gaining knowledge, enlightenment and using media power in their personal, professional, educational and financial lives. Social media plays a very important role among the various media available, for example traditional media, print media and digital media. We have entered an era, where technology is our main priority. This is the norm to interact with costumers and peers. For example, we have changed our newspaper reading habit and now read content from multiple websites. Smart phones handles our all needs whether it is planning our trips, office works, searching for jobs or enhancing our lifestyle. Emails have replaced letters and Webinars have also replaced seminars. The penetration of broadband connections and in-expensive devices has increased the demand and they are the main source of increasing connectivity of social media across the country. Earlier, we were restricted to use only a few technologies which were initially available exclusively to the military and laboratories, now anyone can avail those facilities to set up at homes and offices, like Google Maps, Skype and other digital communication platforms. The best advantage is that use of these social media tools is very affordable and simple. Social media also provides a big platform for recruitment. Many recruiters are much cheaper than the traditional way of recruitments. LinkedIn is a very useful to find candidates and post new jobs. Twitter is another social media tool whose popularity is increasing, which is mainly used to update candidates on new opportunities and staffing professionals. It is a good tool to develop a voice and initiate a conversation with potential and existing customers and keep the relationship alive.

We can divide the Indian media activities (historically) into two periods. From 1947 to 1991, the time when the government was totally dependent on the monopoly of the radio and television broadcasting. This time, the media was free of government control even though the government tried to influence the licensing procedures for importing newsprint. Though government media policies were restricted, but the media was playing a role in influencing media comment on foreign policy. In the late 1990s, the internet was introduced to social media. After 1991, the first Gulf War, TV news took the center stage instead of cable news broadcast. During the Kargil conflict of 1999, journalists were directly interacting with the military personnel or handling news in the war zone area. The whole world could see what was going on at the battle field. This began the process of empowering the media, which was the indication for the authorities that now they will have difficulties in blocking the media from any news development. There are many ways to define social media. For example, you can buy a book on Amazon and are using social media without realizing it. Basically, before we buy a book, we go through what the ratings and views from the comments or user ratings are. This is an example of user -generated content in social media.

Social media tools are allowing individuals and organizations to become more efficient and competitive in communication with their audience. This social media revolution is a symbol of our changing thinking of people. Twitter, YouTube and Wikipedia are the new game changing consequences. The Tea Party, the Arab Spring, and Occupy Wall Street movements were all made possible in one way or another by new media, and the way they empower consumers of information to become producers. Further, as the use of smart phones and tablets has sky rocketed, the ability to write, take photographs, and make videos and send them out to the world is now literally in almost every one's hands. This revolution in communication encompasses all levels of society. The Tea Party movement was well-liked and a lawful movement. Since 2009, it was involved in several protests and supported different political candidates. Although Tea Party was not an authorized party. The party's main agenda was conference call to affiliate against Obama's agenda. The Arab Spring was a series of anti-government protest, uprising, armed rebellions which were against the present government. People were suffering from hunger, lack of education etc. Protests started from Tunisia and revolution spread strongly to different countries like Libya, Egypt, Yemen, Syria and Bahrain where the situation was the same through major uprisings, social violence, riots, civil wars or insurgencies. It was the awakening call for Middle East History who had thrown out the current government with the power of social media. People were facing repression of free speech, human rights, abuses, economic mismanagement, corruption and stifling of political dissent. It was a case of 28-year-old Khaled Mohamad, who was beaten to death by the Egyptian Security thugs in 2010. Photos of his death were posted along with a tag: 'WE all Khaled Said' by one of Google employee Wael Ghonin, online and on Facebook. Soon this post got viral and got hundreds of thousands of followers. Facebook, YouTube and Twitter everywhere people were posting their protest online. Social media helped begin the revolution and overthrew the current government with the power of social media. Over the last 30 years the nature of communication has undergone a significant change. Apart from this over the last few years, social media is the key source of government usage, education, business etc. If we look at last the few years, social media has become a way in which something is usually done with an online perspective where major social networks and social media websites make changes and improvements on a fairly regular basis. These websites offer a way of approaching a problem or making progress towards something through which we communicate with people. In education, social media is playing great and wide role. Email has a profound effect on the way we communicate with people.

The communication is shorter and more frequent than letters which were the norm earlier. The response time has also diminished. Instant messaging has created another method of interaction, where the length of messages is shorter and the interaction is more conversational. For example, broadcast technologies like Twitter transform these shorter bursts of communications from one on one conversation to short news. Social media has the potential to fundamentally change the character of our social lives interpersonal and at a community level. Online communication tools are the main example, which have the potential to increase our awareness of the movements of our professional or social contacts. For example, Twitter, offers us an update of things people happen to be doing at a particular point of time. As social media has become more accessible, it has become a means by which people, non-state actors and even governments can share their foreign policy priorities in an effort to receive feedback, engage in diplomacy, educate people, and attempt to influence foreign policy process. Facebook, Twitter and YouTube created a greater sense of urgency among those who seek a greater understanding of the impact of social media on foreign policy. Social media and foreign policy work can be found in different fields like public diplomacy which is conducted as part of the broader public diplomacy literature and also found in the political communication literature, in working papers and articles generated by foreign policy think tanks such as academic journals dedicated to area studies that often concentrate on specific episodes of social media used to influence foreign policy. Social media has become a critical tool for a wide variety of international actors running the complete range or scope of something from governments to portions of civil society to terrorist groups such as Al-Qaeda and the Islamic state of Iraq Syria (ISIS, also known as the Islamic State of Iraq and the Levant or ISIS based in part on the group's territorial claims). Social media and foreign policy are explored across disciplines and start to deal with (a situation or problem) in a certain way. These are the desirable changes in area of theoretical development. Network theories focus on interactions between parts of a network (in this case a social network); network analysis methods are sometimes employed as part of this theoretical framework. Social media has made diplomacy more accessible to the public. Earlier the role of public remained as receptors but now through social media, they have become prominent actors. India has been focusing on technological advancement as it does not want to be left behind in the race for soft power using mediums of social media (Hall, 2012).

Indian diplomacy is focusing on the true sense of communication, rather than one-way oration it has opened the gates for several actors. India's former Foreign Minister, Sushma Swaraj has made this possible.[1] Prime Minister Modi is a firm believer in the power of technology and social media to communicate worldwide. After winning the 2014 elections, he has gained over 11.9 million followers in the number of followers in a year for an Indian context (8.8 million followers from September 17, 2014, to September 17, 2015) (Twiplomacy). He has set a new benchmark of media world after posting his selfie on Twitter. In foreign policy, Modi imbibed in ideas rather than ideologies. He has demonstrated a skillful approach to motivate public opinion through social media platforms. He is setting trends especially in the contemporary digital field developing itself as a power that takes responsibility, deconstruction and to maintain global issues. His foreign policy is making India shine focusing on three dimensional objectives – economics; political and cultural. His main concern or vision is focused on strengthening economic independence in India. He is exploring bilateral relations with countries those were never part of India's international relations plans or ones where relations were too strained to move ahead. He has rebranded India's "Look East" policy as "Act East" with special emphasis on strengthening economic and security ties with Asian neighbors. Behind his vision is to develop or improve internal ties with key actors (especially East Asian) to increase global standing and influence for India. He used to communicate by tweets in their official language to connect the leaders and the people. For the Indian government, the internet remains the chosen platform for socio-economic empowerment schemes, which also makes India uniquely dependent on internet platforms for its development while, at the same time, it heightens the risks of India's vulnerabilities. In the last few years alone, India has witnessed the potential of the social media in co-ordinating large scale protests across the country with the 'India Against Corruption' movement led by Anna Hazare in 2011. While these protests were largely peaceful, they did test the local security infrastructure in terms of sheer numbers. We saw a repeat of events in the aftermath of the tragic Delhi gang rape incident in 2013 where a large number of protestors mobilized themselves with the help of social media. In a more ugly turn of events, mobile and social network interface was used to send offensive clips and hate messages that triggered panic and mass exodus of north east Indians from large parts of India in the aftermath of the ethnic clashes in Assam in 2012.

In September 2013, a morphed video on YouTube was used to fan communal riots in Muzaffarnagar in Uttar Pradesh and led to mass panic. These incidents snowballed into a cyber-security challenge and exposed a facet of the medium that could be exploited by anti-national elements and required immediate attention. In 2014, the arrest of a Bangalore based executive, Mehdi Masoor Biswas, accused of being the man behind terror group Islamic State's (ISIS) most influential Twitter handle in India, @ShamiWitness brought to surface the extent of the threat posed by the misuse of social media at home.[11] Two years on, a propaganda video released by ISIS shows alleged Indian Jihadists fighting in Syria and calling for more Indian recruits to join the cause.[12] The threat has really come to bear upon India and has proved that social media has become a potent tool for radicalisation by terror groups. In addition to this, we are also witnessing the growth of the "new media phenomena" in India where traditional media (mainly television) is increasingly relying on social media to feed its 24-hour news cycles and picking content and coverage led by social media trends. The 2011 Arab Spring and 2011 London riots are controversial, yet powerful examples of how social media is impacting matters of national security. History shows that terrorists affiliated with Al-Qaeda, extreme right-wing organizations, and otherwise, have long used the Internet to spread propaganda about their ideology and attacks, distribute training guides, and recruit others. They host forums where they discuss how to create bombs, post videos to YouTube demonizing their enemies, and ingratiate themselves with possible recruits by chatting with them over Twitter, Facebook, and even video game worlds like the World of Warcraft. The terrorist's groups and their handles on Twitter such as (@HSMPress-al-Shabaab, @almanarnews-Hezbollah, @Alqassambirgade-Hamas, @aBalkhi-Taliban, @alsomood-Taliban, @MYC_Press-AlShabaab are few such examples. Today technology has enabled both state and non-state actors to misuse the marketplace of ideas and beliefs at the speed of algorithms and this nature has changed the battlefield of war at all level globally. If viewed through the lens of 'hybrid' warfare, the information warfare is becoming an end unto itself.

1.1 SOCIAL MEDIA

"Social media is addictive precisely because it gives us something which the real world lacks: it gives us immediacy, direction, a sense of clarity and value as an individual."

—David Amerland

Figure 1: Social Media

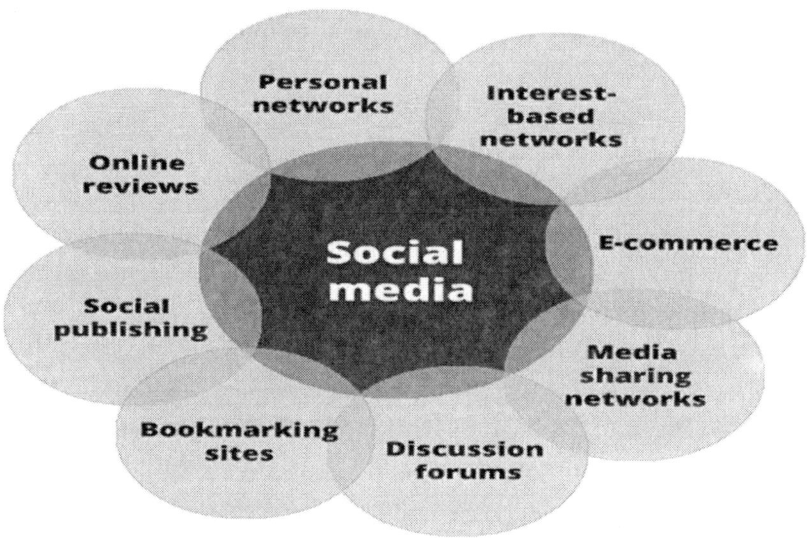

Source: https://www.tes.com/lessons/OioCS800E23GLQ/is-society-becoming-addicted-to-social- media (Accessed on 8th August, 2017)

Social media is changing the way we communicate and the way we perceived, it could be both positive and negative. It connects people on the strength of human values, not identities. Thus social media is a two-way communication where users are allowed to interact with the informing body and use wide variety of online content, videos from various social networking sites like Facebook to interactive encyclopedias like Wikipedia. In fact governments, institutes, business policy and online businesses are taking help of social media to sell their product or taking feedbacks via social media channels. For example, blogging, micro-blogging, online rating, social book-marking, podcasts, forums, message boards, social knowledge, geo-location, multimedia and social networking etc. It involves blogging and forums and any aspect of an interactive presence which allows individuals the ability to engage in conversations with one another, often as a discussion over a particular blog post, news article or event. Nowadays lifestyle has become very fast. People are dependent on technologies. The development of mobile technology has played an important role in shaping the impact of social media. Across the globe, mobile devices dominate in terms of total minutes spent online. This puts the means to connect anywhere, at any time on any device in everyone's hands. Social media applications encourage users to share their experiences, opinions, knowledge, and sometimes their locations.

1.2 What's the Difference Between Social Media and Social Networking?

Social networking is really a subcategory of social media. Media refers to the actual information which we can share with a link to an article, a video, an animated GIF, a PDF document, a status update. Networking needs to have relationships with your audience like friends, relatives, colleagues, anyone from your past, current customers, mentors and even complete strangers. So social networking does include your likes and comments, which we use to send related post. Along with this, we can upload a link on Reddit, which is also a social media platform and helps out the community. We can give our view in the matter without any intention of building relationships with other users. So, we can say social networking, social news, social bookmarking, wikis, blogs and private web messaging are part of the broader social media category.

1.3 Are Traditional Media Also Social Media?

Social media is two-way process. It has the ability to communicate too, but traditional media like television, newspaper or radio is a one-way process only. People can read or watch news, but cannot communicate with it. Conventional media, such as television or newspapers, essentially transmits information in one direction. Users can consume the information the media offers, but they have little or no ability to share their own views on the subject. Social media, however, gives users the ability to interact with the content that is being distributed. This communication may be as simple as allowing users to comment on articles or news stories. It can also be more complex, such as on Wikipedia, where users can dictate and revise the content contained in encyclopedia articles. Other social media sites may offer recommendations to users based on the interests of other users. For example, allows users to share their music tastes and then receive music recommendations based on the listening habits of similar users.

1.4 History of Social Media

Figure 2: History of Social Media

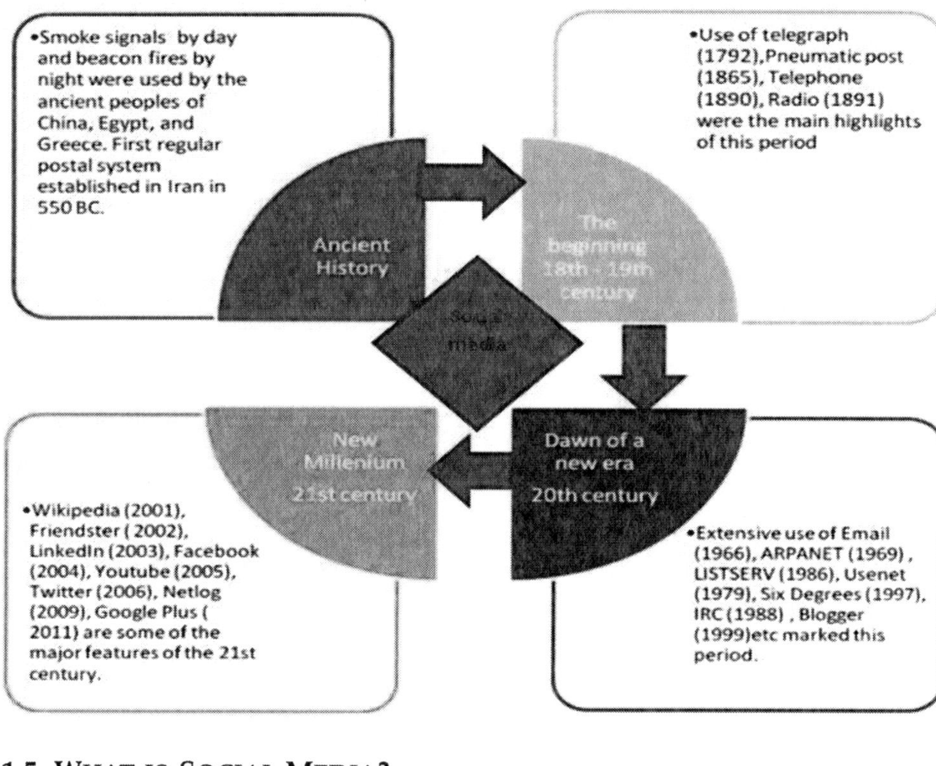

1.5 What is Social Media?

Social media are computer-mediated technologies that facilitate the creation and sharing of information, ideas, career interests and other forms of expression via virtual communities and networks. Social media includes popular networking websites, like Facebook and Twitter; as well as bookmarking sites like Reddit. It involves blogging and forums and any aspect of an interactive presence which allows individuals the ability to engage in conversations with one another, often as a discussion over a particular blog post, news article, or event. Social media is a two-way form of communication that allows users to interact with the information being transmitted. Social media encompasses a wide variety of online content, from social networking sites like Facebook to interactive encyclopedias like Wikipedia. Other examples of social media include social news sites such as Reddit, Propeller and Digg. These sites allow users to interact with one another by sharing content and voting on its quality, which determines the articles that rise to the top of the site. Social video sites like YouTube allow users to share video content and interact through video comments. Social media is a phrase that we throw around a lot these days, often to describe what we post on sites and apps like Facebook, Twitter, Instagram, Snapchat and others. The term is used so vaguely that it can basically be used to describe almost any website on the internet today or maybe not. Some people have more of a restricted view of social media, often equating it to mean the same as social networking (a.k.a. Facebook, Twitter, etc.). Other people don't consider blogs to fall under the social media category.

Figure 3: What is Social Media?

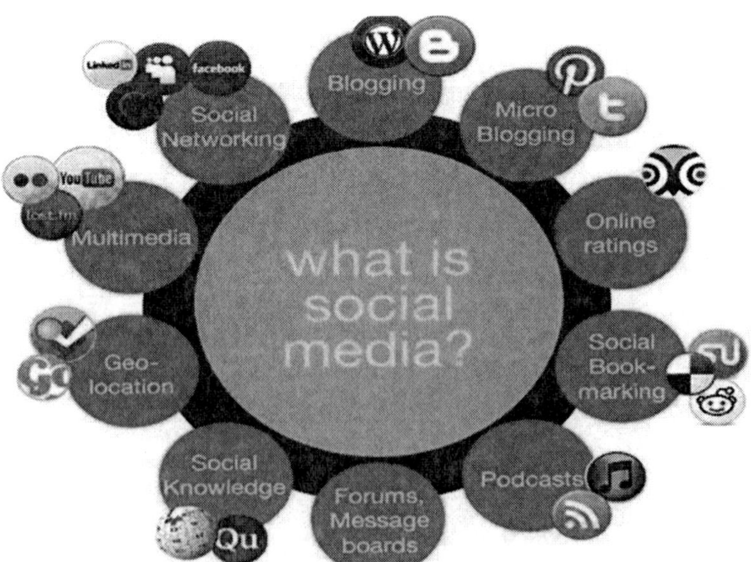

Source: https://www.tes.com/lessons/OioCS800E23GLQ/is-society-becoming-addicted-to-social-me (Accessed on 8th August, 2017)

- The "social" part refers to interacting with other people by sharing information with them and receiving information from them.
- The "media" part refers to an instrument of communication, like the internet (while TV, radio, and newspapers are examples of more traditional forms of media).
- "Social Media is the collection of tools and online spaces available to help individuals and businesses to accelerate their information and communication needs." – *Axel Schultze*
- "Social media are primarily Internet-based tools for sharing and discussing information among human beings." – *Wikipedia*
- Social media is a different type of tool which people are using for different purposes.

As above mentioned about social media, this is the fastest way of communication and sharing ideas, thoughts and knowledge. Today media is considered to be the most effective communication and influential channel. It supports right things on proper time. It gives exposure to the mass viewers about right or wrong process immediately. Whether the issue is local, regional or global, people rely and even trust the information provided to them by the media. Therefore, this dimension/value of media increases its significance as an influential and instrumental tool with regard to building confidence or promoting mistrust among people on issues related to national security. The importance of media can be observed at the times of disasters at national level. Even though, sometimes, media is related to spreading false news, but it is a fact that it helps to inform people about the realities as well. Media, the means of communication that reaches or influences people broadly has a significant position in the statecraft mechanism especially in the period of information rebellion.

1.6 Characteristics of Social Media

Social media has different tools and each tool has a different quality. Social media users are content creators. They can create their own blogs, they can post or express their thoughts on an issue on Facebook or Twitter or post a video blog ("vlog") about their latest travel adventures on

Figure 4: Characteristics of Social Media

Source: https://www.freevector.com/social-media-icons (Accessed on 8th August, 2017)

YouTube. Nowadays companies are also very active on Facebook or other social media tools to engaged Audiences with brand messages because they can provide feedback from the companies, creating a two-way conversation. Another characteristic of social media is instant or immediate communication. Here people do not need to wait for news broadcast to receive information because reporters and media outlets can bring the news directly to social media platforms. The beauty of the technology is that people can easily share and post news content on their networks. Social media is the best mode to interconnectedness and communicate by bringing people across the globe together online. Clusters of like-minded individuals can easily swap ideas and scrutinize data on public matters anytime, anywhere of the world by sitting at home. To understand social media, the core characteristic is its conventional medium that is print, radio and TV media. Social media is a participatory medium for online users. They can participate in online discourse in many ways and open to get feedback too. Podcasting, blogging, tagging RSS-generated syndication, social bookmarking, social networking, wikis, and other collaborative tools, help in participation. Social media is owned and controlled by users only. Social media is a medium of traditional conversational interaction which is for one or one to many interaction. Social media provides new opportunities to access data and information given by social media and Web 2.0 channels. Through these channels users are allow to establish mass collaborations by working together in a many to many context to achieve certain aims. This is a relationship oriented medium where individual are free and easily to use it as per their choices and convenience.

1.7 Role of Social Media

> *"Don't use social media to impress the people; use it to impact the people."*
>
> — **Dav Willis**

Social media has both the positive and negative side. If we will use this in a positive way, this is the best way to use it otherwise it has darker sides too.

Positive Role of Social Media:

- Social media facilitates opportunity.
- Social media is the creation and sharing of information like video conferencing, emails and texting message, Sites like Google, Wikipedia etc are extremely useful to provide knowledge instantly.
- Social media is promoting ideas and career interests.
- Social media is a form of expression via virtual communities and networks.

Social media has two important parts like social networking and media. Media facilitates content and shares it with different tools. Social networking expresses via community, people and through us. Today media is considered to be the most effective communication and influential channel. It supports right things on right time. It gives exposure to the mass viewers about right or wrong process immediately. Whether the issue is local, regional or global, people rely and even trust the information provided to them by the media. Therefore, this dimension / value of media increases its significance as an influential and instrumental tool with regard to building confidence or promoting

Figure 5: Positive Role of Social Media

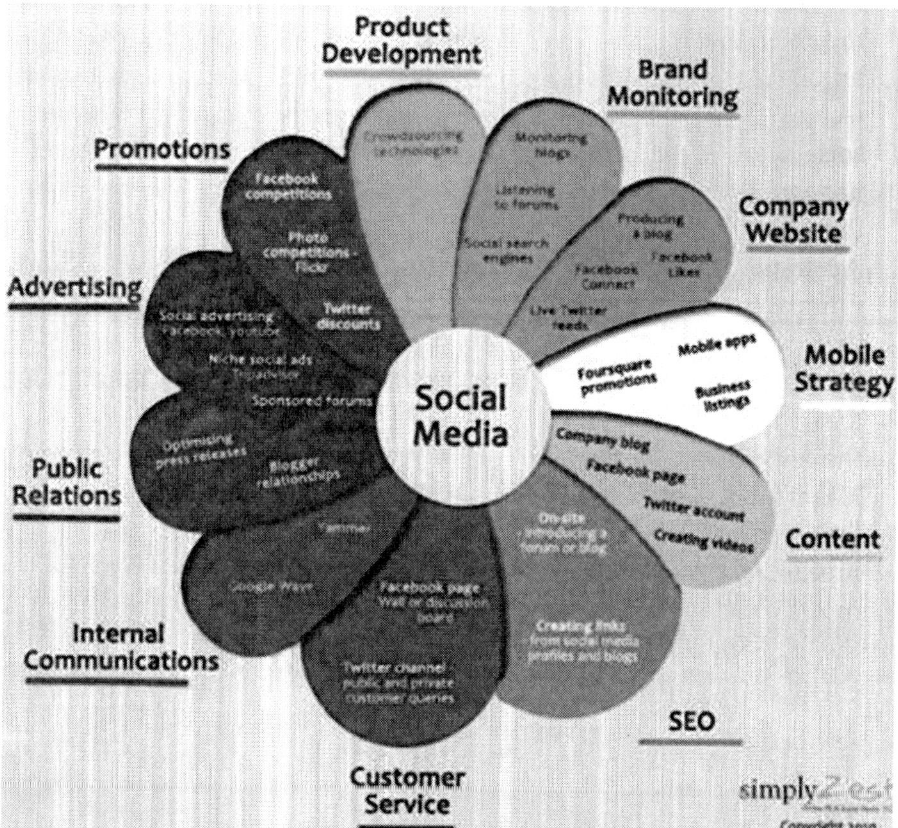

Source: https://hatisolutions.wordpress.com/social-media-hospitality/ Accessed on 10th August, 2017

mistrust among people on issues related to national security. The importance of media can be observed at the times of disasters at national level. Social media – its reach, impact and potential in a globalised world is no longer contested. It is a fascinating phenomenon which presents both challenges and opportunities to governments and law enforcement agencies across the spectrum. An investigation into how India has grappled with the challenges posed by the medium as also whether social media can be harnessed to act as a force multiplier for our enforcement agencies is essential. Issues related to the inadequacy of the Indian legal regime in dealing with social media and fears relating to breach of privacy and censorship of the internet also need to be addressed. Social media is not only confined to us but to politicians as well. Through different activities politics and politicians in India have brought social media into the limelight. It is expected that social media will play a crucial role and influence the coming general elections to a great extent. All the recent lectures by Gujarat Chief Minister, Mr. Narendra Modi, received huge social media attention. He even hosted a political conference on Google+ hangouts and this makes him the third politician across the globe to do this after the Former President of the US, Mr. Obama and the former Australian PM, Julia Gillard. Then there is Anna Hazare's Social Media Campaign against corruption in India. Many researchers have indicated that social media would be stronger and more persuasive than television in influencing people. In the last few years alone, India has witnessed the potential of the social media in coordinating large scale protests across the country with the 'India Against Corruption' movement led by Anna Hazare in 2011. While these protests were largely peaceful, they did test the local security infrastructure in terms of sheer numbers. We saw a repeat of events in the aftermath of the tragic Delhi gang rape incident in 2013 where a large number of protestors mobilised themselves with the help of social media.[2]

Tea Party Movement (2009 in US), Arab Spring Movements are the few best examples of social media's positive role.

1.8 Negative Role of Social Media

- Cyberbullying
- Addiction
- Trolling (online witch hunts, fake news)
- Cyber-terrorism
- Abuse of someone's privacy

There are darker sides of social media too. It is time to be alert and keep an eye open to observe that social media presents enormous risks to individuals, communities, firms, nations and even the society. WhatsApp is proving to be the most challenging for social media. In 2014, Computers in Human Behaviors revealed that the majority of people on social media are not using it as a means of being social. Social networks like Facebook, Twitter, WhatsApp, LinkedIn became a greater

Figure 6: Negative Role of Social Media

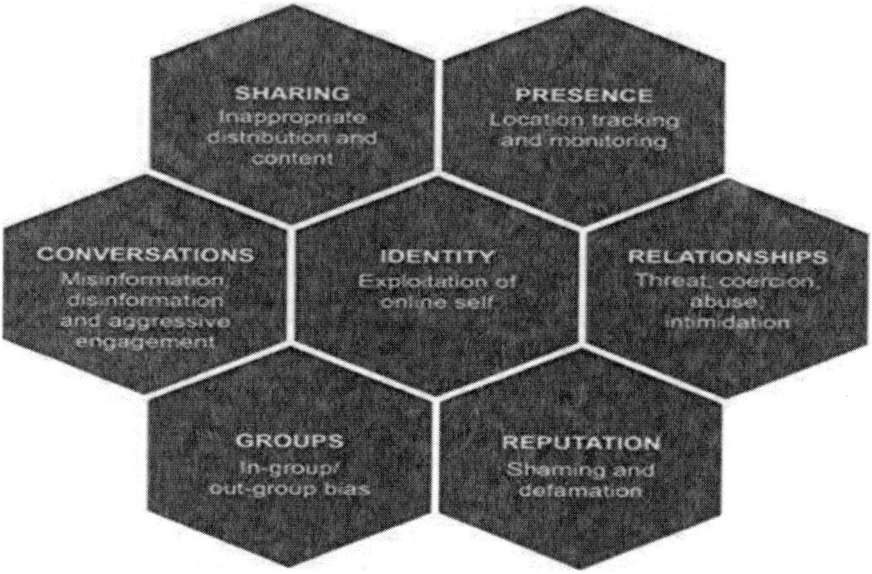

Source: https://www.sciencedirect.com/science/article/pii/S0263237318300781 Accessed on 11th August, 2017

threat to cyber security. Phishing has become a new way of theft for example, Pay Pal scammers – who can trace your login information by sending out an email that instructs users to click on a link in order to fix a discrepancy with their account. Fake or false news are one of the darker sides of social media. Terrorist organizations are using social media tools to spread their ideological, radicalization, recruitment, communication and training. In addition to this, terrorist groups take advantage of Social Media to communicate with cyber-crime organizations and to coordinate along with them for fund-raising activities (from illicit activities) carried out in part (drug smuggling, gunrunning) or completely (e.g. phishing) on the Internet. The link between organized crime and terrorist organizations is increasing considerably in the cyber-world, and this coalition will be able to produce new offensive technologies. Blue whale game was one type of an online suicide. In 2012, the Assam mass exodus occurred because of mobile and social network's offensive clips. It led to hate messages and became the reason of ethnic clashes across the country. Similarly an incident happened after posting a morphed video on YouTube in Muzaffarnagar (Uttar Pradesh) September 2013. There are several incidences of mob lynching because of fake news and video clips. These incidents quickly grow in to a cyber security challenge and spread other social issues of the medium that could be exploited by anti-national elements and require immediate attention.

1.9 Importance of Social Media

Social media has increased its importance strongly during the last few decades by increasing the expanse of its usage. This is a two-way communication channel which has its own pros and cons. It connects people worldwide. This is much cheaper as compared to other traditional recourses of communication. It has a unique facility that anyone can approach or interact at all levels of personality on social media. People can ask their queries to the government and they can use it to share their views on national issues, foreign affairs etc. Social media is a very good source of online brand awareness which goes rapidly viral on media and which makes them successful in a very short amount of time and easily connect to your customers and easily sort their issues. It is also very useful for students as they can enhance their knowledge via Wikipedia and other information sites. With the recent growth of social media in the past ten years as a new staple in our modern culture, social media has also emerged as a growing threat to national security. As the Internet and social media are constantly growing and changing, national security has lagged behind.

National security experts and policy makers must now adapt quickly to emerging threats or face major national security breaches. India's National Security concerns have been attributed to a troubled neighborhood surrounded by failed as well as ill-governed states. India has been subjected to a range of security challenges from both state as well as state sponsored non-state actors. The country has been plagued by a multiplicity of internal and external security challenges in the form of terrorism and emergency movements, unsettled borders, disputed territories, and old treaties that have never been adhered to in spirit create enormous problems for bilateral relations. However, from the decision-making point of view, the challenges are linked to systemize conditions, capacities of institutions, legislations, personalities, policies, politics and economic strength. India's security policy efforts towards erecting a national country terrorism architecture and policy towards the threat of left-wing extremism are included as the international security decision-making sphere. Analyses of the decisions pertaining to national security reveal three distinct trends. First, the decision-making process has become complex with an expansion of the list of influential actors. Second, successful decisions taken still remain personality oriented or are aided by favourable systemic or domestic conditions. In the absence of towering personalities and enabling conditions either no decisions could be taken or the compromised decisions barely fulfilled their stated objectives. And third, the overstretched bureaucracy plays a pivotal role in the process without necessary expertise and competence, and on most occasions, has prevented the emergence of structures that could aid the decision-making apparatus.

1.10 Importance of the Research Topic

In this modern era, people are using mobiles and computers for various purposes. Social media and social networking are very much important for communication to each other and social media tools and social media apps are very popular among public to send videos, files, photos etc. Through social media tools, public is sending messages to their friends. Even many offices are using social media tools like WhatsApp, Facebook, Twitter, etc. for sending official messages to the public or their officers and their followers. The research topic selected for study is very much important to gauge the influence of social media and how social media is used by the public for India's Foreign Policy. Whether social media can be used by the public for contributing their views to India's foreign policy is discussed.

1.11 Importance of Social Media

Social media importance has risen sharply in the last decade because of the increased user base. The importance of social media isn't going to come down anytime soon, as people are using it daily and exploring it more and more. At first companies had not taken social media seriously but consistently, they recognize that it is not something to avoid because of the potential and profits early entrants witnessed. Here are some statistics and facts for providing people with the clear view about how significant social media has grown in current time. Here are some statistics and facts for providing people with the clear view about how significant social media has grown in current times.

1. Active users on different social channels as per 201. (Facebook 2 Billion, YouTube 1.5 Billion, Instagram 700 Million, Twitter 328 Million and Snapchat 255 Million)
2. 97 per cent of customers search about local businesses online of which decisions of 93 per cent get influenced by online search.
3. Volume of users who engage on social media daily. (70 per cent Facebook users, 49 per cent Instagram users and 36 per cent Twitter users).
4. Social media is a two way communication channel which let brands get feedback from consumers in order to constantly transform as per changing consumer needs.
5. Social media is much cheaper as compare to traditional marketing channels.
6. All level of personalities can be easily interacted and approached on social channels irrespective of how big a name is.
7. Social media is great for increasing brand awareness fast, as we can see now many brand ads go viral on social channels which make them a success in relatively much shorter amount of time.
8. Rapid response for consumer queries can be given on social presence so that consumers never go dissatisfied.
9. Constantly being good and serving to your target market on social channels also builds your authority in the industry.

1.12 Definitions Related Terms & Definitions of Social Media by Different Authors

- "Social media are primarily Internet-based tools for sharing and discussing information among human beings." – **Wikipedia**
- "A category of sites that is based on user participation and user-generated content. They include social networking sites like LinkedIn, Facebook, or My Space, social bookmarking sites like Del.icio.us, social news sites like Digg or Simpy, and other sites that are centered on user interaction." – **Lazworld**

- "Online technologies and practices that people use to share opinions, insights, experiences, and perspectives with each other." –**tvb.org**
- "Social media are works of user-created video, audio, text or multimedia that are published and shared in a social environment, such as a blog, wiki or video hosting site." – **Capilanou**
- "An umbrella term that defines the various activities that integrate technology, social interaction, and the construction of words and pictures." – **Anvil Media**
- "Software tools that allow groups to generate content and engage in peer-to-peer conversations and exchange of content (examples are YouTube, Flickr, Facebook, Myspace etc)." – **Bottle PR**
- "Social media is the collection of tools and online spaces available to help individuals and businesses to accelerate their information and communication needs." – **Axel Schultze**[3]

1.13 Social Media Terms

- **Dark Side** (The negative or troubled part of someone or something that is usually concealed)
- **Unintended consequences** (A term used to describe a set of results that was not intended as an outcome. It may be anticipated or un-anticipated, they should be the product of specific actions within the process)
- **Cyber Bullying** (Cyberbullying is the use of cell phones, instant messaging, e-mail, chat rooms or social networking sites such as Facebook and Twitter to harass, threaten or intimidate someone)
- **Trolling** (A social media troll is someone who purposely says something controversial in order to get a rise out of other users)
- **Fake News** (Fake news is news, stories or hoaxes created to deliberately misinform or deceive readers)
- **Inflammatory lines** (Messages in the conversations block)
- **Sharing inappropriate content** (In the sharing block)

1.14 Definitions of Foreign Policy by Different Authors

- Prof. Tailor – "Foreign policy of a sort which will go on so long as are sovereign states".
- George Madlikosi – "Foreign policy is the systematic activities

evolved by communities for changing the behavior of other states for adjusting their own activities in an international environment".

- Prof. Joseph Framkel – "Foreign policy consists of decisions and actions which involves to some appreciable extent relations between state and others".

1.15 Definition of National Security by Different Authors

- A nation has security when it does not have to sacrifice its legitimate interests to avoid war, and is able, if challenged, to maintain them by war." – **Walter Lippmann, 1943**.
- "The distinctive meaning of national security means freedom from foreign dictation." – **Harold Lasswell, 1950.**
- "National security objectively means the absence of threats to acquired values and subjectively, the absence of fear that such values will be attacked." – **Arnold Wolfers, 1960.**
- "National security then is the ability to preserve the nation's physical integrity and territory; to maintain its economic relations with the rest of the world on reasonable terms; to preserve its nature, institution, and governance from disruption from outside; and to control its borders." – **Harold Brown, U.S. Secretary of Defense, 1977-1981.**
- "National security... is best described as a capacity to control those domestic and foreign conditions that the public opinion of a given community believes necessary to enjoy its own self-determination or autonomy, prosperity and wellbeing." – **Charles Maier, 1990**
- "National security is an appropriate and aggressive blend of political resilience and maturity, human resources, economic structure and capacity, technological competence, industrial base and availability of natural resources and finally the military might." – **National Defence Collage of India, 1996.**
- "National security is the measurable state of the capability of a nation to overcome the multi-dimensional threats to the apparent well-being of its people and its survival as a nation-state at any given time, by balancing all instruments of state policy through governance... and is extendable to global security by variables external to it." – **Prabhakaran Paleri, 2008.** [4]

1.16 OBJECTIVES OF THE RESEARCH

1.16.1 To study the social media and its use at various levels

Social media is used as a tool for organization and mobilization on a massive scale. There are a number of communication theories that can help explain this phenomenon. It can also be argued that social media today has become a mode of communication. Harlod Lasswell's functionalist sociology of media gives us an analytical framework to help understand communication. With a sudden boost in communication post World War I, Lasswell's formula is based on a multi-faceted question "who says what in which channel to whom with what effect?" Lasswell's theory therefore favours a content analysis approach, in which, the research technique is "aimed to achieve an objective, systematic and quantitative description of the manifest content of communications" According to Manuel Castella's network theory, we can use it effectively to demonstrate how social networks today are invaluable for political activism. In addition to this, social media also helps us create weak ties which are useful in providing information and opening up opportunities at low costs. In addition to this, social media can also be used to 'form weak ties' with strangers who share common interests or goals. Furthermore, according to Mark Granovetter, the advantage of weak ties over strong ties is their ability to diffuse information and ideas easily across social groups. The best use of social media can be seen with its extensive use during the Arab Spring. The activists during the Arab Spring could spread the word through social media due to their weak ties. Had they relied only on strong ties, it would have been difficult to help spread the message. Facebook and Twitter are two of the social networks which exploit weak ties.

1.16.2 To study the social media tools which have an influence on Indian foreign policy making

With the election of Prime Minister Narendra Modi, there has been a surge in social media interest in his government, domestic policies as well as foreign policy. Since the Modi government came into power, the Twitter handle and Facebook page of the Ministry of External Affairs (MEA) has seen a quantum jump of 400 per cent. In addition to this, the number of visitors on the MEA website has also doubled. The spokesperson of the MEA is responsible for its Twitter handle and is constantly being updated. Through the use of social media, the

MEA has increased its outreach tremendously. During the Prime Minister's visit to the US, the Twitter handle of the spokesperson was a constant source of news and updates of the daily going ons and meetings.

1.16.3 To identify and study the modern technologies used in Social Media

Today, Facebook, YouTube and Twitter are some of the most widely used social media today. Their reach helps connect every nook and corner of the world. This can be better understood looking at the rapid growth of the Internet and the global spread.

1.16.4 Does the Social Media influence and shape the policy agendas?

With the growth of social media, the number of weak ties also grows. With the anonymity that the Internet provides, it is easy for people to use their weak ties to even try and spread false rumours. However, when the government releases certain information, the public could take to social media to express their agreement/displeasure. This in turn could gain momentum and could influence the government's decision. Coming from a democracy, social media could play a vital role in shaping policy agendas. The most recent example of social media shaping policy agendas would be the Arab Spring. Through the use of social media, people from all over the world ensured that their respective governments would shape policies favouring the protesters during the Arab Spring.

1.16.5 If it does, then what is the role and extent of this influence – constructive or otherwise?

Social media today can help influence people's decisions. It has the power to sway governments based on people's preferences. However, social media also has the power to be destructive if certain reports hurt the sentiments of many. Taking India's example, with every terrorist attack, the Indian populace calls for an outright war with Pakistan on every form of social media. However, the similar medium was used by Coca-Cola to bring people from conflicting countries together to 'share a moment over a coke'. The video has received 3,177,391 views on Youtube, and has also been shared and viewed by thousands of others on Facebook. Therefore, we can also argue that social media also has the necessary tools to bring people together and work constructively.

1.16.6 What are the challenges on reporting on foreign policy in India?

One of the main challenges facing India today is its fluid and uncertain concept of national interest. Unlike many countries, India needs to define its national interest with discernment, realism, objectivity and foresight. Therefore, most reports on foreign policy in India are given by Ambassadors to their selected editors and journalists, thus creating a problem with sharing such reports through social media. Historically, reports on Indian Foreign Policy were published either in print or through traditional media. However, with the current government, the avenue of social media is being thoroughly exploited and news blasts/flashes are constantly sent to millions of people globally.

1.17 Limitations of the Study

- We have considered social media tools, however, only popular tools and which are mostly used by users are discussed in this project
- Impact of social media is not measured in terms of statistical figures

1.18 Scope of the Study

- Scope of the study is restricted to foreign policy of India.

1.19 Research Methodology

To solicit the information about usage of social media and its tools, it was decided to conduct a survey of social media usage by different group of stakeholders. A list of stakeholders who use social media for various purposes was prepared and thirty stakeholders were selected for the pilot study. Social media is used by most of the students, teachers, researchers, media personnel, government officials and politicians etc. To test the group, a structured questionnaire designed for this purpose was distributed among these stakeholders and they were requested whether they have any difficulty in understanding the questions. They have been given sufficient time to think and fill in the questionnaire. The researcher did not receive any suggestions to modify the questionnaire. Hence, it was decided to distribute the questionnaire to all thirty stakeholders to conduct the pilot study. Nobody suggested any improvement to the questions asked to them. Questions were designed to keep in mind the objectives of the project. There were twenty-five questions included in the questionnaire. This paper is a part of research project sanctioned by ICSSR to me for a period of two years. To knows the views of various stakeholders who are using social media and social media tools, about the use of social media and its impact on Indian Foreign Policy, a structured questionnaire was developed and distributed to 550 participants which includes post-graduate students, research scholars, defence officers, faculty members etc. Out of which we have received 484 responses from various groups of stakeholders.

1.20 Pilot Study Conducted

Nowadays social media is an essential part of life of users who know how to use the medium for various purposes. We have conducted a pilot study about the use of social media by students, researchers, faculty members etc. We have developed a structured questionnaire for this purpose and to test these questions from these users, a pilot study was conducted. The analysis of these questionnaires is given below:

First six questions are about use of social media, social media tools, purpose of using social media tools, their participation and contributing views on India's Foreign policy through these tools and how they update their knowledge in Indian foreign policy etc.

The stakeholders were asked whether they used social media networking and at what level. 31 per cent stakeholders answered they used social media for personal use, 28 per cent as students, and 11 per cent as research scholars and others are also using social media networking at different levels, but their percentage is low. Second question which was asked to them was which social media tools they used, Facebook was the most popular tool used by majority of people which is used by all and YouTube and Twitter were among the second most used by them. There are other tools like, LinkedIn, Blog, Slideshare,

Instagram, Snapchat, MySpace and Flicker which were also used by a few students.

In the questionnaire it was also asked for what purposes they used these social media tools. Five options were given to them. Out of which they mentioned that they use social media tools to obtain knowledge and information in various subject areas and for their personal use. Stakeholders also said that they use it for updating information and knowledge and also for their personal interest in the Indian foreign policy.

It was further asked them whether their views on various problems or policies is contributed by them through social media tools. 17 per cent stakeholders said that they do contribute their views on international relations; views on national security etc and 11 per cent said that they were not contributing their views. 12 per cent stakeholders expressed their views on India's foreign policy through social media tools, 15 per cent said that they did not express their view, and here the percentage of negative is more than positive responses. It was further asked them whether they visit Govt. of India's Ministry of External Affairs website to get recent updates on India's foreign policy. In response to this, 21 per cent said that they frequently visit the website and get updates.

Another question asked was that many incidents happen in the country and whether these incidents force the government to frame the foreign policy. 76 per cent participants gave positive responses and mentioned that a few cases in which the government has decided the foreign policy for example in the Kashmir valley, new conditions of Kashmir valley is rules and accordingly, the government has changed policy with internal government of Kashmir as well as some border issues where terrorist attacks took place. It was further asked if foreign policy changes when the central government changes. In response to this, 22 (73 per cent) respondents said policy is slightly changed as per situation. 9 (30 per cent) said policy is completely changed in certain cases.

Participants were asked whether use of social media tools could influence and affect our Indian foreign policy, out of 30 participants, 24 (80 per cent) said it could influence and affect it whereas 6 (20 per cent) gave negative responses. In the positive response, participants said that the reactions and feedback from citizens affect the foreign policy, few said that the media has a great impact on citizens in influencing our policy. Whereas one participant said that social media tools only gives information (may be true or false), but the ultimate decision lies with the government. Another person expressed that public opinion of Chinese presence in Doklam has influenced the government to not unilaterally withdraw forces from the region.

It was further asked whether social media has been influenced by or has an impact on Indian national security and IFP. 17 (56 per cent) participants opined that it is influenced and has an impact because all the information is exchanged through social media, because of radicalization of people through social media which has made national security experts to track all social elements. Cyber security is a matter of great concern now that social media is very active and India should implement a cyber security mechanism. 6 (20 per cent) participants said there was no impact on security and FP.

Twenty-three (76 per cent) respondents opined that present government is more active on social media as compared to the previous government and 2 (6 per cent) said they were not active and 5 (16 per cent) did not give their response. Few opinions are that the present government is fully active in social marketing because the previous government failed in connecting with the people that is the reason they were not elected in 2014. Another participant expressed that the present government is posting and tweeting on Twitter their views. Our Prime Minister Mr Modi has one of the largest followers on Twitter, and the existing government advertisement uses all programmes set up as new one on social media.

To seek the opinions, it was asked whether powerful nations like the US, the UK, China, Russia and France are active on social media to influence the foreign policy. 21 participants said yes because these countries are active on social, hence these states are trying to change the third world countries' public opinion and can easily form their foreign policy. Another example is that at the time of the American President election, every country was watching and taking an interest in their election process and everyone got to know about the victory of Trump and are now watching how it is affecting the world and every nation is thinking of changing its FP.

A question was also asked about China playing an important role in international power politics and how it is not actively involved on social media. However, 11 respondents said that it is actively involved social media whereas 10 participants said it is not. Nine respondents did not respond to this question. Some comments on this question are that even China plays an important role in international power politics, however, they do not expose itself or any information on social media which is an external step towards success, China tends to be self-sufficient by having their own social media sites. China has their own social media tools for domestic use and China is developing its human resources focus on technology which is used by social media, but the information provided is limited.

It was asked whether strategic think tanks influence foreign policy through social media. 14 participants replied positively yes whereas 11 participants replied negatively. Think Tanks work on the agenda of the government and think tanks give out performance views and not necessarily what is good for the government.

Social media reflects meaningful political competition over India's Foreign Policy, if so what relationship can social media reveal and its limitation of social media data for the use of research scholars. Only three participants said yes and six participants said no. Majority of the participants (21) did not respond to this question. Here available resources are shared on social media and they are provided to research scholars, but it has a limitation to some extent, without authenticity and the research scholar will drive it by data available on social media.

Further the participants were asked whether social media has an impact on the foreign policy, 20 participants replied positively while four denied. Since social media provides everyone a platform to voice their opinions, miscreants can easily sway public opinion over a certain issue by making false claims. Therefore we can say that social media does play a role in the making of foreign policy.

What criteria do editors and reporters follow while covering sensitive topics such as war and foreign policy? There are certain rules that need to be adhered to, however, at times journalists tend to overlook them. The 26/11 Mumbai terror attacks is one such example.

When asked whether religion, caste, class and poverty affect Indian foreign policy decisions, 18 out of 30 participants responded in the affirmative. Six respondents stated that these criteria do not affect policy.

Participants were asked whether internal security challenges in Kashmir, North East and insurgencies like naxalism play a role in framing foreign policy and whether social media influence affects the same, following were the responses:

- Internal security in Kashmir and North East is a big challenge in India. Public opinion is often influenced by radical extremists, especially in the case of Kashmir and while reviewing Pakistan's foreign policy.
- Scholars of international relations and conflict use social media data to illuminate questions of foreign policy and in particular, understand how structure of social media reflects offline behavior. To this question, a few comments are, yes, scholars and IR researchers of conflict can use social media as they are the new generation and the opinion and suggestions can be useful for foreign policy.

In the questionnaire, participants were also asked how frequently they use social media to understand India's foreign policy. A total of 11 participants said they use it occasionally, seven use social media daily, six use it weekly and five, monthly.

Participants were asked how social media can be related with Indian national security issues. Following are the views submitted for consideration:

1. People can post anything on social media and the content reaches everyone as the medium works as a pressure group.
2. It is important that terrorism, naxalism, insurgency and left wing extremism is kept in mind while formulating Indian national security.
3. National security matters need to be kept a secret.
4. Social media shows public opinions regarding regional cooperation to national security and regional security in areas such as Kashmir.

5. Information whether right or wrong, less significant role, fraud rumors etc. plays a huge role in impacting law and order.

From the above statements we understand that social media is used as a platform to express views regarding a certain topic pertaining to national security, however, naxalite groups use other mediums to circulate information.

Participants were asked if they were aware of the Indo-US strategic partnership in the Nuclear deal. While 11 replied yes, three said no and 16 did not respond to the question. Five options were provided to the participants when asked which social media tools are most effective for this strategic partnership. News channels was selected by 14 respondents, electronic and print media was selected by 12 respondents and social media was labelled the third most effective. Published literature was considered not so effective.

Participants were asked whether they were aware of the Indo-China border dispute, to which 22 replied yes, three said no and five did not respond to the question. The participants were further asked if issues raising this issue on social media influenced policy makers, following were some of the answers:

1. Through social media, people raised their voice to support government. The support of the people boosts the government in forming a policy in this respect.
2. Indo-China border dispute and Doklam issue on social media raised the issue to policy maker and hence it influenced India's foreign policy.
3. The media is not concerned about the border dispute as people from Arunachal Pradesh are under special protection.
4. It is suggested that academic community and intelligent researchers must come forward with such issues and find out solutions.

From the above comments from the participants, it appears that social media is mostly used to support the government or raise a few social issues which can be general, national and international.

The respondents were asked how they are aware about the India-

Pakistan conflict during the Kargil war, Parliament attack, Mumbai attack and other issues. A total of 18 participants said they learnt of it through news channels, whereas 17 participants said they came to know about it through print media. Few people said they knew about it through social media tools like WhatsApp and very few participants knew it through published literature.

1.21 Technical Tools of Social Media

Nowadays people spend most of their time using technology and media. This is enough reason to understand social media's importance in this area of study. Perhaps more significant is the impact of technology and media on human relationships and vice versa. Some popular social media tools are Facebook, Instagram and Twitter; as well as bookmarking sites such as Reddit. These sites promote interaction allowing individuals to engage in conversations, often over a particular blog post, a news article or event. While classifying the various social media tools into categories,

Figure 7: Technical Tools of Social Media

keep in mind that social media is driven by text, photos, video, audio and simulated environments. The goal of social media in a business context is to engage people. For an employee, the desired outcome may be an improvement in efficiency pertaining to workflow, whereas for a customer, the desired outcome may be an additional purchase or a strong recommendation to a friend. As a reminder, the four primary ways to engage people with social media are as follows:

1. Communication
2. Collaboration
3. Education
4. Entertainment

Social media tools provide users with enhanced skills to create and share information to influence society and the global community. However, a key concern is whether the increased usage of social media reflects improved communication using cultural competency. Though theoretical foundations exist in the literature for social media and cultural competency, few studies synthesize these constructs and provide strategies. This presentation presents results of a literature review study to address these issues.

1.22 Social Media Consists of a Variety of Tools and Technologies that Include the Following

1.22.1 Social Networking Sites

There are two versions of social networking sites. One is available publically and other one is using for business purposes. Basically they are used in maintaining or building relationships among people who share similar interests. Social network sites users can create a public or semi-public profile. They can establish friendship link also. Recently Facebook at work social networking site open where cooperate users can create and collaborate publically.

1.22.2 Content Communities

Common tools in this category are YouTube and Flickr. These sites allow you to organise and develop content such as photos, videos etc. The content posted here can be availed by the general public.

1.22.3 Blogs

Blogs allow people to start their own websites. Wordpress and Blogspot are a few examples. People can post text, images, videos, links etc. Here users can express their opinions on personal matters, give feedback and get innovative ideas.

1.22.4 Micro-blogging

The most popular micro-blogging platform is Twitter. Here users can publish or exchange brief messages. They can be in text, images, or links to other websites.

1.22.5 Online Collaborative Projects (Wikipedia and Wikispaces)

Wiki is a good way of communication, collaborating projects, create a websites where users can add, modify or delete content. Ward Cunningham was the one who came up with the concept of Wiki.

Wikipedia is an online encyclopedia where users can upload their articles. Wikipedia has more than 30 million articles in 287 languages written collaboratively by volunteers around the world.

1.22.6 Folksonomies or Tagging (e.g., Delicious)

The term folksonomy is also known as social tagging, social indexing, and collaborative tagging. Here users can tag, organise, classify and share content. Facebook and Flickr also provide tagging services to their users. Since the contents are tagged with useful keywords, social tagging expedites the process of searching and finding relevant content.

1.22.7 Facebook

Facebook is a popular free social networking website that allows registered users to create profiles, upload photos and videos, send messages and keep in touch with friends, family and colleagues.

1.22.8 Twitter

Twitter is a free micro blogging tool where users can broadcast short posts called tweets. Users can read and send short messages. Twitter members can broadcast tweets and follow others tweets too.

1.22.9 Google+ (pronounced Google plus)

This tool is a great source of Google's social networking project, navigation system which users can use offline more closely.

1.22.10 LinkedIn

This site is especially designed for business community. They allow users to registered members to establish and document networks of people they know and trust professionally.

1.22.11 Reddit

Reddit is a social news website or forum where users can promote or publish their stories on topics like technology, politics or music. The site members are known as Redditors and subsites known as subereddits.

1.22.12 Pinterest

This site is used for social curation of visual content. Before uploading any image, user has to take prior permission and it should be taken from an original source.

1.22.13 YouTube & Vimeo

This site is using to upload videos and can get information about the different sites.

1.22.14 Flickr

An image and video hosting website and online community. Photos can be shared on Facebook and Twitter and other social networking sites.

1.22.15 Instagram

A free photo and video sharing app that allows users to apply digital filters, frames and special effects to their photos and then share them on a variety of social networking sites.

1.22.16 Snapchat

A mobile app that lets users send photos and videos to friends or to their "story." Snaps disappear after viewing or after 24 hours. Currently, we are not allowing individual departments to have Snapchat accounts, but asking that they contribute to the Tufts University account.

REFERENCES

1. Allmer, Thomas, *Critical Theory and Social Media, Between Emancipation and Commodification*, Taylor & Francis: Print Publication, April, 2015: Online Publication, 2015
2. Abraham, Rhea, *Media and National Security*, KW Publication Pvt. Ltd, New Delhi, 2011
3. Coombs, Timonthy W., Jesper Falkeimer, Mats Heide, Philip Young, *Strategic Communication, Social Media and Democracy: The challenge of the digital naturals*, Taylor & Francis: Print Publication, August 2015: Online Publication, 2015
4. Cross, Michael, *Social Media Security, 1st Edition, Leveraging Social Networking while Mitigating Risk*, ISBN: 9781597499873: Imprint: Syngress: Published, 15th November 2013, p. 346
5. Jayakumar, Shashi, *State, Society and National Security, Challenges and Opportunities in the 21st Century*, S Rajaratnam School of International Studies, NTU, Singapore, June 2016, p. 296
6. Johnson, Thomas A., *Power, National Security, and Transformational Global Events Challenges Confronting, America, China, and Iran*, Taylor & Francis Group, LLC, 2012
7. Katoch C Dhruv, *Shaping of India's Security Discourse: The Impact of Regional Conflicts*, 28th December, 2016
8. Pandalai, Shruti, *The 'Social Media' Challenge to National Security: Impact and Opportunities: A Conceptual Overview*, Monograph No. 55, 2016
9. Shafi, Abdulhamid, Muhammad, *Privacy and National Security Challenges in Online Social Networks*, LAMBERT Publication, Paperback, Import, 24th January 2013
10. Sharma, Loveleena, "Social Media as A Challenge to Traditional Indian Diplomacy A Medium of Communication or A Mode of Diplomacy?" Accessed through on http://www.jgu.edu.in/JJIA/PDF/vol4/Loveleena-Sharma.pdf, 2nd July, 2017
11. Zavattaro, Staci, Thomas Bryer, *Social Media For Government: Theory and Practice*, Taylor & Francis: Print Publication, March 2016: Online Publication, March 2016

CHAPTER II

Review of Literature

2.1 Introduction

This chapter discusses the review of literature in which we have considered research articles published in various journals. Review is the systematic identification and analysis of document in particular field of study. Literature review is an important step in research and it an integral part of research. It helps find what research has already been done in a particular area of study and what needs to be done. It also gives up-to-date understanding of the subject and its significance. The first input to any research is a detailed literature search on the topic of research concerned, enlightening the work already done, current trends and future research. Literature review is a critical summary of documents scanned on the proposed research topic. The purpose of a literature review is to study past work. Review of literature helps to measure the quality of research work and is useful in conducting research efficiently and effectively. For the sake of convenience review is arranged under various headings.

To understand more about social media and India's foreign policy, the first step is to go through articles/research papers published in various journals, presented at conferences and websites/portals. Searches made on 'Google' and 'Google Scholar' search engine and various journals published by reputed publishers such as Emerald, Oxford University Press, Cambridge University Press, Science Direct, Project Muse, Jstor and journals from open access movement like Indian journals.com, Directory of Open Access Journals (DOAJ) etc, and papers presented in number of international/ national conferences/ workshops yielded few core and relevant literature material. Literature search or literature review is an attempt to identify, locate and synthesise completed research reports, articles, books, and other materials about the specific problems of a research topic. It is a chronological presentation of growth and development of literature in a particular field over a period of time. It helps to narrow down the research problem, suggests new approaches to the planning of investigations and assists investigators to develop firmer understandings of theoretical implications. The researcher gets a guideline to formulate and identify the objectives, hypothesis, methods for collection and analysis of data.

For the present study literature search is carried out to uncover a body of literature appropriate to the study. Key terms are

2.2 Senadheera, Vindaya and others (2017) take the review of social media and technological development and prove disadvantageous for both practice and theory. Further they provide research key gaps and provide dynamism to social media strategy formation for continuous improvement of strategy.

2.3 Penni, Janice (2017) highlighted future of online social networks and created interactive and communicative global phenomenon that enable billions of users to connect with other individuals on Facebook and Twitter but also with media sharing platforms such as Instagram and Pinterest. Furthermore, online activities such as posting video content on social networks also highlighted the online usage patterns and trends of using social media to actively engage with other users more willingly than text. This study examines the current use of social media platforms and explores the factors that help define the long term implications of social media.

2.4 Dahibhate N.B. and Patil, S.K. (2013) express the need of library and information services by using social media tools. Various social media tools Tools like Facebook, Myspace, Flickr, Slideshare, Blogging, Forums, Wikis, Twitter, Ning and YouTube and how these can be used in libraries to provide better services to users of the library are described. This paper made an attempt to use of social media tools for managing library services, however library professionals are required certain skills to provide IT base services using social media tools which are missing in this paper.

2.5 Sukhwabt, Bindra (2004) highlighted foreign and domestic policy issues which are related to our political system which is designed in such a way that define and implement national purposes behind the policies. He has explained in this paper that no single party in the world is the only policy maker, a large number of other parties are also involved in the decision and nobody denying the fact. Further the process of policy making is more complicated than the admitted complications of international relations. While explaining the policy process, it is not possible to the leadership of political system without domestic support. It is true that without keeping pressure on the leadership, they are not willing to form the policy for the nation.

2.6 Schulz, Kerstin (2013) while studying political communication, he recorded that foreign policy process have played minor role because media is acting central mediatory role between political decision makers and the public, however, the media's impact remains contingent across various processes of foreign policy making. Public role is essential in foreign policy making. There is a demand for research on the performance of media in making foreign policy. In this paper an analytical framework for systematic analysis of media – foreign policy relations are explained in the context of foreign policy research variables and the framework is based on the assumptions that the role of media varies across diverse foreign policy context depending on the government involvement in the foreign affairs.

2.7 Chanan, Naveh (2002) explained the media's involvement in all stages of foreign policy formulation process. Political leaders consider media in its national and international aspects. He also explained three main models to create a general model in which role of media will be incorporated. It was further explained that the first model presented by Glenn Snyder and his colleagues (1969). The process of decision making of involvement of media is complex. When internal and external events occurs, leaders learn it from media. Media advice and public relations professionals participate in the process; government officials consult with them and take their advice. In this article Chanan considers past studies of foreign policy decision making and the points it neglected while dealing with the complex role of media. He also provided schematic structure of the foreign policy decision making models, that do not include the media and the next model with incorporation of the media. Both the models are explained very well, considering various aspects like media as environment, political communication, communication policy, political economy, setting of the media, media channels, functions of media etc.

2.8 Mukherjee, Rohan and David M. Malone (2011) India faces numerous contemporary security challenges, many of them internal. Domestic politics play a major role in determining which security challenges are construed by Indian. This article first touches on the evolution of India's domestic politics and foreign policy since independence, then discusses various domestic, regional and global security challenges relevant to India today and concludes by considering whether the country's current foreign policy can hasten its emergence as a great power or conversely, will confine it to its current reach as merely a regional one.

2.9 Barton, William P. (1950) Indian Foreign Policy relying on her immense population, her great economic resources, and on the magnificent army bequeathed to her by Britain, decided on a policy of splendid isolation. She would not ally herself with any power block either in the West or in the East; she would cultivate friendly relations with Russia. She would lead Asia: western imperialism, the western colonial system would no longer be tolerated. Asia was on the march to freedom; Asian nations struggling for self-expression could look to India for leadership and moral and material support. The last vestige of Dutch rule must be swept from Indonesia; with this in view India gave strong moral support to the nascent Republic at Jakarta.

To implement his policy of Asiatic leadership, Pandit Nehru evolved a scheme of an Asian Relations Conference to be summoned from time to time. Unfortunately for India and the world, he made no attempt to establish friendly relations with Pakistan. Had the Indian Prime Minister taken such a step and as a corollary of it avoided the Kashmir adventure his country might have been in a much stronger and happier position today. The halcyon days India had promised herself were of short duration. The Kashmir quarrel and the cold war that followed it absorbed a large proportion of the Indian army, involving a charge on the Indian budget that paralyzed economic enterprise, holding up the great multi-purpose schemes (hydro-electric and irrigation) that had as their object the improvement of the food supply, the shortage of which was involving a huge expenditure in subsidies. Disturbances in the political climate added to the difficulties of India's rulers. Congress supremacy was challenged in many quarters. The socialists aimed at overthrowing it; the high caste Hindu Mahasabha and its militant right-wing (the RSS) were determined to cancel the partition; communism was a growing danger.

2.10 Cui Zhang, Charles and William Meadows (2012) This study employs first- and second-level agenda-setting to investigate how media salience, public opinion, and policy agendas influence the perceptions of foreign countries in the United States. Triangulation of research methods allowed examination of media coverage, public opinion and presidential public papers. Results indicate that salience promotes awareness of inflated significance for foreign countries named in U.S. media. The study identified a strong relationship between the foreign country salience in media coverage and in presidential public papers. The hypothesis for agenda-setting effects of policy agenda on public agenda was not supported. Regarding second-level agenda-setting effects, a correlation was found to exist among a negative tone in news coverage, presidential public papers, and public opinion. In contrast, no correlation was identified pertinent to the positive valence in the three agendas.

2.11 Kapur, Ashok (1971) While Washington and Moscow are trying to manage their political relationship and to carry on an institutionalized dialogue to control the strategic arms race, India, with the fourth largest military force in the world, is contemplating the bomb. Early in 1968, after considerable hesitation, she refused to sign the nuclear Non-Proliferation Treaty. By the beginning of last year press reports were saying that, under pressure from Parliament and the pro-bomb lobby, her leaders were considering cost estimates for a bomb programme, and during the summer the Atomic Energy Department announced a ten-year programme which includes a plan to develop rocket and space technology, guidance systems, and radar and missile-tracking stations.

2.12 Tully, Stephen (2014) In his article "Social Media in the Conflict Between Law and Democracy" says that Twitter and other blogs, Facebook, emails, SMS messages, LinkedIn, Youtube and Flickr are ubiquitous forms of communication within modern society. The role of these tools in enabling individuals to express their political opinions, as well as whether and how social media should be regulated, has emerged as questions of considerable interest. However, the issue of locating social media within a possible conflict between regulation and democracy remains underexplored. Law is just one of the forces or 'regulators' that control and define systems such as the internet, the others being markets, architectures and norms.[2] Civil or political liberties within cyberspace will only be enhanced if these forces are democratic in nature.[3] This chapter will assess two broad propositions: first, that social media has the potential to enhance democratic participation, and secondly, that legal restrictions can curtail this opportunity. These topics are significant because the influence of social media is frequently overstated and, in debates where democracy is at stake, the desirability of regulatory controls is typically overlooked. Part one defines social media and explores the premise that social media is conducive to enhanced democracy. It also identifies some of the risks and dangers of relying on this particular medium as a means of political participation. Part two will illustrate sources of and solutions to contests between law and democracy by reference to the human right to freedom of expression. Permissible limitations and restrictions on the exercise of that right can be identified from the paradigm of international human rights law. Those considerations will inform an analysis of a posited conflict between law and democracy. Particular attention is given to recent developments within the United States, Europe, China, and Australia. There is an observable trend towards greater government regulation of social media within each of these jurisdictions for national security, law enforcement and other reasons. Underlying themes to be addressed include notions of individual liberty, conditions of access to and participation in social media, the permissibility of restrictions within a democratic society, sound regulatory development and ensuring government accountability.

I contend that, in order to accommodate competing policy priorities, the adoption of regulatory measures inevitably but necessarily impairs the enjoyment of human rights and constrains the civic potential offered by social media.

2.13 Chatterjee, Manjiri Miller and Kate Sullivan De Estrada (2017) 'Pragmatism'—and its promise as a medium of change—has a distinctive connotation in the context of India's foreign policy. In the post-Cold War era, a number of scholars within and outside India's foreign policy establishment have both identified and championed greater 'pragmatism'. A 'pragmatic' foreign policy implies a rejection of India's earlier reliance on Nehruvian 'idealism' or 'moral posturing' and, instead, a focus on power and material interests. Many argue that 'idealism', indelibly associated with the premiership of Jawaharlal Nehru, led to major foreign policy failures as well as the entrenchment of redundant policies. Thus, post-Cold War pragmatism is warmly welcomed by these scholars. Indeed, they argue that pragmatism represents the approach that India must follow in order to become a 'normal power that is no longer focused on transforming the world', and to emerge on the world stage as a materially powerful state in the twenty-first century. The discourse on pragmatism in Indian foreign policy—consistent with the post-Cold War scholarship and most evident in sections of India's print media—has experienced a resurgence since the assumption of the premiership by Narendra Modi in May 2014. Modi's election was heralded as a seminal moment for India's foreign policy. As one commentator pronounced: 'There is little question that Modi's foreign policy constitutes a departure from India's stances of the past.' These predictions of change have been based on hopes and alleged signs that Modi's approach to foreign policy-making will be even more pragmatic than that of previous leaders. Not only, it is said, will he bypass the long-held idealistic notions of Nehruvianism, he will also set aside cultural and religious ideologies or entrenched principles, specifically, his own party's Hindutva or Hindu nationalist ideology.

2.14 Kapur, Devesh (2009) Among the many factors that drive a country's foreign policy, the least understood is the role of public opinion. In any democracy, there is a presumption of some link, however weak and indirect, between public policy and public opinion, in so far as the latter represents voter preferences. But public opinion's links to foreign policy are more tenuous. In the Indian case there have been very few attempts to gauge public opinion on foreign policy issues, let alone to examine its effects on the country's foreign policy. This paper measures public opinion on Indian foreign policy through a survey of more than two hundred thousand households (the largest ever in India) and lays out some hypotheses on whether (and how) public opinion might affect Indian foreign policy in the future. The first section summarises key findings of literature on public opinion and foreign policy, which has been developed in the US. The next section examines some of the surveys on public opinion and Indian foreign policy.

2.15 Baum, Matthew A and Philip B K The Relationships Between Mass Media, Public Opinion, and Foreign Policy: Toward a Theoretical Synthesis, Cambridge, Harvard University, Democracy requires that citizens' opinions play some role in shaping policy outcomes, including in foreign policy. Yet, although the literature on public opinion and foreign policy has made great progress in recent decades, scholars have reached no consensus concerning what the public thinks, or thinks about, with respect to foreign policy; how it comes to hold those opinions or whether those opinions influence (or even should influence) foreign policy.

2.16 Rubenzer, Trevor (2017) This article is considered from Oxford Research Encyclopedia of Politics, while explaining social media, it refer to websites and other internet applications that enable users to create and share content with other users, as well as to react to such content in various ways.

As social media has become more accessible, in terms of both internet access and ease of use, it has become one means by which people, non-state actors, and governments can share their foreign policy priorities in an effort to receive feedback, engage in diplomacy, educate people, and attempt to influence foreign policy outcomes. Foreign policy practitioners and scholars have rushed to describe and begin to analyze the ways in which social media has become part of the foreign policy process. The social and political upheaval associated with the Arab Spring, some of which has been traced to both foreign and domestic use of social media outlets such as Facebook, Twitter, and YouTube, created a greater sense of urgency among those who seek a greater understanding of the impact of social media on foreign policy.

Thematically, much of the academic work concerning social media and foreign policy is conducted as part of the broader public diplomacy literature. Public diplomacy, which relates to efforts by international actors to engage with foreign publics in the pursuit of policy goals, can be advanced along a number of paths. However, given their accessibility, low cost, and ease of use, social media has become a critical tool for a wide variety of international actors running the gamut from governments to portions of civil society to terrorist groups such as Al-Qaeda and the Islamic State of Iraq Syria (ISIS, also known as the Islamic State of Iraq and the Levant or ISIS based in part on the group's territorial claims). Social media and foreign policy work can also be found in the political communication literature, in working papers and articles generated by foreign policy think tanks such as the Council on Foreign Relations, and in academic journals dedicated to area studies that often concentrate on specific episodes of social media used to influence foreign policy.

Theoretical development in the area of social media and foreign policy is fragmented across disciplines and approaches. Network theories focus on interactions between parts of a network (in this case a social network); network analysis methods are sometimes employed as part of this theoretical framework. Other theories in this area focus on traditional problems associated with collective action and how these problems can be overcome by removing barriers to communication and lowering the cost of some types of political action. Different theoretical perspectives are often accompanied by different empirical results. Results vary from findings of a profound impact of social media on foreign policy outcomes to skepticism of the role played by social media in the face of other, potentially confounding, factors. Keywords: social media, foreign policy, Arab Spring, public diplomacy, social network theory, YouTube, Facebook, Twitter

2.17 Wynton, El While investigating the impact of social media by Wynton in Japan it consider the cyber security and politics in Japan. This is an Electronic Thesis published by University of Arizona. In this thesis the advancement of technology and social media tools are considered in East Asia. It has created an opportunity for cyber-criminals to access information from individuals and corporations. Three of the most technologically and economically advanced nations in the world lie in East Asia and have a substantial amount of data in cyberspace. A large volume of sensitive and inadequately protected data is in this continuously growing cloud. This suggests the need for governments in the region to establish increased cyber-security legislation in order to protect national security interests. The purpose of this research is to investigate the impact of social media on cyber security and politics in East Asia with an emphasis on Japan. Research suggests that China and South Korea lead Japan in cyber-security, however, Japan is making great efforts in effectively securing its cyberspace. With the help of from the United States and other NATO allies, Japan has the ability and means to create an optimal cyber-defense infrastructure that matches its technology innovations.

2.18 Nurmi, Maria (2012) conducted a survey on social media communication of the Finnish mission abroad for her master thesis, in University of Jyvaskyla. She explained how social media is changing the way people communicate and how it influences the people. She focuses on the issues of stakeholders of communication and how to use social media for public relations. The missions have also implemented social media as a platform for their communication since 2010. She explained the need to evaluate social media and its use and how social media can offer.

She suggested that there is a need for re-evaluation of the theories of public relations due to the rise of social media and various tools, hence there is a need to assess the theories of dialogue. In addition, this research tested the applicability of the Communication Grid (van Ruler 2004) in the context of social media. The purpose is to offer some guidelines about social media communication in the context of public diplomacy. Thus, the theoretical framework in this study is built on public relations in social media and public diplomacy. Research data was collected by using triangulation, interview with the communication specialist from the Ministry for Foreign Affairs. A questionnaire was prepared to the missions and observations on the social media sites.

The results of this study suggest that there is a need for improvement in the dialogue of communication on the missions' social media. At the moment, it seems that the missions use social media rather as traditional media, than utilizing the potential for dialogue. Thus, the strategies of the Communication Grid were applicable in the social media communication of the missions but not fully taken advantage of. Social media is used by the missions mainly for information and persuasion strategies.

2.19 Baru, Sanjaya (2009) The Influence of Business and Media on Indian Foreign Policy, India.

Manmohan Singh was perhaps the first Indian Prime Minister to clearly articulate the rising influence of civil society and business in the making of Indian foreign policy. Turning a nineteenth century aphorism on its head, the Prime Minister seemed to suggest that it is no longer trade that "follows the flag", but "the flag" that follows trade. It is, of course, clear that this view of international relations is intimately related to the nature of society about which we are talking. It is only in democratic societies that civil society has any significant influence on the foreign policy.

Business interests could still influence foreign policy in non-democratic societies, if the regime in question has commercial, business, and wider economic interests to pursue through its foreign policy. But public opinion can shape foreign policy only by influencing domestic politics. Needless to add, business and media have for long been instruments of diplomacy, but this paper is not about diplomacy. Its purpose is to examine the influence of business and media on foreign policy. The interaction between people, in the form of migration, and between businessmen and merchants, through trade, has always been at the center of the relations between nations.

As the Nobel Prize economist and the guru of strategic economics, T. C. Schelling claimed, "Aside from war and preparations for war, and occasionally aside from migration, trade is the most important relationship that most countries have with each other." In an influential essay entitled "Trade Policy is Foreign Policy", Richard Cooper, took the view that whereas traditionally trade policy had dominated "high foreign policy", the Cold War had brought political issues to the fore and reduced the salience of business interests in shaping foreign policy. The end of the Cold War; the economic transformation of China; and the processes of globalization, accelerated by the Uruguay Round of multilateral trade negotiations and the spread of regional trade blocs, have raised the profile of business and economic factors in the foreign and strategic policy considerations of most nations.

The past decade has also witnessed increased global migration and the globalization of media, with new satellite technologies and the Internet making McLuhan's "global village" truly global. These trends have impacted on the choices available to Governments in dealing with national and international issues and bilateral, regional, and multilateral relations.

This has had its inevitable impact on India, which has been transformed this past decade by its increased economic openness. This, in turn, has shaped India's relations with the world economy and global communities.

2.20 Summary

From the above review of literature scanned for this project on the topic, social media and its impact on foreign policy making of India, it has been observed from the literature that social media does not impact India's foreign policy, however, people express their opinions on foreign policy through social media tools. Many times the facts spread on social media by people are fake and it has an impact on the public who are not aware of the fact.

REFERENCES

1. Vindaya Senadheera, Matthew Warren & Shona Leitch (2017), "Social media as an information system: improving the technological agility," *Enterprise Information Systems*, 11:4, 512-533, DOI: 10.1080/17517575.2016.1245872
2. Penni, Janice (2017), "The future of online social networks (OSN): A measurement analysis using social media tools and application," *Telematics and Informatics* 34 (2017) 498–517.
3. Dahibhate N.B. and Patil S.K., "Library and Information services using social media tools: need of the future," *Asia Pacific Journal of Library and Information Science*, Vol. 3, No. 2 (Jul–Dec 2013)
4. Bindra, Sukhwant S. (2004), "Domestic milieu of India and foreign policy making

process: a theoretical perspective," *The Indian Journal of Political Science*, Vol. LXV, No. 2, April-June, 2004

5. Schulz, Kerstin (2013), "Foreign Policy Involvement Matters: Towards an Analytical Framework Examining the Role of the Media in the Making of Foreign Policy," *Global Media Journal*, German Edition ISSN 2196-4807, Vol. 3, No.1, Spring/Summer 2013
6. Chanan, Naveh (2002), "Role of the media in foreign policy decision making: a theoretical framework," *Conflict and Communication online*, Vol. 1, No. 2, 2002 pp. 2-13
7. Mukherjee, Rohan and David M. Malone (2011), "Indian foreign policy and contemporary security challenges," *International Affairs* (Royal Institute of International Affairs 1944-), Vol. 87, No. 1 (January 2011), pp. 87-104, http://www.jstor.org/stable/20869612 (Accessed: 11-04-2017 08:59 UTC)
8. Barton, William P. (1950), "Indian Foreign Policy," *The Australian Quarterly*, Vol. 22, No. 4 (Dec., 1950), pp. 25-34, Published by: Australian Institute of Policy and Science Stable URL: http://www.jstor.org/stable/20633300 .
9. Cui Zhang, Charles and William Meadows (2012), "International Coverage, Foreign Policy, and National Image: Exploring the Complexities of Media Coverage. Public Opinion, and Presidential Agenda," *International Journal of Communication* 6 (2012), 76–95 1932–8036/20120076
10. Kapur, Ashok (1971), "Nuclear Weapons and Indian Foreign Policy: A Perspective," *The World Today*, Vol. 27, No. 9 (Sep., 1971), pp. 379-389 Published by Royal Institute of International Affairs Stable URL: http://www.jstor.org/stable/40394547 Accessed: 05-01-2016 20:12 UTC
11. Tully, Stephen (2014), "Social Media in the Conflict Between Law and Democracy Chapter," in *Law and Democracy* ANU Press, 2014.
12. Chatterjee, Manjiri Miller and Kate Sullivan De Estrada (2017), "Pragmatism in Indian foreign policy: how ideas constrain Modi," *International Affairs* 93: 1 (2017) 27–49, Published by Oxford University Press on behalf of The Royal Institute of International Affairs
13. Kapur, Devesh (2009), "Public opinion and Indian Foreign policy India review," *India Review*, Vol. 8, No. 3, July-September, 2009, pp. 1–27
14. Rubenzer, Trevor (2017), "Social Media and Foreign Policy," *World Politics Online*, Aug, 2017. DOI: 10.1093/acrefore/9780190228637.013.485
15. Wynton, El, *Social Media in Japan: An Investigation of the Impact Social Media Has on Cyber-Security and Politics in Japan*, Electronic Thesis, Publisher: University of Arizona.
16. Nurmi, Maria (2012), *Social media in Public Diplomacy: Survey on the social media communication of the Finnish missions abroad*, Master Thesis, Organizational Communication & Public Relations Department of Communication University of Jyväskylä
17. Baru, Sanjaya (2009), "The Influence of Business and Media on Indian Foreign Policy," *India Review*, Vol. 8, No. 3, July–September, 2009, pp. 266–285

CHAPTER III

An Overview of India's Foreign Policy 1947-2019

"A country that demands moral perfection in its foreign policy will achieve neither perfection nor security"

– Henry Kissinger

Foreign Policy does not exist in a cultural vacuum. It protects and promote its national interest. In the context of national security, it comprises the obligation to defend the country's national security, economic benefits from international trade and commerce, as also to enhance the effectiveness of its 'soft power' through propagation of its core cultural assets. Foreign policy paradigm is as deeply informed by its civilizational heritage as it is by modern ideas about national interest. Even policies that appear to be new contain ethos of themes that recur in history. The tool of Foreign policy is spread of communism. The main objective is to create more space or more options on a global level. Our foreign policy from Chanakya till Prime Minister Modi has developed in two concepts of autonomy and independence in decision making policy. Foreign policy has a keen interest to protect and promote the country's national interests. Basically it comprises the obligation to defend the country's national security and improve the productiveness of its 'soft power' through the action of widely spreading and promoting an idea of its core cultural assets. The goal of the country's foreign policy is to maintain international relations policy, consists of strategies chosen by the state to safeguard its national interests and to achieve its goals in international relations. India's foreign policy has evolved as a result of interplay between personalities, institutions, with theoretical determinants of foreign policy in general. To begin with the leadership responsible for evolution and development of India's foreign policy, the contribution of Pandit Jawaharlal Nehru is universally accepted and highly criticized for some major issues. If Gandhi is the father of modern Indian identity, Jawaharlal Nehru is indisputably the man who shaped India's foreign policy after Independence. The ideals and ambitions of India's first prime minister and foreign minister are referred to as 'Nehruvianism' and have left an indelible mark on India's world view, shaped under Nehru's stewardship from 1947 to 1964.[5]

However, he is known as the sole architect of the foreign policy of independent India. His foreign policy was based on two pillars of peaceful coexistence and non-violence. Mihael Brecher writes, "he was the philosopher, the architect, the engineer and the voice of his country's policy towards the outside world."[6] The making of India's foreign policy can be traced back to the 1920s, when the Congress Party started discussing basic determinants and principles of such a policy. Towards this end a small foreign department was created by the Indian Congress Party in 1925. In the 1920s new political thought on the right to independence of small nations was gaining currency. There were freedom struggles taking shapes in the colonized nations. Prominent freedom fighters identified India's struggle for independence to be in consonance with those of other nations and declared that India's efforts were part of the larger National Congress on international affairs. Jawaharlal Nehru declared that anti-imperialism and anti-racialism was the "kernel of our foreign policy". To understand India's foreign policy is very important to know its genesis, basic determinants and objectives. There are several factors who has played a very significant role in formulating India's foreign policy are its geographical size, location, historical backgrounds, experiences, traditions, state of economy, political institutions and the personality of the country's leadership. At the same time, Indians have had no qualms in anchoring external relations in 'Realism'. From ancient times, realist and idealist philosophies have coexisted in India and the post-Independence era is no exception. Indians reflect a cultural ability to entertain seemingly contradictory thoughts parallel to each other.

Belief in moral principles did not turn Indian leaders into pacifists. Notwithstanding messianic idealism, New Delhi has always recognized the importance of hard power. 'Messianic Idealism', reflecting the mantra of global peace, justice and prosperity has served as the strong moral component of India's foreign policy, inspired by the moral legacy of ancient Indian thought reiterated during the national struggle under Mahatma Gandhi. Proponents of this perspective believe that India is an example for the world and that India has the duty to proclaim that example for other nations. This element of Indian exceptionalism often forms part of India's view of itself and of the world.

3.1 India's Foreign Policy are Discussed into Four Phases

- 1947-1962
- 1962-1990
- 1990s and beyond
- 2014 – A Paradigm Shift?

3.2 1947-1962: Primary Stage of Indian Foreign Policy

Jawahar Lal Nehru India's first Prime Minister articulate independent India's foreign policy as the vice chairman of the Interim government declared: "We propose, as far as possible, to keep away from the power politics of groups, aligned against one another, which have led in the past to world wars and which may again lead to disasters on an even vaster scale...the world in spite of its rivalries and hatreds and inner conflicts, moves invariable towards closer cooperation and the building up of a world commonwealth. It is for this one World that free India will work, a world in which there is the free cooperation of free peoples, and no class or group exploits one another".[7] During his tenure Nehru's main concern was building a unified secular democratic state, own national interests, defending the territorial integrity of the nation, neighborhood policy and to stick on principle of panchsheel. Article 51 of the Indian Constitution also states that India is committed to international peace, security, cooperation and conciliation. By defining the concept of peace, Nehru told in parliament, after all peace is not peace, it is a quality: It is a way of doing things; it is the objective you want to reach. By peace, he did not mean the peace of any particular country, rather he was convinced that the success and failure of any foreign policy was sure to cast its influence on the whole world and from this point of view there was no doubt that India's foreign policy behavior was significant.[8] In short the key pillars of Nehruvianism were the concept of to regenerate India's great civilization, his belief in strong economic autarky, stand for support of international institutions in maintaining global order and world peace. Sarvepalli Gopal, son of India's second President Sarvepalli Radhakrishnan in his words, 'the foreign policy of a newly independent nation does not emerge overnight' and 'with the general directions clear in his mind, Nehru set about building up the foreign policy of India brick by brick, in the process discarding the generalizations which had taken the place of rigorous thought.'[9] Nehru emphasis an independent peaceful foreign policy where national security was the main concern. He use to address his people that our internal party matter divides us so ignore these conflicts and take responsibility of the leadership not only in India else a large part of Asia. In the early 1950s Asia was going through a volatile situation. "Nehru faced the first violent clash of the USA-USSR Cold War with the 1950-1953 Korean War. The French –led conflict in Vietnam was underway at the same time. The Civil war in China had just ended, but the future of the Chinese Nationalist government in Taiwan was unclear. The Chinese occupation of Tibet in 1950 was a potentially destabilizing factor."[10] When China entered Tibet, Nehru made traditional security arrangements with Himalayan kingdoms rather than taking measures to ensure that the Chinese aggression was internationally confronted. Nehru ditched his minded idealism at the global level in favor of pragmatic realism at the regional level. He signed the first three treaties with immediate neighbor's i.e. with Bhutan, Sikkim and Nepal. "Nehru also personally signed a friendship treaty with Afghanistan in 1950. Nehru was signaling India's enduring interest in Afghanistan, notwithstanding the changed geopolitics after the partition."[11]

Beyond the immediate neighborhood, Nehru wanted India to established country not only in Asia infect on the global stage. He confessed that India's military and economically condition is not able to stand in front of superpowers. Nehru's was trying to strengthen peace, disarmament and economic cooperation with his Non-alignment policy.

Non-alignment – the notion of aligning with neither superpower while maintaining friendship with both and adopting positions on different international issues not because of alignment but on a case by case basis- appeared to be the way out. Michael Edwardes refers to non-alignment as Nehru's 'doctrine of defense by friendship', a policy that appealed to Nehru on both practical and moral grounds.[12] Nehru's panchsheel and non-alignment policy were reasonably successful until the India–China War 1962. This war has proved him failed in many contexts. Nehru's foreign policy was thoroughly based on peace and non-violence but the Chinese did not reciprocate him as India wanted. They took advantage of 'Hindi-Chini bhai bhai' rhetoric. It is often argued that Nehru ignore many other major tasks in his foreign policy within the nation like consolidating the new India and ensuring its security. "At the same time, advocating a foreign policy with a moral and idealistic dimension came in direct variance with the existing values of the major powers."[13]

3.3 1962-1990: Idealism to Realism?

After defeat of 1962 war with China Indian policy makers were no choice but to rethink our foreign policy. If we take a broad scenario from 1947 until 1962, we will find few shifts in foreign policy.

- These were India's role in multilateral institutions and particularly in United Nations peacekeeping operations;
- Commitment and propagation of Non-Aligned Movement;
- Significant contribution toward the process of decolonization.

Till the late 1950s Nehru "by virtue of being Prime minister of India, the largest democracy in the world, was able to make a significant contribution to the theory and practice of international relations."[14] Post-1962 policy has changed in different factors like global, regional and personal level. India started search for military hardware from the developed countries and United Nations entertained military cooperation with India after 1962 war. After China attack Indian parliament debated the option of going in for nuclear weapons but Prime Minister Lal Bahadur Shastri was discarded the idea of nuclear weapons. Later on Indira Gandhi, who succeeded Lal Bahadur Shastri, had asked for a nuclear guarantee from the super powers without any success. "In the aftermath of this failure, Prime Minister Gandhi authorized India's Subterranean Nuclear explosions Project (SNEP) which culminated in India's first nuclear test of May 1974."[15] Now India's foreign policy was shifting in two rival sight. India understand military power with the victory in the 1971 war, India established itself as the undisputed dominant power within the subcontinent. The 1980s saw a minor changes to reshape Indian Foreign Policy after Mrs. Indira Gandhi's death. Now scenario is changing. In 1985, Gorbachev, who came to power in the USSR, was willing to reach out and wanted to bond with United States. India still was constrained to reorient its policy towards China. In 1988 the USSR and Afghanistan had a conflict and USSR wanted to throughout Afghanistan and US supported to Afghanistan Jihadis. Soviet has to exited foreseeable. After this in Punjab and Jammu Kashmir terrorist moments happened and Pakistan was responsible for that. Pakistan was establishing nuclear country with the help of China. During the same time Sri Lanka was facing tremendous situation due to the rise of civil war. Now India's foreign policy took various dimensions of world order: continued support for decolonization and leadership of weaker state in the international system. After decisive victory in 1971 war. India established itself as the undisputed dominant power within the subcontinent.

Era of 1980s was a marginal reshape of India's foreign policy towards the internal security situation which was affected after assassination of Mrs. Gandhi in 1984. India and USSR equations affecting after joining Gorbachev in 1985, now previous relationship was getting sour. Apparently, the USSR was willing to work with the United States and also seek to improve relations with China. In 1985 Rajiv Gandhi became the Prime Minister of India with stable government. He was establishing relations in the field of technology and opening new space of foreign relations. His vision was to maintain good relation with US and Soviet. His visit to the U.S. in 1985 enabled clearing of Indo-U.S. mutual apprehensions though it did not very clear in availability of the latest technology. "India and the U.S. maintained minimal realistic and 'positive orientation' right till the end of Gandhi's term in 1989."[16] During Prime Minister Rajiv Gandhi period relations were improving, resulted Moscow enabled access to major military hardware like fighter aircraft, tanks, ships and submarines. But soon relationship with USSR started deteriorating due to difference of opinion on crucial issues like collective security in Asia. Here Soviet was not supportive on Kashmir issue.

Significant reorientation of India's foreign policy was the hallmark of the 80s. Its reoriented India's engagements with the United States as well as with China. "Perhaps the most fundamental shift in foreign policy was Rajiv Gandhi's recognition that India's modernization and economic development required greater and more adroit engagement with the world and that foreign policy had to be geared towards achieving these objectives."[17]

3.4 1990s and Beyond: Constructional Changes

An intense interest has been generated in India's foreign policy over the last one and a half decade. India's actions at global and regional level, especially those which directly affect socio-economic and socio-political level progress are being scrutinized very intensely. So far India was seen as a champion and defender of the developing world. However, a perceptible change started appearing in the orientation of India's foreign policy beginning with 1991. C Raja Mohan describes this change "about the shift from being a leader of the 'Third World' to the recognition of the potential that India could emerge as a great power in its own right."[18]

C. Raja Mohan discover four major structural changes in India's foreign policy orientation post 1991. Those changes are as follows:

- Move towards a capitalist model of society.
- Economic orientation of foreign policy.
- India's rise on the global stage.
- Renunciation of anti-West sentiment.

This period of foreign policy evolution started since 1990-re-engagement with the major powers after the Cold war, rediscovery of the extended neighborhood in Asia, Africa and the Indian Ocean, and an attempted redefinition of its ties to immediate neighbors in the subcontinent. It concludes with a brief discussion of the enduring debate in India on the concepts of non-alignment and strategic autonomy. With the disintegration of the Soviet Union in 1991, India's orientation towards state–socialism began to evaporate. New challenges posed by globalization drew the attention of India's political elite. The balance of payment crisis forced a change in the foreign policy strategy. The collapse of the Soviet system, as well as the economic success of the 'Asian Tigers' forced a re-think of Indian foreign policy and refocused India's attention on the East, at least in principle.

New Delhi newly remembered again Jawaharlal Nehru's reference to Southeast Asia as Greater India."[19] After the collapse of the Soviet Union India started expanding relations with U.S., the European Union, Russia, China, Japan, Israel, Brazil, South Africa as a policy of multi-alignment. In front of Unipolar world India launches new initiatives such as the 'Look East' policy to engage the miracle economies of ASEAN. "Positive initiatives undertaken to boost trade and improve economic relations saw the two way trade with South East Asia grow up to US$ 6 billion in between 1996-97."[20] Nehru believed that India was destined to aspire for its great civilization and gigantic geography in one of the prime regions of the world, the mind-set of policy makers remained rooted in the erstwhile theories of anti-imperialism, universal brotherhood and peaceful coexistence till 1990 primarily due to lack of economic resources. After Oil crisis in 1973 most developing countries had decided to integrate with international market but India still took remained. "Much of the developing world had made considerable economic advances, leaving the South Asia way behind. While the rhetoric on the third world remained popular, the policy orientation in India's external relations increasingly focused on India's own self-interest. There was a growing perception, flowing from the Chinese example, that if India could sustain high growth rates it had a chance to gain a place at the international high table."[21] During 1990 India's foreign policy focuses on three themes to re-engagement with the major power after the Cold War, rediscovery of the extended neighborhood in Asia, Africa and the Indian Ocean, and an attempted redefinition of its ties to immediate neighbors in the subcontinent.

It concludes with a brief discussion of the enduring debate in India on the concepts of non-alignment and strategic autonomy. Prime Minister Rajiv Gandhi opened the space for commercial engagement during the era of state-led socialism. During the Cold War, India's foreign policy was originated, how to deal with the dangers of confrontation and occasional collusion between America and Russia. Past two and a half decades, India still struggling good relations between the US and China. The end of the Cold War ASEAN (Association of South-East Asian Nations) was a good opportunity for India to recast its regional relations to set a benchmark for its own liberalization. Prime Minister P.V. Narshimha Rao turned out to be one of the most successful Indian diplomatic initiatives after the Cold war which was reflected in the Look East policy. After the breakdown of the Soviet Union, Rao also quickly established diplomatic ties with all the new republics in Central Asia.

By the turn of the millennium, all of the subcontinent's adjoin regions acquired a new prominence for India's foreign policy. "Rao was indeed faced with a difficult and troublesome international environment when he became Prime Minister. The de facto strategic alliance with Moscow, that had hitherto guaranteed India's security, was in shambles. The Indo-Soviet link, for long perceived as central to Indian diplomatic behavior, had become history. Worse were Pakistani pretensions, which had been claiming-unofficially since 1987 and officially since 1992—that it possessed all the components of a nuclear bomb, and the know how to assemble one. Though Rao never conducted a nuclear test, there appears to exist a general consensus of opinion that it was he who had really operationalized the nuclear programme."[22] Under supervision in Vajpayee and V.P. Singh, India's commitment with the comprehensive neighborhood widened and strengthened. Indian economy has changed in a good pace, commercial links with all the neighboring regions grew rapidly. India sign free trade agreements with ASEAN, its trade with East Asia overtook that with America and Europe, India signed Comprehensive Economic Partnerships with Singapore, South Korea, and Japan. 'Idealism' to 'realism' has given systemic transitions to India's foreign policy's framework. Initially Indian foreign policy opted whole oppressed humanity, freedom in all aspects, social, cultural, economic, and political. India was trying to keep his policy to becoming a world leader by setting new ideas and principles of peaceful coexistence and multilateralism in order to transform the world. After 1991, India has to changed his ideology and had to take on to the demand of globalization.

Even though Prime Minister Manmohan Singh did attempt to carry on the Vajpayee legacy, the foreign policy orientation did not change much during the UPA regime as the government was constrained by the coalition politics to introduce radical changes in India's international affairs. In ten years UPA governments tried to achieve development and economic integration with the world but wasn't successful. FDI was One of the major reasons marginalization of foreign policy issues by domestic policies and constraints. Party's top leaders was not strong enough to prevail upon the states and regional interests as was seen in the case of west Bengal Chief Minister Mamata Banerjee scutting what could have been a historic deal with Bangladesh on water sharing.

3.5 A Paradigm Shift

In 2014 parliament elections Bhartiya Janta Party came in power with regional party alliances namely NDA. BJP suggests in its election manifesto that they will bring a paradigm shift in the country's foreign policy. "BJP believes a resurgent India must get its rightful place in the comity of nations and international institutions. The vision is to fundamentally reboot and reorient the foreign policy goals, content and process, in a manner that locates India's global strategic engagement in a new paradigm and on a wider canvass, that is not just limited to political diplomacy, but also includes our economic, scientific, cultural, political and security interests, both regional and global, on the principles of equality and mutuality, so that it leads to an economically stronger India, and its voice is heard in the international fora."[23] In a very short time of period Prime Minister Modi has visited most of the countries to give new vision to India's foreign policy. NDA government has redefined India's foreign policy priorities, and the level of external engagement has also gone up. Though prime minister asserted lack of experience in foreign policy but he uplifted India's profile in global affairs. He acceded to a – Neighborhood First policy. Modi said that the future of any country is influenced by the state of its Neighborhood. He understands that unless India's Neighborhood is peaceful, the development goals it sets for itself are unattainable.

Towards this end India is engaging each one of its Neighbors more vigorously. He implemented his idea the first sign was to invite all of the heads of all the SAARC countries to the new government swearing in ceremony in May 2014. Another step he took with Bangladesh India has ratified the long-delayed land boundary agreement putting an end to their disputes over boundary. Prime Minister first visit was Bhutan in 16th-17th June, 2014. He promised to help Bhutan with capacity building in the field of technology and education sector. He also agreed to build another hydroelectric power station in Bhutan. Scholarships worth Rs. 2 crores to Bhutanese students coming to India for higher studies. Modi signed a free trade agreement with Bhutan, exempting their goods from taxes. So, he basically gave them an advantageous access to Indian Markets. Instead of this agreement Bhutanese ensure that they are not a party to the insurgency efforts. Co-Development of 600MW Kholongchu Hydro-electric project which would help India provide power to its north-eastern states. Talented Bhutanese students would come to India and increase our talented human resource base. India signed treaty with Nepal after a gap of 23 years to promote mutual benefits in economic, trade and multiple uses of water resources. India was the key country involved in responding to Nepal earthquake. The 1950's India-Nepal Friendship Treaty had said that, Nepal has to take India's permission in military and foreign policy matters. With this statement, Modi ended that perception of India being the hegemonic meddler in Nepal without having to do much. This was done to keep a check on growing Chinese Influence in Nepal and make Nepal an ally. In return India got Trust of the Nepali political community regarding India's goodwill in helping Nepal and Hydel Power Projects which will help India in its power needs and be beneficial to Nepal in generating revenue. Prime Minister has updated his strategic partnership with Japan in strategic global partnership. Prime Minister vision, to invest in smart cities, industrial corridors, power generation, bullet trains, manufacturing and even nuclear technology for civilian use. Following our 1999 nuclear tests, Japan had banned several Indian Companies. India also build multiple partnerships to develop and maintain its role as an important security guarantor in Indian Ocean. United States of America is emerging as India's most important bilateral relationship. The strategic convergence between the two countries is outlined in the vision for the Indo-pacific which was released during President Obama's second visit to India in January 2015. US is primary security Guarantor in Indian Ocean. Thus, a partnership with the US and its Indo pacific allies – Japan, South Korea and Australia is seen to be beneficial for India's global aspirations.

Economic traction is also growing between the two countries. The US is now India's second largest trade partner. India has an uneasy relationship with China. India's largest trading partner. The territorial dispute remains unsolved and it periodically boils over into incidents of friction. In 2014, China offered to finance 30 per cent of India's targeted infrastructure plan. During China president Xi visit to India 2014, China committed investments worth $20 billion over 5 years. The next important bilateral agreement is with Russia. India has gone beyond most countries in support of Russia. Government of India has started buildup relation towards east to south east Asia. Government of India is trying good relation with Middle East Countries because they are the largest source of energy.

About 70 per cent of oil in India comes from this region. India got new emerging country as Iran in the field of trade. Government has been strengthening its ties with Israel which is an important supplier of defense equipment and technology in India. While government policies are designed to attract foreign capital and technology and seek foreign markets for Indian products. They are also geared towards a closer linkage of regional stability, peace and prosperity.

Despite PM persona and initiative, Indian foreign policy continues to be driven by the bureaucracy, which is not always strategic in its thinking and often ideologically dogmatic. This is perhaps true, especially with respect to the South Asia policy. Policy on South Asian Neighbors such as Bangladesh, Nepal, Sri Lanka, Myanmar and Afghanistan, and even Pakistan, should be reviewed. Indian provinces and states should be encouraged to become critical players in foreign policy. India-China relations will be one of the major challenges for India in the months to come. Relations with Russia also need to be revisited in the light of the changing geo-political landscape. The possible emergence of the G2 (China and US) can pose a significant challenge to Indian interests and therefore should be carefully monitored and handled.

3.6 CONCLUSION

India is going through the transition of becoming a global power from the regional power. Such a transition demands that India improves its relations with regional as well as global powers and at the same time act in a manner that supports its status. A healthy growth of economy for the last two decades have provided maneuver space for the Indian state to chart its independent course in international relations. India's foreign policy is therefore the most important tool to bring about change in perception of the rest of the world by visible actions across the globe.

REFERENCES

1. Bava, Ummu (2018), *India's Role in the Emerging World Order FES Briefing Paper 4*, March 2007, p. 4, (accessed on 24th December, 2018)
2. C. Raja Mohan (2018), "Modernizing the Raj Legacy," http://www.india-seminar.com/2012/629_c_raja_mohan.htm,India Seminar Jan 2012 (accessed on March, 2018)
3. C. Raja Mohan (2006), *India's New Foreign Policy Strategy*, Draft paper presented at a Seminar in Beijing by China Reform Forum and the Carnegie Endowment for International Peace, Beijing, May 26, 2006
4. Country Overview, The World Bank, http://www.worldban.org/en/country/india/overview (accessed on 30th December 2018)
5. Deelip Laxman, and I.S. Vidyasaga (2014), "Contribution of Pandit Jawaharlal Nehru to Indian Foreign Policy," *Golden Research Thoughts Impact Factor*: 2.2052 (UIF), Vol. 3, Issue 11, May 2014
6. Dixit, J.N. (2003), "Jawaharlal Nehru: Architect of India's Foreign Policy," in *Nehru Revisited*, Mumbai: Nehru Centre, 2003, pp. 58-60
7. Dixit, J.N. (2001), *India's Foreign Policy and It's Neighbours*, Gyan Publishing House, New Delhi, 2001, p. 21
8. Gunguli, Sumit and Pardseshi Manleet S. (2018), "Exploring Sixty Years of India's Foreign Policy," http://www.tandfonline.com/loi/find20, (accessed on 19th December, 2018)
9. Harish Kapur (2009), *Foreign Policies of India's Prime Ministers*, New Delhi: Lancer, 2009, http://www.transnational-perpectives.org/transnational/articles495.pdf, (accessed 10 March, 2019)
10. Kumar, Atul (2018), "An Historical Perspective On Indian Foreign Policy," *World Affairs*, Spring 2010, Vol. 14, http://www.India. Journals.com, (accessed on 23rd December, 2018)
11. Michael, Brecher (1966), "Nehru: A Political Biography," cited by V.B. Karnik, in *India's Defence and Foreign Policies*, Bombay, Manaktalas, 1966, p. 10
12. Ministry of External Affairs, INDIA Bilateral Treaties and Agreements, Vol. 7, http://www.mea.gov.in/Portal?legal/Treaties Doc/RU7181557.pdf, (accessed on 21st December, 2018)
13. Mishra, Pramod (2003), India and South East Asia: Relevance of Look East Policy, in *India's Foreign Policy Emerging Challenges and Paradigms*, Vol. 2, Kalinga Publications 2003, p. 313.
14. Mukherjee Rohan and David M. Malone, "Indian Foreign Policy and Contemporary Security Challenges," *International Affairs* 87:1, 2011 p. 87, https://scholar.princeton.edu/sites/default/files/Mukherjee_IA_0.pdf, (accessed on 23rd March, 2018)

15. Pande, Aprana (2018), *From Chanakya to Modi, Evaluation of India's Foreign Policy*, Harper Collins Publishers, 2017, pp. 25-26 (accessed on 21st December, 2018)
16. Pandya, Archana and David M. Malone, *India's Asia Policy: A Late Look East*, ISAS Special Report No.02-25 August 2010
17. Publication Division, Govt. of India (1967), *Jawaharlal Nehru's Speeches*, Vol. 1 (September 1946-May 1949), Publications Division, Government of India, 1967, pp. 2-3
18. Raghavan Srinath, "At the Cusp of Transformation: The Rajiv Gandhi Years, 1984-1989," The Oxford Handbook of Indian Foreign Policy, p. 118
19. Shah, A.B. (2018), India's Defense and Foreign Policy: Realism and Idealism-in-international-affairs-history-essay.php. (accessed on March 30th 2018)

CHAPTER IV

Foreign Policy Decision Making in India

4.1 INTRODUCTION

Decision making in foreign policy is the very complex and multi -stage procedure. To make this process successful multiple agencies, institutions and factors are working and each are dealing range of issues of different subjects and agendas. The Prime Minister plays a key role in decision making process being an important factors. He/she has been the centre figure in foreign policy decision making. During the time of Nehru, The Prime Minister's Secretariat (as PMO was called earlier) became the centre of Foreign policy Decision making, as Nehru was handling both the MEA and PMO simultaneously. In addition, the leadership of Nehru was so influential, that the role of the cabinet was minimal and mostly accepted Nehru's views on administration. Basically, political parties (ruling party) are the main actors who plays a very decisive role in foreign policy decision making process. Later on, in the next government several changes in the government. In spite of these changes, it continues to remain the centre of governance and plays an important role in the planning and formulation of national and international policies, security (internal and external) issues of India.

Apart from this there are various institutions and agencies are involved the process of foreign policy making and their multiple role. In this chapter will discuss how actors, agencies and institutions are playing a critical role and how they can affect nations foreign policy? Though the Ministry of External Affairs is playing a crucial role in India's external relation, there are other agencies such as The Cabinet and Cabinet Committees, The Prime Minister's Office, The National Security Council, The Strategic Policy Group, The National Security Advisory Board, Joint Intelligence Committee, Ministry of Commerce and Industry, Parliament and Pressure Groups and Media. Along with these various institutions NGOs and Think tanks are also contributing their enormous part.

4.2 Actors of Foreign Policy

Actors of foreign policy are multiple and well defined. It can be as a person, political parties, interest groups and trade association's foreign policy making. Usually foreign policy actors are divided into two categories-state actors and non-state actors.

1. **States actors** – have typically been considered the main (and for a long period, the only) actors in Foreign Policy.
2. **Non-state actors** – Non-state actors comprises various actors such as Sub-State actors, International Non-Governmental Organisations (INGOs), International Governmental Organisations (IGOs), Economic Agents and Media.
3. **INGOs** – They operate as actors in Foreign Policy mainly through their ability to influence other Foreign Policy actors. They can be divided into different categories: Regional Organizations-These include the European Union (EU), the African Union (AU), the Organisation of American States (OAS), the Association of South-East Asian Nations (ASEAN), etc.
4. **Ethno-cultural organizations** – Open to members sharing a common cultural, linguistic, ethnic, religious or historical background such as the Commonwealth of Nations (CoN), the Organization of the Islamic Conference (OIC), the League of Arab States (LAS) etc.
5. **Economic organizations** – The economic organizations are IGOs composed of sovereign States and that have as their primary goal that of promoting certain economic objectives. These organisations include the International Monetary Fund (IMF), The World Bank (WB), World Trade Organisation (WTO) and the Organisation for Economic Cooperation and Development (OECD), amongst others.

6. **Collective Security Organizations** – These organizations work to the prevention of and counteraction to military threats or attacks to its members. As a consequence, if a third State or party attacks one of the members of the organization, all other Member States are committed to support the attacked member, the degree of commitment depending on the organization. The list of Collective Security Organisations includes the North Atlantic Treaty Organisation (NATO), the Organisation for Security and Cooperation in Europe (OSCE), the Collective Security Treaty Organisation (CSTO), the Shanghai Cooperation Organisation (SCO), etc. Additionally, some global or regional IGOs may have a security dimension, as is the case of the United Nations or the European Union.
7. **Media** – The role of media is essential to shape national/trans-national public opinion. Last year traditional media have been complemented and social networks such as Twitter, Facebook, etc are playing very important role in today's scenario. Thus, actors and non-actors plays very important and multiple role in foreign policy decision making. There are few more non-actors, who are not falling directly in the above mentioned list but they have contributed to shape, along history and essential developments in the subject of Foreign policy. These include criminal, ethnic and religious groupings. Apparently, those organizations have shaped international developments for more than a decade now. The most prominent examples are Al-Qaeda, global Islamist organization.

4.3 INSTITUTIONS INVOLVED IN FOREIGN POLICY IN INDIA

There are various Institutions are working for India's Foreign policy decision making process. Their nature of work is to deal with comprehensive account on the structure, functions and the role of these agencies on India's foreign policy decision making process. Ministry of External Affairs is the primary institution of foreign policy decision making in India. Along with this other important agencies such as the Cabinet, Ministry of Defense, Ministry of Commerce and Industry, National Security Council, Prime Minister's Office and Parliament also are contributing significantly for the planning and formulation of India's foreign policy.

4.4 Ministry of External Affairs

It is the primary institution of foreign policy decision making in India. It is the oldest and foremost department of Government and dealing external affairs of the country. It is involved in foreign policy decision making process, evaluation of Ministry of External Affairs structure and organizing of Ministry of External Affairs, territorial division, how ministry of affairs functions like any other foreign office, ministry of external affairs functions like other foreign office, ministry of external affairs formulate plan and manage India's external relations with other nations and taking care of India's national interest at the global stage from the other nations. Planning and formulation of foreign policy is the department where external affairs deal with the increasing complexity of contemporary international relations in foreign policy devolvement's policy planning. However, until 1663 there was no such dedicated foreign policy planning section in India under the Ministry of External Affairs. After the Military disaster of 1962 war, the East Asia Research and Coordination Division was created in 1963 to conduct research and planning on China, which was later institutionalized as the current research division in 1965. Since then, the Policy Planning and Research–Division (As it is called now) is engaged in planning and formulation of India's foreign and strategic policy. Through the division, the MEA awards research projects to the academia, think-tanks, research organizations, and foreign policy institutes of India And assists them financially to organize seminars, conferences and studies to deliberate on various facets of India's external relations. The MEA prepares a Monthly Summary of important developments and global events for the Cabinet and senior officials of Government of India, on which the government prepares its future policy.

4.5 The Cabinet and Cabinet Committees

The important decision on issues of national and international affairs are decided by the cabinet in the Parliamentary system by the Indian government. Ruling party's senior most members selected for the

Council of Ministers, including the Prime Minister itself. Here cabinet decides to takes decisions on subjects of national importance and approves the policy proposals. Prime Minister, he /she use to calls the meeting of the cabinet members to discuss major issues and follow the policy accordingly. The composition of the cabinet is the premier section of the Council of minister, selected from both the houses of the parliament. Cabinet Secretary is the head of the Cabinet Secretariat who is rather a senior civil servant of the Government of India appointed to assist the cabinet in policy making and implementation. Cabinet secretary deals all matters related to the cabinet committees and promote the inter-ministerial matters which is divided into four different categories such as to get approvals and draft legislations require the Cabinet's approval before implementations or carry out necessary changes to the draft-proposal. Recommended all major appointments –Cabinet appoints the head of the major administrative and judicial institutions including Governors, Ambassadors, Chief Justice and other judges of the Supreme courts, Attorney–General and various top most appointment done by the cabinet. Other important task of Cabinet is to Settle Interdepartmental Disputes. The cabinet is to resolve facilitate interdepartmental coordination which generally, the cabinet adopts the middle path or the synthesized approaches to please both during the time of dispute settlement. Coordination of Developmental Activities is the core of the Council of Ministers and the senior most executive body, Cabinet is directly involved and failure of government policies. The 'sails together and sinks together' provision leaves no option for the cabinet than to lead the government and guide the developmental activities. Hence, the cabinet coordinates between the departments and ministries and provides all necessary helps to complete the pending tasks. It supervises recent ongoing works and guides them for its implementation.

4.6 Role of Cabinet in Foreign Policy Decision Making

The role of the Cabinet is very essential in foreign policy making and to clear up (solve) the foreign policy crisis. Apart from this India's internal and external security issues in alliance with Ministry of Home Affairs and Ministry of Defense respectively. The formation and policy making of the cabinet has become the product of political bargaining and negotiation. This is the top most decision making body of the government, which control the external and internal relations of the country by giving necessary directions. Prime Minister has the most trustworthy members in his /her cabinet committee, where he/she use to call urgent meetings to discuss in any crisis where the issues are put up for discussion and the members put their views and opinions. After the discussion the cabinet takes the appropriate decision to resolve the issues. Cabinet Committees have been setup the cabinet in policy formulation, coordination and supervision of the government. Committees are responsible to resolve the inter departmental conflict and ensure greater cooperation among the ministers and departments. Cabinets are the main source, who will decide to pass suggestions and recommendations for decision making to reject and incorporate the suggestions.

4.7 Role of the Cabinet Committees on Foreign Policy

Though none of the cabinet committee deals with the subject of foreign affairs directly, it does not mean that foreign affairs remain out of its preview. Moreover, Administrative Reform Commission used recommendation to setup a Cabinet Committee of Foreign Affairs, which was eventually played down by the government. In spite of that cabinet committees are indirectly involved to deal with the issues related to foreign policy and take important steps on the matter of India's external relations. Economic and national security issues, which are bound to affect the conduct of India's foreign relations, cabinet committees take care of issues too. The weapon procurement or technology transfer which is the subject of external security committees is directly linked to the foreign affairs, where the diplomatic negotiations are highly essential. On the further side the cabinet committees also work together to resolve the despites and promote India's national interest by making several policies. Officially cabinet committee does not near to been formed to look after the issues of foreign affairs but indirectly they have challenges to deal with it. Committee keeps an eye on matters of World trade organisation to resolve issues related to India's concern at WTO, development on the field of global trade and takes action accordingly to promote India's Foreign Trade. Hence, indirectly committee keeps an eye related to the matter of foreign economic affairs. Instead of handling and dealing with the enormous and significant issues, cabinet committees were not shown positive results. Their meetings are not organized regularly and most of the important matter were not discussed. Therefore, the cabinet committees gradually become less institutionalized and more polarized infect it has lost its importance in today's scenario.

4.8 The Prime Minister's Office

The Prime Minister plays a crucial role in the politico-administrative system of the country and oversees the day-to-day function of the Union Government. Prime Minister is assisted by the Prime Minister's Office (PMO). Observing the progress of development activates, the PMO passes necessary information to Prime Minister so that he/she can take his own decision at time of need.

4.9 Role of Prime Minister in Foreign Policy Decision Making

The Prime Minister and his office one of the most powerful institutions in Indian foreign policy decision making process mechanism. Prime Minister is responsible for the planning, formulating and execution of all internal and external policies. Prime Minister remains his/her decision as a deciding factor on any policy formulation. Country's successful foreign policy depends on the degree of the Ministry of the administrative coordinator between the PMO is to coordinate the different ministries and put extra efforts to clear administrate obstacles on clear administrate obstacles on the matters of foreign affairs and ensures the action of making the best resources of the national gain. Before implementation of foreign policy and national security matters, Prime Minister use to go through and after his approval, cabinet pass those matters for implementation. PMO is put in charge to approve the proposals for the appointment of Indian heads of Missions aboard. The Prime Minister becomes the center of the diplomatic relations He/she signs the international treaties and agreements with other nations. The National Security advisory who used to be the Principal Secretary to the Prime Minister provides necessary advice to the Prime Minister in matters of foreign and security affairs. Thus, Prime Minister is, in the matter of foreign policy, becomes the central figure when he/she shows personal interest in international affairs and the decision-making constraint within the PMO.

4.10 The National Security Council

The National Security Council (NSC) is the apex advisory body to the Government of India which gives advice to the Prime Minister on the matter related to the security issues, foreign policy, defense policies. Those policies directly or indirectly affect India's national interest, like policies on economic and energy security.

4.11 The Strategic Policy Group

This is the top most decision-making body group who is responsible for formulating and implementing India's strategic policies. Top most bureaucrats of who take the major decision at the time of crisis. They are responsible to formulate India's long- and short-term strategic blueprints also it coordinates different ministries, departments and agencies with respect to national security matters.

4.12 The National Security Advisory Board

The National Security Advisory Board is formed to give advice to the government for national security and developments matter. Prime minister and consists of persons use to head this board where they talk on strategic policy, Defense and national security, economic development, science and technology.

4.13 Joint Intelligence Commerce and Industry

Intelligence plays a very crucial role in the successful formulation of an effective Foreign Policy. These intelligence agencies are almost every modern world has who collects much firsthand information on various matters related to foreign policy. To control security threats with its neighbours as well terrorist organizations, India has set up multiple intelligence agencies to control internal and external threats.

4.14 Ministry of Defense

Ministry of Defense (MoD) is actively participates in decision making process and the government has to take permission before taking any decision on matters related to defense and national security issues from MoD.

4.15 THE PARLIAMENT

As per the Indian Constitution, Parliament is the supreme legislative body has the absolute power to make policies on any item under the union list, including foreign affairs. Parliament is the centre of governance and plays an important role in shaping India's external relation in the context of foreign policy making.

4.16 ROLE OF THE PARLIAMENT ON FOREIGN POLICY MAKING

Parliament is the supreme position who plays a unique role in the administrative and institutional hierarchy. Defense and foreign affairs, can pass any law to facilitate the implementation of International irrespective of the distribution of power between center and states, controlling budgetary allotment and passing necessary resolution along with these Parliament has several standing committees that play a major role in formulating the better country's administrative, keeping tracking record of the performance of the ministry Parliament has setup two important committees – the Standing Committee of the External Affairs (SCEA) and the Standing Committee on Defense (SCD), who has many ways to influence the external policies of India. In current scenario along with so many responsibilities and lengthy process, it seems that the role of Parliament has been neglected and pushed to play the role of a secondary agency in decision making.

4.17 PRESSURE GROUPS AND MEDIA

Pressure Groups and Media are the voice of non-political groups, associations and organizations. They are an important source of influence in shaping government policies like other political process to make policy formulation. Groups like business houses, arms lobby groups, International Non-Governmental Organizations, overseas Indian religious and cultural associations are some of the organizations that actively work to influence India's Foreign policy.

4.18 Procedures of Making Foreign Policy in India

Process of decision making in foreign policy is a very complex in nature and needs interplay between various institutions and agencies along with the number of individual actors. It is a very tough to reach a conclusion on any matter in today's scenario because the process of foreign policy decision making is politicized. In policy making process all the decision is taken out of consensus of the agencies / organizations instead of logical outcome. Sometimes in few cases decision can be rational and effective. Even policy makers say that India's foreign policy behavior has been reactive rather than proactive. Hence, the Decision-Making policies came out to be defensive. Domestic, international environments and leadership quality are also very influential on this process. At the time of Independent India Nehru was whole soul of Foreign Policy decision making process. He had a small group of members to assist him. It was globally visible during the 1950s and 1960s when Nehruvian ideology was the driving force of India's foreign policy. This time foreign policy decision mostly driven by ideology. But gradually time changed, instead of ideology democratic and pluralistic trend took over the previous policy process. Slowly agencies, organizations are involved. Now today's modern time they are the main components of the process of decision making. Through the PMO and the Prime Minister remain the most important institutions of India's foreign policy decision making Process passes through three important stages while making policy-decisions. At first stage collection and input of information, later the assessment and analysis of the data and the final stage is the decision making and its implementation. Agencies have very important role of core foreign policy decision making process. Various institutions view the issues from various angles and give necessary inputs to the policy proposals to make the decision more comprehensive. These agencies are PMO and Cabinet, National Security Council, Policy, Planning and Research Division etc.

4.19 Conclusion

After Independence the legacy of the Foreign Policy management has been successfully carried out by the Indian government. As a result, India has been at the forefront of the third world movements including the Non-Alignment Movement (NAM). Initially, Foreign policy decision making in India was Prime Minister centric. Nehru, the chief architect of India's Foreign Policy used to take all the decision as a foreign minister. He was the main decision maker though all the stakeholders of the decision-making body express their view, as per Prime Minister's decision. Later on, democratic and pluralistic trend took over the previous policy process. Now the bureaucrats, departments, organizations and other players are dominating. Therefore, the decision outcomes are out of consensus and balanced. However, in this situation the government sometimes takes hard steps to take rational decisions during the crisis. Though many agencies and factors have tried to jeopardize the foreign policy decision making process in India, still the process remains his effectiveness and working successfully throughout the years. Different governments taken different decisions bold, surprising steps to give maximum national interest. Ideological to pragmatic decision-making process is the time of need that's why India still remains one of the vibrant players of world politics.

REFERENCES

1. Aday, Sean (2017), "The US Media, Foreign Policy, and Public Support for War," *The Oxford Handbook of Political Communication*, edited by Kate Kenski and Kathleen Hall Jamieson, Online Publication, Jul 2014 DOI: 10.1093/oxfordhb/9780199793471.013.025_update_001
2. Coban, Filiz (2016), "The Role of the Media in International Relations: From the CNN Effect to the Al-Jazeere Effect," *Journal of International Relations and Foreign Policy*, Vol. 4, No. 2, December 2016, pp. 45-61, Published by American Research Institute for Policy Development DOI: 10.15640/jirfp.v4n2a3
3. Hallin, D. (1986), The "Uncensored War": The Media and Vietnam. Berkeley: University of California Press. Google Scholar. Hammond, P. (2003), "The Media War on Terrorism", *Journal of Crime, Conflict and the Media* 1(1): 23-36.
4. Seib, Philip (2011), *The Al Jazeera Effect: How the New Global Media Are Reshaping World Politics,* California, Published by Al Jazeera Centre for Studies and Arab Scientific Publishers, 2011 p. 255
5. Wikipedia (n.d.), Retrieved May 21, 2019, from Russian interference in the 2016 United States elections: https://en.wikipedia.org/wiki/Russian_interference_in_the_ 2016_United_States_elections

CHAPTER V

Comparative Study: Indian Foreign Policy and P5 Countries:

(China, France, USA, UK, Russia) in the Context of Social Media Use and its Effect on Foreign Policy

5.1 Chinese Foreign Policy and Social Media

In recent years, the relationship between the media and the foreign policy-making process in China has become more interactive and even a typical symbiosis. Though very conservative, Chinese media gives narrative and agenda and narrows its down and shapes its foreign policy through decision-makers. Chinese media is strictly controlled by the Communist Party. As a milestone of media convergence, the Internet is altering every aspect of politics, economy, society, and interaction among human beings. Moreover, foreign policy decision-making (FPDM), a traditional arena of elite politics in China, is also slowly becoming more and more influenced by the Internet in a networked world. The increased diversity, velocity and free flow of foreign policy information, has raised public attention to foreign policy issues. This, combined with the widespread public discussion facilitated by the Internet, changes the context of, and exerts pressure on, the process of Chinese FPDM. Media right from 2000 BC onwards remained under the state's control where reports and articles and their writers were directed by the Kings and now the Communist party of China, which controls the media. The media in China has its manifestation by way of Internet, social media, messaging apps, Twitter and movies. The government can monitor all these apps and either remove the content or penalize the source through the **'Great Fireball'.** China has the world's largest and biggest media populace. Alibaba and its subsidiaries support the government agenda and gain financial support from the government. Any adverse propaganda harming the Chinese interest is curbed ruthlessly.

The 'Reporter without Borders' gives Chinese media abyssal rankings; free media is only on paper here. The reportage of Tiananmen Square is still banned which students, intellectuals rose against the hypocrisy of the rulers at the helm of the affairs. Thousands were mercilessly killed and fair analysis still remains banned in China. China due to 'Open market economy' has to have relatively free media and its interest has to be protected in hegemonic communist China. China is the biggest in terms of media internet users and government has to feed them with their version of stories whether in Xinjiang, Tibet or Yellow Sea. Domestic media is rewarded by way of advertisements and government funding to the 'pliable media'. Media including social media, is constantly monitored in China. The Communist leaders are shapers of the agenda and its foreign policy through aggressive bombardment of information and so significant is the Chinese media that US had to call 'national emergency' because of the Chinese 'Huawei'.

5.1.1 Analysis of Chinese Foreign Policy

5.1.1.1 Socialist Foreign Policy

People within the U.S. understand their government dominating and incursive different countries. The U.S. government serves the requirements of the large firms and banks, which require to economically and politically management different countries to create profits. China doesn't have a capitalist category. As a socialist country, China has no ought to exploit or dominate others. China needs a peaceful world so as to develop its economy and to trade with others. As party 1st secretary Hu Yaobang aforementioned at the twelfth Party Congress:

> "We don't station one soldier abroad, nor have we tended to occupied one in of foreign land. We've ne'er infringed upon the sovereignty of another country, or obligatory associate

unequal relationship upon it. In no circumstances can we tend to get form of government." China has diplomatic relations with one hundred twenty-five countries, most of that aren't socialist. It's willing to measure in peace with different countries if there's mutual respect for sovereignty and territorial integrity, mutual foreign policy, foreign policy in every other's internal affairs, equality and mutual profit, and peaceful being ness. How do these principles of socialist policy apply to today's world?

5.1.1.2 Mideast

China has taken a powerful change opposing Israeli aggression and supporting the Palestine Liberation Organisation (PLO). China has opposed every of Israel's school of thought wars and needs the withdrawal of Israel from all occupied Arab lands. It terribly powerfully condemned the role of U.S. imperialism in backing Israel. The Chinese support the formation of a Palestinian state within the Near East. At a time once the Palestine Liberation Organisation was facing a brutal Israeli attack in Lebanese Republic, the Chinese gave $1 million to the Palestine Liberation Organisation to use for no matter purpose they selected.

The Chinese government has long had a politician, a political candidate Palestine Liberation Organization delegation office in Beijing and has refused to with diplomacy acknowledge Israel. (Marxists on-line, 1982)[24]

5.1.1.3 Asia

The Chinese emphatically contradict superpower obstructions in Asia. They condemned the 1979 Soviet-backed Vietnamese intrusion of Cambodia. The Vietnamese proceed to station over 200,000 troops in that nation and introduced a manikin government within the capital. The Chinese allow solid political and financial bolster to the resistance strengths battling the Vietnamese intrusion. They have supported the recently shaped Amalgamation Government of Democratic Kampuchea and battled to preserve it situate at the UN. Their bolster of the national freedom strengths is being demonstrated adjust in hone, as the Vietnamese-installed administration faces expanded issues and instability. Similarly, the Chinese unequivocally criticized the 1980 Soviet intrusion of Afghanistan, and back the guerrillas battling for the independence of their nation. U.S. troops have proceeded to possess South Korea since the early 1950's. U.S. and other colonialist powers rule the economy of that nation. The Chinese have continuously called for the withdrawal of U.S. troops, an end to imperialist domination, and reunification of north and South Korea. The Chinese enjoy close relations with the government and communist party in Korea. The Chinese also oppose any other imperialist domination in the region. For example, they consider the Marcos regime in the Philippines to be a right-wing military government and they politically support the resistance forces there led by the Communist Party of the Philippines.

5.1.1.4 Latin America

Latin America continues to be mostly underneath the domination of U.S. imperialism, though the Soviet Union and its agent, Cuba, cause a growing threat to the region. The Chinese support peoples' movements and countries' efforts to stay freelance of either world power. Throughout the Malvinas (Falklands) crisis, China condemned land invasion. It joined most Latin American countries in recognizing Argentine sovereignty over the Malvinas and needed a peaceful settlement of the dispute. In yankee country, Central American nation, and alternative Central American countries, China supports the popular forces fighting for independence and democracy against U.S. imperialism. Some western newspapers according that China had sent government observers to the Salvadoran elections earlier this year during which a right inner circle came to power. In fact, China solely sent 2 Xinhua wire service reporters to hide the elections. China expresses its commonality with the Revolutionary Democratic Front (FDR) of Republic of El Salvador.

5.1.2 Global Supremacy

"The quest after political system by the superpowers and also the resultant international group action between them are the most supply of the unrest and turmoil within the world," Chinese minister Harkat ul-Mujahedeenng Hua told the international organization Oct four. The Chinese imply that the U.S. may be an old imperialist commonwealth that's well-known for its domination of geographic area, the geographical area and different elements of the planet. The USSR, on the opposite hand, may be a new and hungry commonwealth. It covers up its actions with verbalize "socialist solidarity" and "supporting national liberation movements." In precisely the last 2 years, the USSR has backed the invasion of Asian nation, directly invaded Islamic State of Afghanistan, and instigated jurisprudence in the Republic of Poland. On a worldwide scale, the USSR is on the offensive, whereas the US is on the defensive. The USSR is that the main supply of war.

The Chinese oppose the aggressive actions of either commonwealth and oppose their competition with each other. For instance, the Chinese have condemned the commonwealth nuclear race. China requires nuclear disarming and has offered to eliminate all of its own nuclear weapons. Since the 2 superpowers management the overwhelming majority of nuclear weapons, China calls on the US and USSR to scale back their weapons, to be followed by reductions by different nuclear powers and ultimate elimination of all nuclear weapons. The Chinese additionally oppose commonwealth domination and competition in Europe. For instance, they oppose all foreign intervention in the Republic of Poland – each Soviet and US. The Union of Soviet Socialist Republics clearly interferes on a bigger scale. They believe that things in Poland should be resolved by the Polish folks themselves in order that Poland will relish bigger independence. Over the previous couple of months, the western press has noted hyperbolic cultural exchanges between the USSR and China. China has hyperbolic public criticisms of US policy. The press speculates that there is also a thaw in Chinese-Soviet relations. The communist and Chinese invariably create it clear to the planet that they're against hegemonism and imperialism and need world peace.

5.1.3 Chinese Foreign Policy Decision-making Process

China's Foreign Minister is often seen as the face of the country's foreign policy but his actual say in foreign policy decision-making is much smaller than in many other countries. The Ministry of Foreign Affairs is not the most authoritative or influential actor in foreign policy formulation in China. Instead, a wide range of Communist Party organs and government departments, plus the military, may be involved in the process. The one-party state's supreme body – the Politburo Standing Committee – has the ultimate decision-making power on all matters, including foreign policy. Below it is a Central Leading Group on Foreign Affairs, which convenes on an ad hoc basis to deliberate on major issues.

Its members are some of the major foreign policy actors in China. The group is led by the president, who has direct oversight over foreign policy, with the vice-president as deputy leader. Its secretary general is the state councilor in charge of foreign affairs, who outranks the foreign minister as the country's top professional diplomat. Other members include the heads of party, government and military departments that may be involved in shaping foreign policy. They include the head of the party's propaganda department and its international liaison department, which is in charge of ties with foreign political parties and plays a special role in Beijing's efforts to reduce tensions over North Korea's nuclear programme. Members also include the ministers of foreign affairs, national defence, public security, state security and commerce. But some bodies not included in the central leading group can also wield considerable influence, including the party's Central Research Office, the National Development and Reform Commission and the Ministry of Finance. The party's powerful National Security Commission, set up in late 2013, was also given a major role in foreign policy formulation. That is a lot of voices seeking to influence the top leadership's decisions, and their perspectives and standpoints are often not aligned and can even class.

5.1.4 Media and China's Foreign Policy

With modern science and technology constantly evolving and with increased public participation in politics, significant changes have occurred in the relationship among the media, public opinion, and diplomacy. Media has an increasingly significant impact on diplomatic activities: public opinion has become an important factor in shaping the government's policymaking and the media play an important role in guiding public opinion and exerting influence on foreign affairs. (Chuanjie, 2011)[25]

5.1.5 Public Opinion

Like ancient media round the world, the Chinese media aren't exempt from the pressures created by the status of the supposed "new media," together with the net and social media. Citizen Journalism: the net, photography, blogging, and different sorts of new media enable voters to become correspondents, news on native likewise as international events. The results of this national journalism square measure for the most part positive, because the growing range of discussions provide the creation of a better-informed public. Increased Reporting: because the role of media is increasing, their impact on policymaking is dynamical. Chinese media have evidenced desperate to report on problems that the govt. itself has not determined its policy, particularly on once the media see such news as in China's national interest.

5.1.6 Perception of Chinese Media Abroad

Despite the fact that opportunity of the press is an issue for Westerners watching the Chinese media, the discussants concurred that Western popular governments should indicate limitation while evaluating the degree of restriction, given that this wonder is available in the West too.

> **Weight and Reporting**: It is a typical confusion in the West that Chinese news organizations at times purposely abstain from giving an account of touchy issues. Western media regularly face comparable, if not constantly obvious, weights from their administrations. Chinese media apply incredible exertion to improve the opportunity of data inside the nation.

> **Worldwide Reputation**: The Chinese media assume a significant job in forming universal impression of China. Remote media frequently watch the Chinese media to evaluate the circumstance inside the nation. For instance, how Indian media regularly refer to the comments of Chinese media to underline Chinese patriotism and hostile to Indian supposition. Thus, Chinese media must recognize the obligation they share for the impression of China abroad.

5.1.7 Challenges

The challenges that Chinese media face are not, in fact, very different from the issues facing media in the West and in other developing countries, panelists agreed.

> **International Reporting**: Due to limited budgeting and resources, Chinese media agencies do not possess a strong foundation for reporting on international events. They are often forced to rely on reports from foreign media without confirming the accuracy of the information.

Market Pressure: The need to keep viewers and sponsors creates pressure on media agencies to cater to the majority opinion. Sponsorship and advertisement revenue are crucial for Chinese media, and these factors play too large of a role in shaping programming and editorial content.

The Chinese media moving forward should emphasize quality of information to better serve the public interest, while at the same time fend off pressure from interest groups.

5.1.8 Internet in China

From Bitcoin to YouTube, the internet has greatly altered the way humans behave and interact. This is particularly the case in China – the largest online community in the world where everything from online payments to shopping has been pioneered and taken up with gusto. While foreign policy may be thought of as being largely immune to this phenomena, public sentiment amplified through online social media channels is increasingly sculpting Chinese statecraft. Recent examples of what has been described by as "tantrum diplomacy" show that official responses by the government are often echoed by just as bellicose reactions on social media platforms.

5.1.9 Huawei and Foreign Governments

One noteworthy recent example of this is the very public confrontations between Huawei and foreign governments. In response to the arrest of Huawei executive Meng Wenzhou in Canada, the Chinese government responded by arresting several Canadians in China. This diplomatic punishment by the Chinese government was mirrored by social media users in China that encouraged a mass boycott of both Apple iPhones and the clothing company, Canada Goose, as a response. This proved to be a major hit to Canada Goose, its stock price dropping by 20 per cent in the following days. (Griffiths, 2018)[26] This was a response that was very much in line with government policy. Yet the fact that it came from members of the public meant that the influence was cordoned off from official action while still punishing Canada. While such a social media campaign serves the purpose of the Chinese government, there are other examples where social media sentiment is forcing the hand of the Chinese government in a way that may not necessarily be in line with government policy.

5.1.10 Stockholm Hotel Syndrome

The breakdown in Chinese-Swedish relations a year ago was one such precedent. After a group of Chinese was expelled from a Stockholm lodging, this generally harmless occasion caused an online tempest in China and wound up a standout amongst the most discussed subjects on Chinese web-based life in 2018. As per one specialist on the Chinese web-based social networking stage Weibo, two hashtags, approximately meant "Chinese Tourists Abused by Swedish Police" and "Swedish TV Show Insults China", got in excess of 220 million perspectives, making it a standout amongst the most perused issues on the stage for the year. Fantastically, the internet-based life furor provoked an official reaction from the Chinese government. Portrayals were made to the Swedish government and an announcement discharged, blaming the police for fierceness and having "seriously jeopardized the life and damaged the fundamental human privileges of the Chinese natives". The planning of the announcement clarified this was a reaction produced because of weight from internet-based life, undeniably more than worries for the wellbeing of family included. What presented the defense of the Stockholm inn episode so educational was it gives off an impression of being one of the main instances of the Chinese government responding to web-based life impact, free of any more extensive point or methodology.

So what causes this feeling of shock via web-based networking media, either genuine or fanciful? The issue is undoubtedly twofold. To start with, treachery as a chronicled story in China has a long, and much of the time, defended history. The feeling of bad form and mortification that was delivered upon China by Western powers all through the nineteenth and twentieth hundred of years isn't just felt by Chinese political elites however nearly the whole nation. Having opium constrained upon the people, alongside unequal bargains and enduring unmitigated land snatches has genuine heritage, which slants discourse of occasions to make the feeling that the world is as yet endeavoring to curb and mortify China. The second clarification for this online life wonder can be sheet home to the Chinese political framework. In a nation where articulation, especially of a political sort, is blue-penciled and exceedingly confined, the political class and the open appear to have gone into an implicit understanding with regards to remarking on these sorts of issues. The gathering will endure venting dissatisfaction towards remote elements that can't ordinarily be freely explained towards their own administration. The majority of this may seem, by all accounts, to be another obstacle for remote governments when endeavoring to creating arrangements for overseeing relations with China. Notwithstanding, this can likewise be believed to be a chance. Calls to put more in creating online life channels would be very much paid attention to. Growing increasingly web-based social networking joins legitimately to the general population of China can be a chance to influence informing, something that up until now, the Communist Party holds a close syndication over.

5.1.11 Soft Power Influence Globally

Beijing is expanding its soft power influence in a range of ways, none more important than its growing influence in the Western press. As part of Beijing's attempt to exert influence in foreign affairs, its state-run media companies are expanding their integration with Western news outlets. The CCP has rapidly expanded its efforts to influence the discussion about China beyond its borders to attempt to suppress criticism of the Chinese government and mold international media to refer to China in a positive light. In 2018, Xinhua, China's largest state-run news agency, announced that it was expanding cooperation with the US news service the Associated Press (AP), declaring that the two news agencies had established broad cooperation in such areas as new media, economic information, and the application of AI. At the time, the US-China Economic and Security Review Commission warned that Xinhua was rapidly expanding globally in an effort to discredit Western media outlets. The AP maintained, in response to a Congressional inquiry on the scope of the agreement between the AP and Xinhua, that Xinhua would not influence its reporting or have access to sensitive information in AP's possession.

In the wake of Russia's interference in the 2016 US presidential elections, no US media outlet would subsequently agree to partner up with RT or Sputnik. Some US members of Congress were of the view that Beijing's influence operations inside the US represented a similar threat. Like other powerful countries (including, first and foremost, of course, the US), China utilizes aid, cultural programming, and the media to boost its global image. But for Beijing, the current influence offensive is on a much greater scale. Beijing can more easily shape global narratives through state media that reaches hundreds of millions of people around the world. It is pouring money into such outlets as the China Global Television Network, turning them into major global media players, as Russia did with RT and Sputnik. Chinese social media and messaging platforms have also spread globally, making it easier for Beijing to push Xinhua and other state-run platforms onto more social media users outside China. Beijing is also seeking to shape media coverage of China by using state-owned media to train foreign journalists, especially from developing countries, inviting reporters from Southeast Asia and Latin America to visit China to participate in workshops and courses that offer an officially sanctioned view of Chinese foreign and economic policies. Recent purchases of local media outlets in South Africa, for example, by pro-China business tycoons are providing Beijing with direct access to target markets. Pro-China business owners are donating funds to influence research institutes, universities and think tanks abroad. China's Confucius Institute project, run by the Ministry of Education, helps set up Chinese language and culture studies programmes at universities around the world, including many in the US. It appears to have been successful not only in promoting language and cultural studies but also in creating a climate of self-censorship at many universities around issues deemed sensitive to Beijing. A 2017 report concluded that the arrival of more than 100 Confucius Institutes in the US had led schools to self-censor programming about Taiwan, Tibet, and the 1989 Tiananmen crackdown.

All the more star Beijing think tanks are likewise being made everywhere throughout the world, some straightforwardly financed by the legislature and others blessed by expert Beijing organizations. No place has China been progressively effective in influencing research foundations and business associations than in Southeast Asia. In Thailand, for instance, the Chinese government office has built up close connects to a few noticeable business and social associations that, over the previous decade, have turned out to be standard mouthpieces for Beijing's arrangement destinations in the kingdom and around the district. The German government exacted that charge against China in 2017, guaranteeing that Beijing had utilized LinkedIn and other web-based life to target more than 10,000 of its residents, including administrators and other government workers, acting like pioneers of research organizations and talent scouts, and offering all-costs paid treks to China and gatherings with compelling customers. Numerous nations burn through cash anticipating delicate power likewise. The test is to separate between generous kinds of social and political advancement versus more straightforward and conceivably intrusive impact selling and impedance. While numerous Western knowledge organizations are centered around Russia's data fighting, relatively few of them are probably giving a comparative size of assets to comprehend China's impact activities and how the nation is anticipating its delicate power abroad. One could undoubtedly contend that Beijing's impact activities are undeniably progressively significant, given this is China's century. Notwithstanding punching over its weight in impact hawking, Beijing is additionally punching over its weight in science. Achievement in present day science requires establishments of advanced education, proficient specialists, and a ton of cash. Since China has all the essential fixings, it is quickly climbing the rankings of logical accomplishment. Aside from its accomplishment on the clouded side of the moon, Beijing has spent a huge number of dollars to recognize dim issue, make incredible advances in quantum correspondences, and become a pioneer in sustainable power source and propelled materials. In 2018, Nikkei and Elsevier found that more logical papers began from China than from some other nation in 23 of the 30 most dynamic fields of study. While the nature of American research has been reliably higher, China is nipping at its heels.

The looming prospect of a dominant China in science alarms Western governments not only because of the new weaponry Beijing is in the process of developing, but because of the implications for how else it may be used—whether for repression at home, AI development, or purposes of spying. Science may end up changing China, and the world, in ways no one is anticipating, but for China to be all it can be in the scientific realm implies granting its scientists an unprecedented degree of freedom to be all that they can be. That implies that President Xi and the CCP will need to ease up on the reins of the scientific community in China. Are they capable of doing that? It remains to be seen, but President Xi has already proven himself to be masterful at adapting when needed to accommodate new realities and keep his vision of an omnipotent China on course. Based on his deft projection of China's soft power, there is little reason to believe that he will not be successful in doing so.

**(International policy digest)*

5.1.12 Media Control by Chinese Communists: Special Emphasis Tiananmen Square

The Year of the Pig is replete with politically sensitive anniversaries: 60 years since the Dalai Lama's flight from Tibet in March, a century since the launch of the influential May 4 student movement, 30 years since the June 4 crackdown on pro-democracy protesters in Tiananmen Square. June 4, 1989, will be termed as the turning point in China. Here thousands of protesters especially students and intellectuals are killed in the brutal suppression of 'Freedom of Speech' and 'Free Media'. These unarmed civilian students and intellectuals were protesting against the economic policy of Communalist leaders amassing wealth and entire population facing the brunt of low employment, growth and high inflation and rampant corruption. Then came intensified restrictions in Xinjiang in early July, 20 years since the party launched its campaign against the Falun Gong spiritual movement later that month, and the 70th anniversary of the founding of the People's Republic in October. Those dates often bring extra censorship even on less significant anniversaries, and regulators seem especially keen to preempt any potential expressions of dissent in 2019. On Jan. 3, the Cyberspace Administration of China announced the launch of a new campaign against vaguely defined "negative and harmful information" online. It is set to last six months and has already included instructions to the web portals Baidu and Sohu to suspend their news services for one week this month in order to "root out undesirable content." As the various anniversaries pass, spikes in censorship will be tracked by monitors such as Weiboscope; localized internet shutdowns and travel restrictions will affect regions such as Tibet and Xinjiang; and arrests or involuntary "vacations" will be imposed on prominent democracy advocates, grassroots activists, and ordinary Falun Gong, Tibetan Buddhist, and Uighur Muslim believers. If the past is any indication, at least some of the repressive measures deployed and the jail sentences imposed will last far beyond the anniversary year itself. Thirty years later, Tiananmen Square cannot be discussed freely in Chinese media, so strict is the Chinese control that is can be called the 'darkest suppression of freedom of expression.

5.1.13 First iCloud Arrest

The 2017 Cybersecurity Law stipulates that foreign companies must store Chinese users' cloud data on servers located in China. To meet this requirement, Apple announced last January that iCloud data would be transferred to servers run by a company called Guizhou on the Cloud Big Data (GCBD), which is owned by the Guizhou provincial government. Apple and GCBD now both have access to iCloud data, including photos and other content. Personal communications and information from platforms such as WeChat, QQ, Twitter, and Skype have increasingly been used by Chinese authorities to detain or convict people for their peaceful political or religious speech. This makes it only a matter of time before foreign companies with localized data centers become complicit in a politicized arrest. Apple has already proved its willingness to comply with Chinese government demands that violate basic freedoms by removing hundreds of apps used to circumvent censorship or access foreign news services from its mobile store in China. Other companies to watch include the U.S.-based note-taking app Evernote, which transferred user data to Tencent Cloud last year, and various blockchain platforms, which as of next month will be required to implement real – name registration, monitor content, and store user data.

5.1.14 Financial News Frozen

Chinese censors intensified their focus on controlling business and economic news—usually relatively openly reported topics compared with political or cultural issues—amid a trade war with the United States and slowing growth at home. Propaganda and censorship authorities actively intervened to suppress negative reporting on a staggering economy by suspending online portals' financial news channels, issuing regular directives to editors to carefully manage their coverage, and providing monthly ideological trainings to journalists at financial news outlets. This year, censors have already told the media not to report information on layoffs in the tech sector and restricted the circulation of a speech by a prominent economist, who said the government had made serious economic miscalculations in 2018. As the slowdown intensifies and its impact is felt across a wider range of sectors, the authorities can be expected to tighten their control over the news and work to prevent— or even prosecute— leaks of negative financial data and analysis.

5.1.15 Technological Advancement in Data Technology

Reports emerge weekly of pilot initiatives in which Chinese authorities attempt to incorporate artificial intelligence and other technological aids into existing control mechanisms. The more benign examples include efforts to identify and fine jaywalkers, limit illegal subletting in public housing, encourage good manners on public transportation, and improve student attendance at school. Yet even these cases involve considerable restrictions on privacy, possible false positives, and enormous potential for abuse. And in other instances, similar technologies are being deployed for more obviously repressive purposes, such as censoring politically sensitive images on WeChat or identifying potential targets for forced re-education in Xinjiang. Previous cases have been experimental or limited to certain geographical locations. But as these advanced systems for social and political control are refined, and as the government proceeds with its plans for a national social credit system, centralized surveillance is becoming the new norm.

5.1.16 Conclusion

Every country tries to control the media whether its social media or free press. Chinese have the dubious distinction of controlling the media from 2000 BC and now the only vibrant Communist country in the world. The agenda is set by the media populace i.e., China and its pliable media houses like Alibaba and Huawei leading to US declaring the national emergency, plays and tows the government line. China, especially in trade war and hegemonic aggression to further its national interest like in Xinjiang, Tibet and Yellow sea had to control the media and feed to its populace what the Chinese line of action is which is righteous. It always supports especially in Africa, Asia and third world countries to spread its business interest and accordingly takes decisions based on targeted population in china and third world countries. China putting its foot down on several occasions in declaring Azhar Masood as global terrorist points in that direction. China as a member of the United Nations Security Council always calculates and entire decision is ultimately in furtherance of its foreign policy agenda. The Chinese are very concerned about its image being fed to the world and the classic example is 'Winnie the Pooh' which was banned because the main character looked like 'Xi Jinping'. Thus, the Chinese media advertently is being controlled by the Communist Part of china and its furtherance of foreign policy.

5.2 France Foreign Policy and Social Media

Several factors shape French Foreign Policy. France has a self-identity that calls for efforts to spread French values and views, many rooted in democracy and human rights. France prefers to engage most international issues in a multilateral framework, above all through the European Union (EU). France is also a highly secular society, a characteristic that influences views on the state's relation to religion. The Internet revolution has affected all aspects of life, including International relations. Diplomacy as a tool of foreign policy has also being transformed by this revolution. Media offers opportunities and challenges for diplomatic activities, and countries cannot afford to be left behind in this era of digital diplomacy as they can greatly benefit from these emerging diplomatic trends. Digital diplomacy and Internet activities as a whole can greatly assist in projecting a state's foreign policy positions to domestic and foreign audiences. (Westcott, 2008)[27] France has a very wide and diverse range of publications, radio and television stations, blogs, and websites. For a population of 63 million, it has about 600 local and national mainstream publications, at least 1,100 radio stations and more than 100 TV channels (including satellite, cable, and digital). The French media are generally independent, but many of them are owned by groups which have interests in other industries. Libel laws are also particularly strict by Western standards.

5.2.1 History

For two decades after 1871 France had remained strategically secluded in Europe. Bismarck, to avert potential French thoughts of vengeance, had insightfully urged the republic's legislatures to leave on frontier success abroad and had arranged unions with every one of those European powers the French may somehow or another have pursued. He, subsequently, kept Austria-Hungary, Russia, and Italy close by, while Britain stayed standoffish in "awesome separation." Upon Bismarck's fall in 1890, the German ruler William II (Kaiser Wilhelm) ended the mystery bargain among Germany and Russia. The Russians started to cast about for companions and looked with some dislike toward Paris. French approach creators urged French investors to make credits to the Russian government and opened dealings for an understanding. In 1891 a free understanding accommodated common discussion in emergency; in 1894 this was expanded into a military coalition by whose terms each accomplice guaranteed to help the other if there should be an occurrence of assault by Germany or Germany's partners. For 10 years the Franco-Russian partnership had minimal commonsense impact (however French credits continued to stream to Russia). French negotiators went to winning the Italians from the Triple Alliance, and a Franco-Italian mystery understanding in 1902 generously debilitated the responsibility Italy had made to Germany and Austria-Hungary in 1882. Of progressively focal significance all through the 1890s was repetitive pressure among France and Britain, who had been inconsistent in different pieces of the world and whose provincial challenge now and again appeared to compromise war. England's South African (Boer) War included further sick inclination, and some British heads started to encourage a conclusion to "amazing separation" for an understanding with a Continental power—most likely Germany, which was viewed as a major aspect of an Anglo-Saxon racial coalition. In any case, the German government reacted coolly to suggestions toward this path, in this manner encouraging the feelings of dread of British pioneers who considered Germany to be a risk to British interests.

The British went to France rather and found a ready accomplice in the outside clergyman Théophile Delcassé. A visit to Paris by King Edward VII in 1903 helped make ready to the Anglo-French Entente

Cordiale of 1904, which settled all remarkable pilgrim clashes between the two powers however held back before military collusion. The new understanding was merged a year later, when French moves to assume control over Morocco as a protectorate were disliked by the Germans, who thought they saw a chance to separate the new understanding. Kaiser Wilhelm offered Germany's help to the sultan of Morocco; this activity chafed the British and drove them to guarantee France solid help. In the gathering of forces that pursued at Algeciras, Spain, in 1906, France must be content with extraordinary benefits instead of a protectorate in Morocco; however, the Entente Cordiale was strengthened, and it was Germany that thus started to grumble of segregation.

5.2.2 The pre-war years

From 1899 to 1905 a fairly coherent coalition of left-wing and center parties (the so-called Bloc Republicans) provided France with stable government. The cabinets headed by Waldeck-Rousseau in 1899–1902 and Émile Combes in 1902–05 managed to liquidate the Dreyfus Affair and to carry through the anticlerical reforms that culminated in the separation of church and state. The Entente Cordiale and the Russian alliance ensured France a more influential voice in European affairs. France possessed a colonial empire second only to Britain's in size. A new period of economic growth set in after the mid-1890s. Not surprisingly, later generations were to look back on the pre-1914 decade as la belle époque ("the beautiful age"). There were indications of a changing scholarly state of mind in the nation, particularly among youthful Frenchmen. A patriot recovery influenced numerous Frenchmen who for 10 years had become progressively on edge about what they viewed as the bewildering and undermining disposition of Germany's post-Bismarckian authority; they looked again to the military as the country's rampart, and its renown was on the ascent. These patriot inclinations found their exemplification in Poincaré, whose uncompromising nationalism and assurance to confront Germany were certain. As head in 1912–13 Poincaré gave himself to fortifying the military and to reviving France's partnership framework. A concurrence with the British accommodated another sharing of maritime duties: the French moving in the Mediterranean, the British in the North Sea.

Poincaré made a state visit to Russia to resuscitate the drooping Franco-Russian union. In January 1913 he was chosen to the administration of the republic, where, he trusted, he could guarantee progression of arrangement amid his seven-year term. In 1913 the measure of the standing armed force was expanded by extending the enrollment time frame from a few years. The elements that shape French remote arrangement have changed since the finish of the Cold War. The nation's government has grasped the chance to construct steadiness in Europe through an extended European Union. France has perceived that fear mongering and the expansion of weapons of mass annihilation are the most significant dangers to their security today.

5.2.3 Factors which Shape French Foreign Policy

France normally wishes to "legitimize" actions ranging from economic sanctions to political censure to military action in the United Nations. Bush Administration officials have at times reacted with hostility to such efforts, charging that French efforts to ensure "multipolarity" in the world are a euphemism for organizing opposition to U.S. initiatives. Trade and investment ties between the United States and France are extensive, and provide each government a large stake in the vitality and openness of their respective economies. Through trade in goods and services, and, most importantly, through foreign direct investment, the economies of France and the United States have become increasingly integrated. Other areas of complementarily include the Balkans peace operations, the stabilization of Afghanistan, and the fight against terrorism—all challenges where France has played a central role. A major split occurred over Iraq, however, with many countries either supporting or independently sharing French ideas of greater international involvement. Developments in the Middle East affect French foreign and domestic policy. France has a long history of involvement in the region, and a population of 5-6 million Muslims. Paris believes that resolution of the Arab-Israeli conflict is key to bringing peace to the region and that the United States too strongly favors the Israeli government, a U.S. tendency that impedes peace, in the French view. Surges in violence in the Middle East have led to anti-Semitic acts in France, mostly undertaken by young Muslims. (Belkin, 2011)[28]

5.2.4 A Global Perspective

France, similar to the United States, trusts that it has an exceptional job on the planet. The center of the view of France's job on the planet originates from the Revolution that started in 1789. The Revolution was an occasion of expansive mainstream inclusion: far reaching carnage, seizure of property, and execution of the ruler nourished the idea that there could be no going back to monarchical government. Not exclusively was the government ousted and a ground-breaking church structure persuasively destroyed, yet French militaries, and eventually French chairmen afterward, changed a significant part of the landmass into social orders where increasingly agent, vote based foundations and the standard of law could at last flourish.

The Revolution was hence a focal, developmental component in present day European history, quite in Europe's advancement from monarchical to law-based foundations. The social accomplishments of France previously and since the revolution have added to French impact. French turned into the language of the élite in numerous European nations. By 1900, French political figures of the left and the privilege imparted the insight that France was and should keep on being an enlightening signal for the remainder of the world. The view that France has a "humanizing mission" (la mission civilisatrice) on the planet suffers today. For a long time, the French government has underlined the message of human rights and majority rule government, especially in the creating scene and in focal Europe and Eurasia. Many French authorities, especially Gaullists, have been profoundly decisive in looking to spread French qualities all through the world. Head administrator Dominiquede Villepin, has composed that "at the core of our national personality, there is a changeless scan for qualities that may be shared by others." Gaullists have looked to implant French perspectives in EU activities, here and there working together with Germany and in some cases alone. In 1996, the previous Gaullist Prime Minister Alain Juppé required an "internal hover" in the EU, characterized as "few states around France and Germany" that must push ahead to verify EMU, a typical remote and security approach, and a military power ready to ensure the Union's advantages. His remote clergyman included that such arrangements, "a long way from debilitating France's impact and specialist in the world...will increment their effect and gathering of people." France's position and impact on the planet are imperative to French policymakers. Enrollment on the U.N. Security Council, close relations with parts of the Arab world and previous overall settlements, parts of intensity, for example, atomic weapons, and inspiration of human rights are integral to France's self-character in worldwide issues.

Others here and there challenge France's summoning of qualities. By the mid-20th century, some French settlements, for example, Algeria and Morocco, strongly questioned whether genuine French strategy met the goals of Paris' message. Algeria battled a twenty-year war for freedom. Today, a few Europeans acclaim the scholarly underpinnings of French "reason and great sense" that battle "preference and obsession." However, they see infrequent logical inconsistencies in French approach, as when France tried to lift sanctions against Iraq when U.N. WMD investigations briefly finished there in 1998, at that point just belatedly acknowledged another examinations routine in 2002, despite the fact that French authorities had secretly been expressing their conviction that Iraqi WMD programmes were likely proceeding, or when France dismisses what some view as increasingly vote based power-partaking in the growing European Union.

5.2.5 The European Union

France was one of the founding members of the European Union (initially known as the European Coal and Steel Community) in 1952. Improved trade and economic development were central objectives of member states in a Europe still struggling from the dislocation caused by the Second World War, but overarching objectives from the beginning were political rapprochement between Germany and its former enemies, and political stability on the continent. The EU was conceived in this context, with strong U.S. support. France has been a catalyst in achieving greater political unity and economic strength in the European Union. President Chirac has altered the traditional Gaullist view that France could act alone as a global power and be the Union's most important member. Rather, today, the Gaullists believe that France can best exert its power through the EU, acting in tandem with Germany and occasionally with

Britain. At the same time, the defeat of a referendum in spring 2005 endorsing the EU "constitution" meant to make EU decision-making more effective may be a sign of popular doubts about the direction and strength of the Union. Some European governments object to the view that France, Germany, and Britain can guide EU policies. They describe the claim for leadership of the three countries as a nascent "Directoire," or initiative to dominate the EU and push smaller member states to follow the three governments' lead. The French officials dispute the idea of a "Directoire." In their view, initiatives in the Union should not be held back by governments that wish to proceed more slowly. President Chiracde scribes the efforts of France and Germany, and occasionally Britain, as those of a "pioneer group" that wishes "to go faster and further in European integration." In 2003 and 2004, France, Germany, and Britain played the key role in persuading Iran to accept International Atomic Energy Agency (IAEA) inspections of its nuclear energy sites for possible evidence of nuclear weapons production. French officials state that they want the EU to have a strong Commission and a strong President of the Commission, although the Council, where ministers from member states meet, must remain paramount in decision-making. Officials in some EU governments believe that France's leadership is constrained by policies occasionally viewed as erratic. In one example, France, with Germany, was a principal progenitor of EMU, conceived to bind the EU economies more closely together by subjecting them to legal strictures over debt and a range of monetary policies. France initially described EMU as above all a political measure, in which EU member states agreed upon joint economic policies for the good of all. When France (and Germany) decided to abrogate the "Stability Pact" governing these policies in late 2003, some member states complained that Paris was acting in its own political interest, at the expense of others. (Belkin, 2011)[29]

5.2.6 Multilateralism

For the Europeans, decision-making in international institutions can lend legitimacy to governmental policies. Globally, Europeans perceive the UN as the locus for decision-making that can provide an international imprimatur for member states' actions in international security. The UN carries special significance for European governments that experienced two world wars. Europeans see the EU and the UN as belonging to a civilizing evolution towards cooperation rather than confrontation in world affairs. France is in a key position in the framework of multilateral institutions. It enjoys a permanent seat and holds a veto in the UN Security Council. Importantly EU policies are not possible without French support. French officials play central roles on the European Commission, in the European Central Bank, and the IMF, and are eligible to lead, and have led, each of these institutions. At the same time, France believes that an anti-terror foreign policy must include a comprehensive multilateral effort to diminish the prevalence of poverty in the developing world and to encourage the spread of literacy, democracy, and human rights. While military action may also be a tool against terrorism for Paris, French leaders prefer to begin any effort to confront an international threat in a multilateral framework.

5.2.7 Use of Force and the UN

For the French government, the contention in Iraq in 2003 brought up issues about the authentic utilization of power. France, together with a few other European governments, has been reproachful of the Bush Administration's national security precept that embraces "preemptive activity" notwithstanding up and coming threat. While the French government does not dismiss the utilization of power, it keeps up that specific criteria must be met for military activity to gain authenticity. In the expressions of Prime Minister de Villepin, dread of psychological oppression and different dangers make "the utilization of power... enticing. [Use of force] is reasonable if aggregate security or a helpful emergency requires it. Yet, it should just be a last plan of action, when every single other arrangement are depleted and the worldwide network, through the Security Council, settles on the inquiry." For instance, France, alongside different nations, since 1990 has gotten a U.N. goals for the potential or genuine utilization of power for mediations in the primary Gulf War, Bosnia, Afghanistan, Congo, the Ivory Coast, and Haiti. One prominent exemption came in 1999, when France joined its NATO partners in doing battle against Serbia with an end goal to forestall ethnic purifying in Kosovo. All things considered, until the eleventh hour, the French government looked for a U.N. goals for NATO's utilization of power. In the meantime, despite an inexorably likely Russian veto, French authorities and partners from a few other European partners started showing that Serbian activities had achieved a phase where utilizing power to counteract a philanthropic fiasco in Kosovo would be legitimate without a U.N. goals. At the point when a Russian veto turned into sure, there was an agreement in NATO that the utilization of power was legitimate in this example even without a U.N. goals.

5.2.8 Multipolarity

France and the United States have clashed over Paris's pursuit of "multipolarity" in economic, military, and political affairs. The French government describes multipolarity as a system of balance in international affairs, in part a natural outgrowth of trading blocs and regional global differences, in part a value that is in principled opposition to global domination by one power or bloc. Some U.S. officials, notably Condoleezza Rice, disparage the concept as a means to thwart U.S. foreign policy. In June 2003, she said that it was troubling that "some have spoken admiringly—almost nostalgically—of 'multipolarity,' as if it were a good thing to be desired for its own sake." She said that France seemed intent upon "checking" the United States and that Paris appeared to consider "the United States more dangerous than Saddam Hussein." Some Administration supporters in the neo-conservative movement are more pointed and claim that France wishes to reclaim the "grandeur" of an earlier era and deny the United States its "unipolar moment"; in this view, multipolarity is a concept employed specifically to subvert U.S. foreign policy. The idea of multipolarity is not new, nor is it French in origin. In recent times, it was a common sentiment in the European Union of the 1990s. It was seen at that time as a means for Europeans, acting together, to put forward their commercial interests in negotiations and reach equitable trade agreements with the United States. French officials have usually tended to describe multipolarity as taking effect across a range of policies. They say that the world is "unipolar" in a military sense, given the U.S.'s overwhelming military power. But they also note that given the proliferation of crises around the globe, the development by the EU of military institutions and units can provide complementary forces in the effort to build order and stability. Chirac has used "multipolarity" in economic terms as well, noting that not only the EU, but the rise of China, India, and Mercosur in Latin America have created global commercial competitors.

5.2.9 Religion and the State

"Le Foulard" France has a long history of religious violence. Political factions went to war in the 16th century over religious differences and dynastic claims; the conflict left many thousands dead and the society badly divided. One cause of the Revolution was a desire by many to end the Catholic Church's grip on elements of society and dismantle a church hierarchy widely viewed as corrupt and poorly educated. In the late 19th and early 20th centuries, the government sought to ensure that public schools did not become embroiled in religious controversies. Parliament passed a law in 1905 intended to ensure separation between religion and politics. The law enshrined "laïcité" as a principle of French life. "Laïcité" is not simply secularism, but rather an attempt to balance religious freedom and public order. A current controversy in France has pitted elements of the Muslim community against the government. Approximately 36 per cent of France's Muslim community describe themselves as "practicing." Within this group are Muslims who seek to ensure that their children may pursue what they view as traditional Islamic practices in France's public school system. Some French Muslim families require their girls to wear head scarves ("le foulard") to school. French public schools are co-educational. Some Muslim families object to elements of co-education; for example, they do not want their female children to take physical education, nor do they want them to take biology classes where reproduction is discussed. The French government believes that such families are causing disruption in the public school system, especially in a period of increased tensions between Muslims and Jews in France, and a period of political tensions with the Muslim world over the issue of terrorism. After an extended debate, the government presented a bill to Parliament to ban "conspicuous" religious symbols in schools through secondary-school level. The law prohibits the wearing of head scarves; it also bans religious symbols such as large crosses and the yarmulke. Moderate Muslim groups in France supported it as a means to reduce tensions in the school system and in broader society. The bill passed by a wide margin in March 2004, with government parties and elements of the left supporting it. (Belkin, 2011)[30]

5.2.10 Anti-Semitism in France

Since 2000, there has been a noticeable increase in anti-Semitic acts of violence in France. Most of the acts have occurred in the suburbs around Paris, and in southern cities such as Marseille and Montpellier. France has a total population of 59.8 million, of whom approximately 600,000 are Jewish. According to a 2002 study by a French Jewish community organization, most French Jews today are white collar professionals, and are well integrated into French society. "Mixed" marriages with non-Jews have become increasingly common in the past two decades, but a strong community sense remains. Over the past decade, there has been a close correlation between surges in violence in the Middle East and increases in anti-Semitic acts in France. The Gulf War of 1991, the Palestinian Intifada since fall 2000, and Israeli military action on the West Bank and in Gaza since spring 2002 have all been followed by increases in anti-Semitic violence in France.

The history of Jews in France is replete with important political milestones and a strong measure of controversy. In 1791, during the Revolution, France was the first European country to extend citizenship to its Jewish population. There have been three Jewish prime ministers (Léon Blum in 1936-1937, Pierre Mendès-France in 1954-1955, and Laurent Fabius in 1984-1986). Some American commentators have responded to the acts of anti-Semitic violence in France by charging that the country as a whole is anti-Semitic. Israeli officials have charged that the French government's Middle East policies create an atmosphere where anti-Semitism can grow. Some prominent French Jews intimate that the French government's criticism of Israel is a cloak for anti-Semitism. (Belkin, 2011)[31]

5.2.11 French Broadcasting

France's overseas broadcasting is an essential component of its policy of soft diplomacy as a means of disseminating its values and culture overseas, of sharing its vision of the world but also of engaging in dialogue with other cultures. French cultural diplomacy in the audiovisual field relies on two main channels: major international media channels such as TV5Monde (broadcasting to over 220 million homes, 24 hours a day), France 24 (close on 200 million homes, also 24 hours a day) or radio stations RFI and its Arabic language subsidiary Monte Carlo Doualiya (close on 50 million listeners a week).

5.2.12 Media Development in the Global South

Overseas broadcasting is also a key component of our cultural cooperation and development aid policy, through which France aims to promote cultural diversity and freedom of expression and creation. France supports its Global South partners by backing their development of their media and their cultural sector. These missions are also closely linked to overarching objectives of supporting processes leading to greater democracy and good governance by States and achieving the Millennium Development Goals.

The importance that the French Ministry of Foreign Affairs places on overseas broadcasting was underscored in 1984 by the creation of a network of some sixty audiovisual attachés. They are in the front line of France's overseas broadcasting, with five main areas of responsibility: gathering market intelligence, commercial promotion, organisation of specific operations in close collaboration with professionals, coordinating film distribution and setting up cooperation projects.

5.2.13 Emmanuel Macron and Media

Amid a year ago's presidential race crusade, Emmanuel Macron was the dear of the French media. His guarantees of "another world" and another French upset appeared customized for the occasions. He cleared to control with 66 percent of the vote, destroying his adversary of the extreme right. Be that as it may, his sentiment with the media has since gone bad. "We all around once in a while observe Macron," says RTL political manager Elizabeth Martichoux. "The Elysee Palace is a significant invulnerable post. Macron does not have lunch meetings with writers like his antecedent, Francois Hollande, used to. He quit doing all that. There will never be a 'confidentially' minute, he is a president who is dependably 'on the record." From his most punctual days in office, Macron clarified which writers he needed covering his story. At the beginning, Macron here and there appeared as though he was part president, part task manager. (Jazeera, 2018)[32] "Just a couple of days into his command, the president chose to venture out to Mali. He at that point reached certain news sources to tell them he just needed columnists who spent significant time in guard and outside approach, not political columnists," clarifies Jean-Jerome Bertolus, a political essayist at

L'Opinion. "This drummed up very some excitement among news sources, who properly said the president ought not be permitted to pick which writers to have close by. It was a first show of solidarity. It's a work of art, political strategy: Court the news media on your approach to control. Set aside a few minutes for them and grin for the cameras. At that point, when you're sworn into office, build up an abrupt abhorrence for columnists. However, as indicated by Sorbonne University educator Francois Jost, Macron does in reality converse with columnists, "yet they are for the most part remote, and that bothers French writers a ton... It isn't so much that he doesn't talk. It's simply that he converses with others. The [French] media must choose the option to utilize bits of these experiences. In any case, none of these discourses is straightforwardly routed to the French press." Whenever Macron allowed his first French TV meet after right around five months, he picked the biggest exclusive channel, TF1, rather than France's state supporter. When he at long last addressed state TV, Macron and columnist Laurent Delahousse walked around the Elysee Palace. It struck French writers and gatherings of people as an American style of light-contact meeting. Today, Macron never again gives French columnists the quiet treatment, however the relationship is a long way from welcoming. He has scrutinized past presidents for being excessively near columnists, blamed the French media for narcissism, and purportedly called the state supporter "la honte de la Republique"—the disgrace of the republic.

He's clarified that state-possessed media are expected for an update, flagging spending cuts and rebuilding. Investigators state that the change recommendations could result in less open administration reporting and, at last, less individuals considering power responsible. "The entire history of French presidents and supporters – regardless of whether with Mitterrand, Chirac, Sarkozy, somewhat less with Hollande – has been tied in with holding open TV and radio under their control," as indicated by Daniel Schneidermann, a media examiner at Arret Sur Images." I think Macron is extremely 'old world' in that he supposes he ought to have unlimited oversight over open telecom." With regards to the media, Macron's aims are not too unique in relation to his ancestors', regardless of whether the strategies and the talk are. In the event that the French president pulls off it, his supposed "transformation" will be broadcast – his way.

5.2.14 2017: France Elections and Media

A newly-translated-to-English report reflects on how the country handled misinformation and politically motivated document leaks in its 2017 presidential election and offers 50 recommendations for how governments, civil society and individuals could tackle similar problems. The findings are compiled in a hefty 200 pages from a working group between France's foreign affairs minister's policy planning staff and France's research institute of the Ministry for the Armed Forces. The group originally convened to explore developing an inter-agency task force dealing with information manipulation, their preferred term for fake news, defined as "the intentional and massive dissemination of false or biased news for hostile political purposes." This report comes from the researchers' approximately 100 interviews with national authorities, academics, and journalists in visits to 20 countries in Europe, Asia, and North America. Their guiding principle: (SCHMIDT, 2018)[33]
Information is increasingly seen as a common good, the protection of which falls into all citizens concerned with the quality of public debate. Above all, it is the duty of civil society to develop its own resilience. Governments can and should come to the aid of civil society. They should not be in the lead, but their role is nonetheless crucial, for they cannot afford to ignore a threat that undermines the foundations of democracy and national security. The report is chunky and full of deeper details on information manipulation and France's response to early indications. Here are some of the highlights:

5.2.15 Why did Macron Gate not Work?

On Friday, May 5, 2017—two days before the second round of the French presidential election—someone(s) hacked 9 GB of data from the campaign of Emmanuel Macron, the eventual victor against right-wing leader Marine Le Pen. Two days before that, and two hours before the final televised debate between Le Pen and Macron, a user with a Latvian IP address posted fake documents on 4chan about Macron's alleged offshore account—which were soon amplified by pro-Trump Twitter accounts using #MacronGate and #MacronCacheCash. But there is good news. "The leak did not significantly influence French voters, despite the efforts of the aforementioned actors. Why? French success resulted from a combination of structural factors, luck, as well as the effective anticipation and reaction of the Macron campaign staff, the government and civil society, especially the mainstream media," the researchers concluded. Cultural clumsiness by the hackers and less reliance on 'alternative' websites helped, but so did the preparation and response of Macron's campaign, existing government, and the mainstream media:

5.2.16 How France Prepared

1) *Don't do what the U.S. did:* Paris had already observed the Democratic National Committee's miserable response to its own hacking, plus American intelligence services had warned its French counterparts about Russian interference attempts during the French campaign.
2) *Rely on the proper administrative actors:* France has two agencies in particular that were robust in watchdogging the campaigns, monitoring cybersecurity, and ensuring the integrity of the electoral results.
3) *Raising awareness via the media, political parties, and the public before and after the hacking:* One of the aforementioned administrative actors even offered an open workshop on cybersecurity for the campaigns.
4) *Signal a united front:* The government already in power showed its resolve and determination to stem foreign interference, both in its words and actions.
5) *Take technical precautions:* The administrative actor heightened security at each step of the electoral process, even ending electronic voting for citizens abroad because of risk of cyberattacks.
6) *Pressure digital platforms to act:* Facebook removed 70,000 suspicious accounts in France as recently as ten days before the vote took place, thanks to pressure from the government and from the public.

5.2.17 How France Responded

1) *Highlight all hacking attempts:* Macron's campaign had already been talking about its susceptibility to hacking and responded in hours with a press release when the leaked documents were dropped.
2) *Beat the hackers at their own game:* The campaign also placed traps along the way, using fake passwords, email addresses, and documents to throw them off, making the hackers explain why

they stole and leaked information "which seemed, at best, useless and, at worst, false or misleading."

3) *Hit back on social media:* Campaign staff systematically and quickly responded to Macron Leaks posts or comments.
4) *Use humor:* Dry, dull government-speak isn't exactly as viral as being funny in responding.
5) *Call out actual propaganda outlets:* Macron's campaign ceased offering RT and Sputnik press credentials in late April and continuing in Macron's presidency. Macron even highlighted their work as "organs of influence, of propaganda and of lying propaganda" during a joint press conference with Vladimir Putin.
6) *Compartmentalize communication as a rule of thumb:* Use email only for trivial and logistic matters, use encrypted apps for confidential items, and save sensitive conversations for face-to-face.
7) *Call on the media to behave responsibly:* On Friday night, Macron's team referred the case to the CNCCEP [one of the administrative actors] which issued a press release the following day, requesting 'the media not to report on the content of this data, especially on their websites, [and] reminding the media that the dissemination of false information is a breach of law, above all criminal law.' The majority of traditional media sources responded to this call by choosing not to report on the content of the leaks. Some have even gone one step further by denouncing an electoral interference attempt and calling upon their readers to not let themselves be manipulated.

5.2.18 What's the Media's Role in this?

As mentioned above, the researchers make 50 recommendations for governing bodies, the general public, and private actors. Here are the top ones relevant to journalism:

1) *Don't underestimate the threat:* The Finnish Security Strategy for Society insists that a good preparation against information manipulation depends on an accurate evaluation of the threat.
2) *Do not surrender the internet to extremists:* Conspiracy theories prosper all the more easily if they are not contradicted…It is necessary, however, to also give due consideration to the risk of

the 'boomerang effect,' for to refute is also to reiterate. Every correction indirectly increases the circulation of the false information. This propagation effect cannot be avoided and it is therefore important to pick one's battles, that is, to focus on counteracting those instances of information manipulation that are most dangerous."

3) *Find a balance with government oversight:* Civil society (journalists, the media, online platforms, NGOs, etc.) must remain the first shield against information manipulation in liberal, democratic societies. The most important recommendation for governments is that they should make sure they retain as light a footprint as possible—not just in keeping with our values, but also out of a concern for effectiveness. As one of the roots of the problem is distrust of elites, any 'top down' approach is inherently limited. It is preferable to champion horizontal, collaborative approaches, relying on the participation of civil society.
4) *Governments should hold digital platforms accountable, but also share information with them when helpful in a public-private cooperation:* Make the sources of their advertising public—by demanding the same level of transparency as is required of traditional media; implement adequate measures with which to fight information manipulation on their websites and contribute to the improvement of media literacy and the awareness of the general public of these issues.
5) *Practice effective fact-checking: Firstly,* the correction must not directly undercut one's vision of the world (otherwise it can even have the perverse effect of reinforcing the person's primary beliefs—this was observed in the case of Iraq's weapons of mass destruction, and discussions on climate change and vaccination). *Secondly,* the correction must entail an explanation of why and how disinformation was spread.
6) Adopt an international charter of journalistic ethics in a collaborative manner, involving both major traditional and online media. Train journalists on how to cover a massive leak, detecting a fake profile, reacting to extremist content.

5.2.19 Facebook and French Government

What might have sounded like an oxymoron to most people was, in reality, a simple statement of fact: the era of social media's voluntary self-regulation is over. Macron's remarks followed the announcement of a new, "experimental" partnership between the French government and Facebook. The cooperation, slated to take place in the first half of 2019, will see a delegation of French investigators work closely with the social network to monitor to how it tackles online hate. It is the first time that the normally wary technology company opens its door to regulators in such a way. (Grant, 2004)[34] This unprecedented move marks Facebook's latest effort to stave off criticism of how it is combating abuse and the spread of hate and disinformation on its platform. For the social media giant, it also signals a tactical shift away from exhorting self-regulation as the only means to police the industry to actually fighting for a seat at the regulatory table.

In recent years, European lawmakers have ramped up legislative efforts to rein in big tech. France is not only embedding itself inside social media companies but is also seeking new "fake news" laws to have courts to rule over the accuracy of media reports during elections. If passed, it would grant authority to the French national broadcasting agency to take any foreign TV station suspected to spread "false information" to alter the course of an election off the air. And on January 1st, 2018, Germany's controversial Network Enforcement Law or NetzDG entered into force, requiring that sites remove "illegal" content, including defamation, incitements to violence, and hate speech within twenty-four hours of it being reported, or face fines up to fifty million euros.

Since the global outcry over data breaches and foreign election meddling, Facebook and others have taken non-negligible steps toward to addressing these issues, including shutting down accounts linked to Kremlin-backed trolls and increasing transparency around digital advertising and research shows that some of these initiatives have paid off in stemming the wave of nefarious content on the social network. In September, an alliance of tech and advertising companies that includes Google, Facebook and Mozilla also pledged to abide by a code of conduct and work together to fight online disinformation. The group committed, for instance, to restrict advertising services to legitimate individuals and parties, prioritize truthful information in feeds and search results, and demote false content. But these strategies are far from foolproof. The Oxford Internet Institute recently found that 25 percent of content shared on Twitter ahead of the U.S. midterm elections came from "junk news" sites—that is polarizing, misleading or conspiratorial sources that try to pass as professional news—up from 20 percent in 2016. Moreover, larger audiences than before interacted with junk content on Facebook. The type of rhetoric once only embraced by the more extreme fringes of the political spectrum has seemingly become more mainstream. (Grant, 2004)[35] Following mounting pressures from policymakers worldwide, tech companies have been pushed to enforce murky and, at times, inconsistent content moderation policies on their platforms, often at the expense of legitimate political expression. Importantly, in the absence of a broader framework of public oversight to monitor their decision making processes and practices, social networks have an incentive to remove content in an ad hoc fashion to avoid facing legal, reputational or financial consequences. In that sense, a trend toward a French method of "cooperative" regulation that would involve formal consultations with government and advocacy groups should be welcomed.

5.2.20 Yellow Vests Protests

France opened a probe into possible Russian interference behind the country's Yellow Vest protests, after reports that social-media accounts linked to Moscow have increasingly targeted the movement. According to the Alliance for Securing Democracy, about 600 Twitter accounts known to promote Kremlin views have begun focusing on France, boosting their use of the hashtag #giletsjaunes, the French name for the Yellow Vest movement. French security services are looking at the situation, Foreign Minister Jean-Yves Le Drian said Sunday in a radio interview with RTL. Russia has been criticized for using social media to influence elections in the U.S. and elsewhere. Attempts to use fake news reports and cyberattacks to undercut the 2017 campaign of French President Emmanuel Macron failed, but Russian-linked sites have pushed questionable reports of a mutiny among police, and of officers' support for the protests. (Matlack & Williams, 2018)[36] The Twitter accounts monitored by the alliance usually feature U.S. or British news.

But the French protests "have been at or near the top" of their activity for at least a week, according to Bret Schafer, the alliance's Washington-based social media analyst. "That's a pretty strong indication that there is interest in amplifying the conflict" for audiences outside France. The Alliance for Securing Democracy is a unit of the German Marshall Fund of the U.S., which monitors pro-Kremlin activity.

5.2.21 Russian State Media

Much of the tweeted material comes from Russian state media outlets including the Sputnik news website, the RT television network, and Ruptly, a German-based video news agency that belongs to RT. These outlets are covering the French crisis closely; RT has said that 12 of its journalists have been injured in the protests, far more than any other news organization. Sputnik and RT have reported in recent days that most French police no longer support Macron and are siding with the protesters. Their sources: representatives of two small police unions that together won less than 4 percent of votes in nationwide union elections this month. Sputnik and RT also have shown a video – widely shared on French social media – of police in the southwestern town of Pau removing their helmets in what was described as a sign of solidarity with protesters. Local police and journalists on the scene said the description was untrue. They said some officers had briefly removed their helmets to talk with protesters before putting them back on. In response to questions from Bloomberg News, Sputnik later corrected its article about police in Pau showing solidarity with protesters, to say the report "hasn't been backed by evidence so far." RT said its article about police siding with protesters, based on comments by the head of a minor police union, was justified because he had been quoted by other news outlets. Macron complained repeatedly during his 2017 campaign that Kremlin-controlled media outlets were spreading fake news about him, because he took a tougher stance on Russia than his chief rivals, Marine Le Pen of the far-right National Front and François Fillon of the conservative Republicans. But negative stories, such as a Sputnik report claiming Macron lived a "double life" and was backed by a "wealthy gay lobby," never gained traction. (Matlack& Williams, 2018)[37] In one instance, a bogus website resembling the site of a Belgian newspaper reported that Macron's campaign was being bankrolled by Saudi Arabia. The source of the hoax was never determined, but the European Union's East Stratcom Task Force, which tracks Russian disinformation efforts, said it bore striking similarities to an earlier incident traced to a Russian "troll factory." Separately, the Macron campaign was hit with repeated email phishing attacks resembling those used by Russia against Democratic Party organizations in the U.S. The Kremlin said it had no involvement in any fake news or cyberattacks on Macron, describing such accusations as "slander."

5.2.22 Conclusion

Taking everything into account, the news-media holds critical power in the situation of a delegate between a state's outside arrangement contraption and the state's polis. Globalization and the internationalization of popular supposition make for this relationship to be never-endingly moving. France demonstrated in 2008 that its delicate power depended on computerized advances. In spite of the fact that somewhat the French demonstrated their publicity associations on those of the British, it is likewise evident that all extensively law based nations reacted to the strains of the war along these lines. The investigation of wartime promulgation for France has been to a great extent worried about the final result, especially issues of wartime oversight, and with the opposition of French intelligent people (and the expected obstruction of the mass of the populace) to their own side's residential publicity, later rejected as bourrage de crâne ("mind stuffing"). In spite of the declaration of the local political ceasefire or Union sacrée toward the beginning of the war, progressive French governments and the French Army were suspicious of the national press as being exceptionally politicized and degenerate. Oversight was managed by enacting old nineteenth century laws administering security and direct amid a condition of attack, refreshed in October 1913, and the Ministry of War made a Press Commission incorporating paper delegates in August 1914 to supervise its activity. From the beginning of the war, France had unmistakable control of its national and local press, with a few papers being briefly suspended for infringement of press guidelines, and stories showing up with areas blanked out by the edit. This was apparently done on military grounds, including endeavors to supplant all provincial non-military personnel blue pencils with military work force; yet there were likewise contentions that progressive governments were controlling or stifling their political rivals. By the center of 1917, after the stun of the French Army uprisings, the legislature and the press worked out a businesslike methodology like that of the British, with the press left to be to a great extent automatic inside acknowledged wartime rules. Most formal authority purposeful publicity was delivered or coordinated by the Ministry of War as a feature of the more extensive French excellent methodology. In October 1914 the Army made an Information Section to give the press ordinary dispatches from the front. In January 1916 the Maison de la Presse (press agency) was built up in Paris to organize official publicity abroad. By mid-1917, the Army had additionally permitted authority war journalists at the front, in addition to picture takers and cine-cameramen who delivered an official newsreel, trading material with the British. Most as of late, India on Wednesday joined a France drove activity to receive an announcement to counter psychological oppression and radicalisation web based incorporating internet-based life in the setting of Christchurch mosque assault. The truth of the matter is that French strategy has commonly not been professed to be impacted by the media and this makes it substantially more intriguing, empowering work to be done on what counter forces may exist in French political life that would hinder the proposed systems of media weight and impact.

5.3 The United States of America and Social Media

The world acknowledged it from before and now the US citizens realize and acknowledge it that its media is biased. They with impunity distort and manipulate through its reportage with omissions, distortions and blatant bias, coverage like 'Invasion of Iraq' by the way of chemical stockpile by Iraq. US believes and recognizes that media control or influence is critical to their unipolar power in geopolitical scenario. It is pertinent to have an independent media for any vibrant democracy. The conflict with expansionist and foreign policy, US tends to manipulate the media to gain support of its allies and maintain its efficacy in the unipolar world. Invasion of Vietnam, Iraq and numerous other events famously uttered words of President Bush 'Either you are with US or with the terrorists' and ultimately the elimination of Osama. The US uses its media including social media to the hilt. The manipulation is so very common that even the right wing US citizens realize this fact. The Wikileaks are examples of how US meddles in internal affairs of sovereign countries. The corporate houses and the owners of 'free press' tend to lend their support in line with their ease of doing business. Political communication scholars have long been interested in the role of the news media in shaping and reporting on the foreign policy of the United States and how that coverage (or lack of it) influences domestic public opinion and policymakers' priorities and decisions. That said, the amount of scholarly attention to this area has increased markedly in the last 25 years, and—undoubtedly owing to the United States waging two wars (and a "global war on terror") in the aftermath of the 9/11 terrorist attacks—the area has seen an even greater quantity and quality of theoretical, empirical, and qualitative contributions over the last 10 years. Still, in many ways it would be fair to say that political communication scholars' understanding of media, foreign policy, and war is still in its relative infancy, certainly as compared with other areas such as American politics, domestic public opinion, social movements, and media influence generally. Yet as the area has grown, it has become clear that what scholars have learned about media coverage, source-journalist dynamics, and media influence sometimes but not always maps from the domestic to foreign policy domains. The media flow from the U.S. to the rest of the world, so-called CNN effect, constituted a soft power and made the U.S. a global hegemonic power in the 1990s. In the 2000s, the broader range of information technology frames and new networks have been taking place in the form of contra flows against American hegemony. As another remarkable success, in 1991 CNN could broadcast from the frontlines of the war zone during the Persian Gulf War. CNN's coverage helped the international society to figure out what was happening in Iraq. It began to take attention to conflict areas and change people's minds. For instance, it is known that the pictures of starving children in the Somalia crisis pushed President Bush toward action.

5.3.1 US Press Freedom

Press freedom index as acknowledged by reporters without borders is very low than as often assumed to be high. The US media is President centric like Obama believed in free press as compared to Bush and now Trump. Trump even manipulated his presidentship through manipulation of social media. It is normally thought—and expected—that US press freedom would rank top in the world. Yet, for many years, it has been a lot lower than the high expectation. For 2011, the US ranked just 47th. It has been around these low numbers for a number of years, especially during the Bush Administration's "War on Terror". For a while, under the Obama Administration it was looking better, but recent events such as the various occupy protest movements and how journalists have been treated has resulted in the recent drops in the rankings. As Josh Stearns from Free Press and the Free Press Action Fund worries, the cherished US First Amendment is being taken for granted.

5.3.2 Political Pressure on Media, too

Political bias can also creep in too. Media watchdog, Fairness and Accuracy in reporting (FAIR) did a study of ABC World News Tonight, CBS Evening News and NBC Nightly News in 2001 in which they found that "92 percent of all U.S. sources interviewed were white, 85 percent were male and, where party affiliation was identifiable, 75 percent were Republican." While of course this is not a complete study of the mainstream media, it does show that there can be heavy political biases on even the most popular mainstream media outlets. Media and media houses pay a significant role seeing its own profitability and businesses thus jeopardizing the very essence of 'free press'. (Shah, 2012)[38]

5.3.3 Media Power is Political Power

Concentrated ownership of media results in less diversity. This means that the political discourse that shapes the nation is also affected. And, given the prominence of the United States in the world, this is obviously an important issue. However, politicians can often be hesitant about criticizing the media too much, as the following from Ben H. Bagdikian summarizes:

> Media power is political power. Politicians hesitate to offend the handful of media operators who control how those politicians will be presented—or not presented—to the voters. Media political power has always been a fixture in American history. But today the combination of the media industry and traditional corporate power has reached dimensions former generations could not match. ... Today ... political variety among

the mainstream media has disappeared. As the country enters the twenty-first century, the news and analyses of progressive ideas and groups are close to absent in the major media. Similarly absent is commentary on dangers of this political one-sidedness to American democracy.

5.3.4 Chomsky/Herman Propaganda Model

Using their propaganda model, Chomsky and Herman, attempt to demonstrate how "money and power are able to filter out the news, ... marginalize dissent, and allow the government and dominant private interests to get their message across to the public."

- Size, concentrated ownership, owner wealth, and profit orientation of the dominant mass-media firms
- Advertising as the primary income source of the mass media
- Reliance of the media on information provided by government, business and "experts" funded and approved by these primary sources and agents of power
- "Flak" as a means of disciplining the media
- "Anticommunism" as a national religion and control mechanism.

5.3.5 Size and Concentrated Ownership

These corporate media houses play a significant role in shaping public opinion throughout the world. It has its negative impact as well. Everything is dictated by its businesses in this open market economy as to what is best for US and its corporate houses. When studied deeply its an open secret that there is no permanent friend in this market driven world. The dumping of Pakistan best illustrated US's geopolitical moves.

5.3.6 Advertising as primary income source encourages dumbing down

On the advertising ingredient, Chomsky and Herman also point out that the pressures to show a continual series of programmes that will encourage "audience flow" (watching from programme to programme so that advertising rates and revenues are sustained) results from advertisers wanting, in general, "to avoid programs with serious complexities and disturbing controversies that interfere with the "buying mood." (Herman & Chomsky, 1988)[39]

5.3.7 Reliance on Official Sources and the Powerful

On the reliance upon official sources ingredient, Chomsky and Herman point out that because sources such as the government and businesses are often well known, they are deemed reputable and therefore not questioned much. However, when another government offers news items, we are often able to recognize it as possible propaganda, or at least treat it with some scrutiny that requires further verification.

5.3.8 US Media and Cold War

Specifically, during the Cold War the United States had used the media in getting its ideological message out in the rest of the world. Together with its hard power and economical means, the media had contributed to the empowerment of US hegemony. The media flows from the US to the other countries worked to spread its anti-communist propaganda and to provide reassurance to its alliances that the transatlantic perspective was valid against the Soviet threat. Tactical disinformation about opposing forces undermined the Soviet attempts and manipulated international public opinion. Media made an important contribution to international relations as the tools of distribution of political actors' images. CNN began in the 1980s with a goal of the 24 hour span of international news available with the local reporters from the different parts of the world. During China's Tiananmen Square uprising in 1989, CNN deserved respect through its 24-hour report.

5.3.9 CNN Effect

Since the 1990s, the dominant debate on the media-politics relationships has centered on the so-called "CNN effect". Media would act as a pitfall agenda setting agent in related to the choice and selection for the sake of national interests. They would become an accelerant in shortening response time for decision and policy making or they would move as an impediment actor that operates through the impact of public opinion. As an agenda setting agent, the news media have an important job in defining issues, primarily to help the public understand the newest array of priorities and alliances. In this context, the news coverage can be useful for justifying state actions by shaping what people around the world think of it. For instance, in 2003 the U.S. war against Iraq was defined as a war of liberation by the White House and produced media campaign to support that idea. In this case, modern media acted as considerable allies in selling the war and sustaining public support for it. When the media become an accelerant, they influence the strategies and behavior of those in power by creating sense of urgency, increasing public awareness and anxiety, leading to pressure to "do something". As the third approach of the CNN effect, when the media act as an impediment actor, they help to spread multiple frames, bring third parties into conflict and help to shape public opinion which in turn affect policymakers' decisions on political conflicts. The opposition to government's foreign policy can be an outcome of the media coverage which is sourced by the domestic political division. In this circumstance, the media's power to distribute the reaction against official policy in public, pressure and interest groups can led the change of balance of power due to administration fail into control the process of the crises management. For an illustration, it can be argued that the collapse of America's will to fight in Vietnam resulted from the media's reporting of foreign policy. In this case, the media coverage was affected by the domestic political divisions and spread a demoralization of involving in an unsuccessful limited war. The media caused the Johnson administration's failure to explain to the American public and Congress why the U.S. troops were fighting in Vietnam; thus the strong public reaction occurred against the government's foreign policy.

5.3.10 US Media and War on Terror

In the academic literature the role of American media in the Bush administration's "the war on terror" and how the national media constructed a link with the events and Saddam regime in Iraq were indicated in the various attempts. Washington's surge morality tale offered all the components of a complete and substantive frame to gain the public support for the Iraq war. The era of post-9/11 has provided Western leaders a preventative measure to pre-empt possible risks and threats which has produced rationale new forms of humanitarian and human rights-based intervention. In doing so, they hoped to recapture a sense of purpose and meaning for themselves and their society.

Therefore, it can be argued that the staging war or acts of terrorism as the media events feed the change in the character of war. This fundamental shift in the politics of Western societies has given rise to importance of media coverage by intensive emphasis on image, spectacle and media presentation.

5.3.11 US Media and Vietnam War

Vietnam became a subject of large-scale news coverage in the United States only after substantial numbers of U.S. combat troops had been committed to the war in the spring of 1965. Prior to that time, the number of American newsmen in Indochina had been small— fewer than two dozen even as late as 1964. By 1968, at the height of the war, there were about 600 accredited journalists of all nationalities in Vietnam, reporting for U.S. wire services, radio and television networks, and the major newspaper chains and news magazines. The U.S. Military Assistance Command, Vietnam (MACV) made military transportation readily available to news people, and some took advantage of this frequently to venture into the field and get their stories first-hand. The media's tendency toward negative reporting helped to undermine support for the war in the United States while its uncensored coverage provided valuable information to the enemy in Vietnam. In any case, American disillusionment with the war was a product of many causes, of which the media was only one. What most undermined support for the war was simply the level of American casualties: the greater the increase in casualties, the lower the level of public support for the war. In the words of Richard Nixon, "The Vietnam War was complicated by factors that had never before occurred in America's conduct of a war... The American news media had come to dominate domestic opinion about its purpose and conduct... In each night's TV news and each morning's paper the war was reported battle by battle, but little or no sense of the underlying purpose of the fighting was conveyed. Eventually this contributed to the impression that we were fighting in military and moral quicksand, rather than toward an important and worthwhile objective. More than ever before, television showed the terrible human suffering and sacrifice of war. Whatever the intention behind such relentless and literal reporting of the war, the result was a serious demoralization of the home front, raising the question whether America would ever again be able to fight an enemy abroad with unity and strength of purpose at home."

And James Reston, writing on the day Communist forces completed their triumphant final drive on Saigon, concluded, "Maybe the historians will agree that the reporters and the cameras were decisive in the end. They brought the issue of the war to the people, before the Congress or the courts, and forced the withdrawal of American power from Vietnam." (Hallin, 1986)[40] Public opinion polls are never perfect, but they provide a useful tool for measuring the public's view of the Vietnam War. In 1965, Americans were largely supportive. Fully 64 percent believed that America was right to send troops to Vietnam and only 21 percent disagreed. These numbers did not change dramatically until May 1966, when the percentage of Americans who saw the Vietnam War as "a mistake" jumped ten points, likely due to increasing casualties. The polls fluctuated over the next year but showed increasing disenchantment with the war. Americans were shocked to see Marines battling Vietcong commandos for the U.S. embassy in Saigon, the center of the American presence in Vietnam. A now-famous photo of a South Vietnamese general executing a Vietcong prisoner forced Americans to question their allies. Evidence indicates the press is responsible for revealing the naked, uncensored truth regarding war to the American public. As news reports became increasingly negative, public opinion compelled the government to down size troop deployment; therefore, forcing an adjustment to America's policy in Vietnam.

5.3.12 Social Media and Foreign Policy

Social media has created an environment which both empowers citizens, and puts diplomats under public scrutiny in a way that the mainstream media was unable to do previously. Social media and the internet have changed the way that information is disseminated to the public. Once upon a time, information was only accessible through the institutions of the State and the flow of information between governments and citizens tightly controlled. Since the internet we have seen this model turned on its head completely, as the costs of recording and distributing information dramatically dropped and the steady rise of citizen journalists, bloggers and online activists began. As the growing use of digital devices and social media platforms spilled over from the private to the public sector, the use of social media in aiding governments in achieving their policy goals both at home and abroad became a widely adopted strategy. Over the last decade we've seen social media help create radical change and shift countries towards equality and democracy, such as the role of Twitter in the 2011 Arab Spring.

5.3.13 Trump and Social Media

The Trump presidency has given us a robust selection of Twitter diplomacy examples, as heated exchanges have played out between government officials and foreign dignitaries for the world to follow, and all in 120 characters or less. First there was the war over the wall between Trump and former Mexican President Vicente Fox, with the latter using social media to attack Trump's oft repeated campaign promise to build a border wall (and make Mexico pay for it.)

The most recent example, is the escalation of hostile language between Trump and North Korea's Kim Jong Un, with North Korean officials declaring the President's tweets amount to a declaration of war.

5.3.14 Social Media and 2016 Presidential Elections

There is considerable concern about the role that social media, such as Facebook and Twitter, play in promoting misperceptions during political campaigns. These technologies are widely used, and inaccurate information flowing across them has a high profile. On November 19, 2016, *the New York Times* editorial board published a scathing critique of Face book's failure to stop the spread of falsehoods in the lead up to the 2016 US Presidential Election. Mark Zuckerberg, the founder and chief executive of Facebook, has dismissed the notion that fake news is prevalent on his platform or that it had an influence on the election. But according to a Buzz Feed News analysis, during the last three months of the presidential campaign, the 20 top fake news stories on Facebook generated more engagement—shares, likes and comments—than the 20 top stories from real news websites. These hoaxes are not just bouncing around among like-minded conspiracy theorists; candidates and elected officials are sharing them, too. Senator Ben Sasse, The Republican of Nebraska, on Thursday tweeted about people who have been paid to riot against Mr. Trump—an idea propagated by fake news stories. A man who wrote a number of false news reports told The Washington

Post that Trump supporters and campaign officials often shared his false anti-Clinton posts without bothering to confirm the facts and that he believes his work may have helped elect the Republican nominee.

The Russian government interfered in the 2016 US presidential election with the goal of harming the campaign of Hillary Clinton, boosting the candidacy of Donald Trump, and increasing political or social discord in the United States. Russia's covert activities were first publicly disclosed by members of the United States Congress on September 22, 2016, confirmed by the United States Intelligence Community on October 7, 2016, and further detailed by the Director of National Intelligence office three months later. According to US intelligence agencies, the operation was ordered directly by Russian President Vladimir Putin. Former FBI director Robert Mueller led the Special Counsel investigation into the interference from May 2017 to March 2019. (Wikipedia)[41] The clandestine influence campaign involved the Internet Research Agency "troll farm" creating thousands of social media accounts that impersonated Americans supporting radical groups, planning and promoting pro-Trump and anti-Clinton rallies, and reached millions of social media users between 2013 and 2017. According to criminal indictments by the Special Counsel, those messages and activities "spread distrust towards the candidates and the political system in general", for example by discouraging African Americans from voting or by motivating conservative voters wary of Trump. Additionally, hackers affiliated with the Russian military intelligence service (GRU) penetrated computer systems of the Democratic National Committee (DNC), the Democratic Congressional Campaign Committee (DCCC), and Clinton campaign officials, notably chairman John Podesta. Tens of thousands of private emails and attachments were released to the public during the final months of the campaign, via DCLeaks, Guccifer 2.0 and Wikileaks. The exposed information exacerbated tensions within the Democratic Party, leading to the resignation of DNC chairwoman Debbie Wasserman Schultz and reduced voter support for Clinton. Russia-connected individuals also reached out to various Trump campaign associates, offering business opportunities to the Trump Organisation and damaging information on Clinton. Russian government officials have repeatedly denied involvement in any of the hacks or leaks. The Russian interference activities triggered strong statements from

American intelligence agencies, a direct warning by then-US president Barack Obama to Russian president Vladimir Putin, renewed economic sanctions against Russia, closures of Russian diplomatic facilities and expulsion of their staff. The Senate and House Intelligence Committees have conducted their own investigations into the matter.

Trump denied that the interference occurred, contending that it was a "hoax" perpetrated by Democrats to explain Clinton's loss. He dismissed FBI Director James Comey in part over his investigation of Russian meddling. The Special Counsel investigation, which concluded in March 2019, stated that the Russia interference "violated U.S. criminal law" and resulted in indictments of twenty-six Russian citizens and three Russian organizations. The investigation also led to indictments and convictions of Trump campaign officials and associated Americans, although none of the charges involved coordination or conspiracy with Russian interference efforts. The Special Counsel's report, made public on April 18, 2019, examined numerous contacts between the Trump campaign and Russian officials but concluded that there was insufficient evidence to bring any conspiracy or coordination charges against Trump or his associates.

5.3.15 US Government disseminating prepackaged, even fake news

In March 2005, *the New York Times* revealed that there has been a large amount of fake and prepackaged news created by US government departments, such as the Pentagon, the State Department and others, and disseminated through the mainstream media. *The New York Times* noted a number of important issues including:

- The US Bush administration has "aggressively" used public relations to prepackage news. Issues with this have included that:
- A number of these government-made news segments are made to look like local news (either by the government department or by the receiving broadcaster);
- Often fake reporters when a ""reporter" covering airport safety was actually a public relations professional working under a false name for the Transportation Security Administration";
- Often a video segment is produced by the government; which

is still taken by public as reportage of media;

- Where there is some attribution, news stations simply rebroadcast them but sometimes without attributing the source.
- These segments have reached millions;
- This benefit both the government and the broadcaster;
- This could amount to propaganda within the United States as well as internationally.

Effectively, American tax payers have paid to be subjected to propaganda disseminated through these massaged messaged.

5.3.16 Cultural Bias

Cultural bias (as with perhaps any country) has an effect on how something is reported as well. For example, look at how we in Europe and USA perceive the Muslim/Islamic world and the "threat" of Islam, due to media concentration on certain aspects of the news. (Since writing the above, around 1999, we of course have witnessed a horrible series of terrorist attacks on the US. The resulting war on terror and various attitudes towards the Muslim world has also become negative too. For more on these issues see this see this site's war on terror section.) The USA media coverage of President Clinton's historic tour of Africa (the first tour by an American President) came under a bit of scrutiny. The previous link mentions how some right-winged politicians made comments on TV about how embarrassed they were when Clinton made some unofficial "apologies" relating to black slavery. Instead, they blamed Africans for the slave trade! America has also had to contend with the legacy of the Cold War. An ideological battle that required a "counter" propaganda effort against communist propaganda. Propaganda battles often involve over-simplifying. Furthermore, the decades of this meant generations were indoctrinated into a specific way of thinking. As such, even though the Cold War is now over, the mainstream struggles to rid itself of those ways of thinking and talking; whether it is how the rest of the world is viewed, or whether cherished principles and issues are oversimplified, it permeates throughout media and culture.

5.3.17 Al Jazeera Effect

"The Al Jazeera Effect," introduced by Philip Seib from the University of Southern California, discusses "new" media, in particular satellite television and the Internet. Seib posits that the media are indeed able to change the status quo of foreign policy by shaping international and domestic public opinion. Seib's main idea is the "virtual state:" disperse communities achieve an unprecedented cohesion that puts them on the political map internationally. Satellite media and the Internet foster "virtual sovereignty" by cultivating a shared identity among disperse members of ethnic or religious communities. This is relevant for foreign policy because virtual states can affect the stability of traditional states and regions. Media can also alleviate tensions and conflict by providing new perspectives to an unprecedentedly large audience. Seib recommends that, if policymakers want to take advantage of the media's power to create communities, cooperation is a better approach than competition, and international media, such as Voice of America and Deutsche Welle, become relevant tools of foreign politics. (Seib, 2011)[42]

5.3.18 Conclusion

It is evident that US uses its media to maintain its unipolarity and floods the information technology world and its allies with social, internet, emails, Twitter with information to get the resultant effect of the US action against its challenges. The use of media, social media and information technology to term any state as rogue like Iran, media was used to term North Korea and Trump meeting as historic and even the entire world was led to believe that Trump should be nominated for noble peace prize. Such is the power of media/information technology. World is led to believe the day in day out 24x7 reportage and social media uses that even a distorted fact seems real. Its creation of information mirage. The world is waking up to this rude shock and ultimately it will information i.e., media/social media which is able to manipulate the world population. The emergence of social media has changed the way in which political communication takes place in the United States. Political institutions such as politicians, political parties, foundations, institutions, and political think tanks are all using social media platforms, like Facebook and Twitter, to communicate with and engage voters. Regular individuals, politicians, "pundits" and thought leaders alike are able to voice their opinions, engage with a wide network, and connect with other likeminded individuals.[1] The active participation of social media users has been an increasingly important element in political communication, especially during political elections in the 2000s. Social media are changing the nature of political communication because they are tools that can be used to inform and mobilize users in new ways.

Users are able to connect directly to politicians and campaign managers and engage in political activities in new ways. Each social media platform is programmed in code by developers, creating a unique digital architecture that influences how politicians and citizens can use the platform for political ends.[3] For example, by simply pressing the "like button" on Facebook or by following someone on Twitter, users have the ability to connect with others and express their views in new ways. The option for users to share, like, or retweet political messages instantly has opened up a new avenue for politicians to reach out to voters. At the same time, social media campaigns can carry risks that are not present on traditional platforms, such as TV or newspaper ads. Whereas the political party controls all of the messaging on a TV or newspaper ad, in a social media campaign, critics and opposing party supporters can post negative comments immediately below campaign messages. Five major conclusions about media and foreign affairs are well grounded in past work: (1) the press-state power dynamic clearly favors political elites, especially the president; (2) coverage of foreign policy outside of war tends to be scarce, elite-driven, ethnocentric, and uncritical; (3) war coverage is all of those things, only more so, plus casualty-free and tactically/episodically driven rather than focusing on geostrategic or more thematic issues and implications; (4) media coverage, especially in crises, can contribute to rallies in public opinion; and (5) these trends have become exacerbated since the early 1980s as news organizations have cut their foreign news budgets and overseas bureaus drastically. (Aday, 2017)[43] At the same time, at least five areas of research political communication scholars are still in an embryonic stage: First, the role of emotion in both the processing of foreign policy events and media coverage of them. Emotion clearly plays a role in how people make sense of international events and news, especially in crises, but we are only beginning to understand how and why. Second, this area of inquiry has a long way to go in explaining what, if any, effects exposure to casualty images produces. Because it involves the wide variety of variables at play, this topic, which is highly relevant to policy and newsroom ethics' debates and policies, is ideally suited to a rich research agenda. Third, despite frequent punditry to the contrary, we know precious little about the effects and role of new and social media on collective action, system support, democracy building, and message reception, to name just a few dependent variables. Fourth, political communication needs to pay more attention to foreign policy not involving wars or crises. Fifth, more attention needs to be paid in coming years to how the transition to online news, both for new and traditional media organizations, influences the media-state-public dynamic. It could be, for instance, that cheaper forms of producing and distributing international news (e.g., "backpacker" journalism and cell phone video cameras), including by amateurs, will arrest the downward spiral in the amount and caliber of foreign news available to American audiences. At this point, however, it is fair to say that despite the existence of some insightful foreign policy and war reporters, a strong argument can be made in favor of the notion that the press is failing to meet its Fourth Estate challenge when it comes to foreign affairs coverage.

It can be argued that in the linkage between the media and foreign policy, public opinion is the key component in the media's effectiveness on a certain foreign policy decision. The media's contribution in conduct of policy is its power to create a favorable climate for the officials in decision making by the coverage of certain issues which can attract large audience attention to gain public support. (Coban, 2016)[44]

5.4 UK Foreign Policy and Social Media

5.4.1 Introduction

Foreign policy is not made in a political vacuum but is shaped by domestic factors (such as public opinion), globalizing pressures (such as communications technologies), integrative tendencies (especially within the European Union) and transnational forces (such as lobbying from NGOs). The logic underlying the UK's foreign policy process, however has changed remarkably little over the past century. Ideally, ministers, officials and outsiders with relevant expertise should formulate policy on the basis of informed discussion of the possible; alternatives and after taking due account of the relevant history and precedents, the positions of the institutions involved and the legality of what is proposed. Once formulated, policy needs to be interpreted by official agents and implemented in order to achieve the desired objectives. During all three phases, policy also needs to be presented or 'sold' to a variety of audiences both at home and abroad. Formulation, interpretation, implementation and presentation are thus integral stages of the policy-making process; indeed, it is often difficult to judge where one stops and another begins. The combination of actors, institutions and external pressures involved in this process vary depending on the issue in question, but this ideal of how to make policy appears to have remained constant. It is also possible to identify some general characteristics of the process in the UK that apply irrespective of which political party is in office. First, while the same goals and commitments can persist for long periods, foreign policy-making is best conceptualized as a dynamic process that exists in a dialectical relationship with the outside world. Second, at times, the process is wide-ranging, involving officials from all areas of government and a (growing) number of outsiders from both foreign governments and NGOs. Nevertheless, the process remains among the most secret in government. It is not just the public who have difficulty in finding out where and when foreign policy decisions were taken or what the rationale behind them is. (Williams, 2004)[45] The Internet revolution has affected all aspects of life, including International relations. Diplomacy as a tool of foreign policy has also being transformed by this revolution. Digital diplomacy and Internet activities as a whole can greatly assist in projecting a state's foreign policy positions to domestic and foreign audiences.

5.4.2 Definition

The United Kingdom's Foreign and Commonwealth Office (FCO) elaborates its definition of digital diplomacy on its website thus: Digital diplomacy is solving foreign policy problems using the internet. It is conventional diplomacy through a different medium. Through the web we can listen, publish, engage and evaluate in new and interesting ways. Crucially, we can also widen our reach and communicate directly with civil society as well as governments and influential individuals ... Why are we doing it? Because we have to ... Those whose ideals and objectives we oppose are active and highly effective at using the web. If we don't take up the digital debate, we lose our argument by default. Many of our partners, particularly those outside government, have an established digital presence, engaged audiences and expertise in achieving goals online. If we don't work with them, we're missing a huge opportunity. Our shift from one—way web publishing into active digital diplomacy reflects the changing way we all use the web—as a multi—way social medium as well as a source of information. We lose credibility and cannot claim to be an open organization if we don't take part. The Internet has its effects in foreign policy as it does in every other area of government policy. The technology now controls the way in which information flows around the globe. This has enabled the "news", which is the base material of foreign policy and the way governments interact with each other, to become faster, more readily available, and able to reach almost every part of the world. The interactions of governments, which are the purpose of diplomacy, are being affected by these developments in significant ways. The prospect for even faster, and potentially more far-reaching, changes in the future will require foreign ministries to be nimble and informed in their responses. Thus, diplomacy has always had to adapt and change to the particular communication forms of its environment. In a world where everyone is increasingly connected, the ability to gather and share information to wide audiences at unprecedented rates has created new opportunities for policy leaders and government departments to share messages and set political agendas beyond traditional channels. While conventional forms of diplomacy still dominate both the domestic and foreign policy landscape, an increasing number of governments are utilizing technology as a new tool for communication, information gathering, and the promotion of values both at home and abroad. The UK @Foreign Office has probably the largest "twiplomatic" network and maintains a public Twitter list with a record 237 ambassadors, embassies and missions on Twitter. The UK FCO have an Office of Digital Diplomacy that is involved in a range of ediplomacy activities. Sweden has also been active in the promotion of digital diplomacy, especially through the online communication strategy of its foreign minister Carl Bildt who soon became "best connected Twitter leader". The UK Prime Minister @Number10gov is the most followed EU leader with more than three million followers ahead of Italy's @MatteoRenzi with 1.7 million followers. The influence of the

British media on British foreign policy is largely hinged upon the changing culture of politics whereby the means of international thinking and action are changing as they become progressively shaped by digitization and the Internet especially in Western Europe and North America. Furthermore, in the age of globalization and contemporary media, "top-down" communications have changed and become more lateral between people around the world.

5.4.3 History of British Foreign Policy

5.4.3.1 Policy of Isolation

After oust of Napoleon in the Battle of Waterloo in 1815, England pursued a strategy of reserved quality from European legislative issues. The facts confirm that from 1815 to 1822 she co-worked with different individuals from the Quadruple Alliance to keep up harmony in Europe, however after the demise of Clastlereagh in 1822, Canning came to control. He was not captivated of universal co-task, and subsequently the period of Congresses finished after the Congress of Verona in 1822. In 1877, the renowned "Bulgarian abominations" occurred. A large number of Christians were killed by the Turks. Gladstone engaged Disraeli to go to the assistance of the abused Christians, yet the last wouldn't do as such. Russia went to the assistance of Bulgaria and pronounced war against Turkey. The last was vanquished and compelled to sign the Treaty of San Stefano in 1878. By this arrangement, Russia came to have an overwhelming position in the Balkans. This couldn't go on without serious consequences by Great Britain and Austria. The outcome was that they asked her either to present the Treaty of San Stefano to Congress of European statesmen or face the results of rebelliousness. At the point when Russia found that Great Britain and Austria were making military arrangements on a huge scale and there was each probability of war being pronounced, she chose to submit. She was at that point depleted and couldn't bear to battle against the new troopers of Austria and Great Britain. At the Congress of Berlin, Great Britain had the option to deny Russia of her additions by the Treaty of San Stefano. She additionally got the Island of Cyprus. At the point when Disraeli returned from Berlin to London, he announced that he had brought "harmony with respect". In general, Great Britain pursued an arrangement of detachment towards

European issues. This approach was viewed as to the greatest advantage of the nation. There was no need of constantly meddling in European legislative issues when a similar reason could be served by periodic impedance. Notwithstanding, it turned out to be obvious to the British statesmen towards the finish of the nineteenth century that it was difficult to keep on following an arrangement of amazing confinement. An increasingly positive approach was made essential by specific improvements in European issues since 1870.

5.4.3.2 Anglo-Japanese Alliance (1902)

The first breach in the policy of splendid isolation was made in 1902 when Great Britain entered into a Treaty of Alliance with Japan. The treaty declared that Great Britain and Japan were actuated "solely by a desire to maintain the status quo and general peace in the extreme East." Their object was to uphold "the independence and territorial integrity of the Empire of China and the Empire of Korea." Equal opportunities for commerce and industry were to be guaranteed to all nations. England was stated to have special interests in China, and Japan both in China and Korea.

It was provided that if either Japan or England was involved in a war with any other power in defence of her interests, the other country was to remain neutral. If Japan or England was involved in a war with two or more Powers, the other country was to join the war. The result of this treaty was that Japan got the protection of British sea-power against the hostile intervention of France or Germany or both in the case of a Russo-Japanese war.

5.4.3.3 Foreign Policy of Sir Edward Grey (1905-16)

After the renunciation of Lord Lansdowne, Sir Edward Gray ended up Foreign Minister of England in December 1905. He was England's Foreign Minister when she was going through a basic period. It goes to the credit of Sir Edward Gray that he took care of the circumstance in a skillful way and did every one of those things which empowered England to win the World War I. If one somehow managed to pose the inquiry with respect to what precisely was the strategy which decided Gray's mentality at the Foreign Office, one can't show improvement over statement Gray himself. According to him, "If all insider facts were known, it would most likely be discovered that British Foreign Ministers have been guided by what appeared to them the prompt interests of this nation when making elaborate figurings for the future." If that was the explanation which he made about the British Foreign Ministers as a rule, he himself was no exemption to the general standard. He was never contradicted to the Triple Alliance, yet might want to have compromise between the Triple Alliance and the Triple Entente. There was one distinct article which could be found in the entirety of his activities. He was resolved to discover partners for England. He was not a devotee of the arrangement of segregation. He didn't need war, however his approach was to see that if war came, England was not in solitude. He coordinated his remote arrangement with that objective in view.

5.4.3.4 *Britain's Boer War and Media*

A wealth of information and historical analysis show that throughout the last century the British media, well capable of shaping public opinion, mostly shaped it in favour of the government's foreign policy. This seemed to have been especially the case during times Britain was engaged in war—while journalists may have had some shaping influence on foreign policy in the build-up to armed conflicts, during the actual crisis military censors and government ideology prevailed throughout media and population. The acquiescence of the media has changed, however, with the advent of the Murdoch empire in Britain. His dailies have been known—and feared—for their clamorous response to politicians and policies, especially during election times, and are assumed to have substantial influence on their readers.

5.4.3.5 *Britan's Foreign Policy and Brexit Impact*

When Britain leaves the European Union, the country will suffer its biggest loss of foreign policy influence in centuries. One of the under discussed aspects of Brexit is the immense damage it will do to Britain's standing as a global foreign policy player. Many commentators concentrate on the UK's future relationship with the EU single market and customs union, the status of EU citizens in Britain or of Brits in Europe, or what role the European Court of Justice will have in the UK. But the biggest change when Britain leaves the EU will be London voluntarily giving up its seat in the forum that decides on the future of

Europe. For centuries, Britain expended blood and treasure to ensure that Europe was open for British commerce; that no dominant continental power, ideology, or faith took over; and that the values of liberalism, democracy, and the rule of law spread across the continent. In recent decades, Britain has had a seat, a vote, and a voice in all the big-ticket decisions on Europe's direction of travel. British diplomats, officials, and stellar leaders like Margaret Thatcher and Tony Blair magnified their influence by cajoling, persuading, and nudging the rest of Europe in a desired direction for Britain. This meant building alliances and accepting some pushback, but Britain has had more power and influence in Europe in recent decades than at any previous time in history. In every world capital, at the WTO, and in other international bodies, British diplomats would meet with fellow EU colleagues and try to push an agenda close to desired British interests. All this comes to a shuddering stop with Brexit—irrespective of whether Britain's exit from the EU will be hard or soft or follow the Norwegian or Swiss model. Overnight, Britain will become an international policy player that has to cool its heels in the waiting rooms of EU deciders, from the European Council to the European Commission to the European External Action Service. There will be no point in anyone in Washington, Beijing, New Delhi, Lagos, or Brasília asking the British ambassador what Europe is going to do or say on key global issues, because the answer can only be "Search me!" (Macshane, 2017)[16] Indeed, this enfeebled post-EU Britain will hold its seat as a lasting individual from the UN Security Council. London can in any case join the line of guests from Berlin, Paris, and Warsaw in looking for a crowd of people with the U.S. president. The Commonwealth will be dependably there. England will stay in NATO, the Organization for Security and Cooperation in Europe, and the Council of Europe. These are on the whole beneficial associations, however none has anything like the significance of the countries of Europe that work in show on a perpetual regulated premise as individuals from the European Union. So the UK will return to reciprocal strategy. Fantasists trust this will mean an arrival to brilliance for the Foreign and Commonwealth Office (FCO), yet the cash isn't and won't be there. On the playing field on which Britain has tried to be available, practice impact, shape the standards, and protect its center advantages, the UK will from now on be on the touchline. From Islamist psychological warfare to ecological approaches to the security of Europe's fringes, Britain will be disengaged from all the primary EU players.

Obviously, there will be amenable invites for the British PM and outside secretary, however the UK's third-nation status will mean London's emissaries have a similar position as those from Mexico, Turkey, or South Korea. London will stop to be the remote approach talk focus of the world outside Washington. Set up London-based remote strategy think tanks like Chatham House, the International Institute for Security Studies, and the Royal United Services Institute or newcomers like the Center for European Reform and the European Council on Foreign Relations have high notorieties. They will turn out to be less significant and pull in less worldwide financing as the UK cuts off itself from EU remote approach choices since its outside clergymen and authorities are never again bolted into center European policymaking. Outside the EU, Britain will look in as the EU part states continue ahead with settling on everything from European policing and equity arrangements to organizations of the EU furnished intercessions to disturbed districts of Africa or Arab nations. Brexit is the greatest impact lessening move at any point found in Britain's history of global relations. It is astounding that the UK remote approach foundation has not communicated concern. The mind-boggling center in the Brexit banter around exchange and movement has sidelined the coming loss of British impact, which is unprecedented in British history. The nation has a long history of unequivocal partisanship in its news coverage. While there has dependably been a prevalence of conservative papers (now and again, exceptionally conservative: the Daily Mail broadly upheld ace Fascist gatherings amid the 1930s), previously, this was incompletely adjusted by the mass flow of the Mirror papers. Be that as it may, the Mirror's decrease has been encourage; the Mail's online strength, then again, determined by its grip of big name news and pictures (generally of young ladies in different conditions of disrobe), has improved its mainstream and political impact. Driven by the Murdoch-claimed Sun, the Daily Mail, the Daily Express, and the Telegraph, with the Times (likewise Murdoch-possessed) in a supporting job, the factional right presently overpowers the similarly unimportant nearness of the Daily Mirror and Guardian on the left, particularly with the left-inclining Independent currently consigned to an online-just nearness. Amid the choice crusade, this lethal mix of firm dedication to a political reason and hatred for reality assumed a noteworthy job in driving Britain down the Brexit street.

5.4.3.6 Britain and Migrant Policy

In a June 18 blog entry, news-casting blogger Liz Gerard arranged a montage of first page features so as to exhibit how the steady emphasis of words, for example, "vagrants" and "outskirts" in huge, strong text style methodically increase the xenophobic message. "Turks, Romanians, Iraqis, Syrians, Afghans, Albanians: a large number of them evidently need to forsake their countries and settle in the English farmland—and just leaving the EU will stop them," Gerard composed. "No case was excessively over the top, no figure too colossal to even consider printing." The newspaper battle against the EU itself—its nondescript pen-pushing officials, its silly guidelines, and the amount it costs the U.K. as an establishment—loaned itself impeccably to the oft-rehashed Leave mantra of "Reclaim control." Maybe the most intolerable model was a first page Daily Mail feature on June 16 (unavoidably rehashed by the Sun) guaranteeing that a truckload of transients had touched base in the U.K. requesting, "We're from Europe – let us in!" The story kept running in spite of video film that plainly showed the fresh introductions had educated authorities that they were, truth be told, exiles from Iraq and Kuwait. In a vain endeavour to show that they sought to some idea of journalistic honesty, the next day's paper conveyed a "revision" comprising of 54 words at the base of Page 2. This was a much-rehashed design all through the choice battle: Journalist Hugo Dixon, who established a star Remain certainty checking site called In Facts, attracted consideration regarding both the quantity of mistaken stories and the constantly deficient "revisions" consigned to inside pages. The issue was aggravated by the sheer weight of hostile to EU press. As indicated by a Loughborough University contemplate, when paper dissemination is considered, only 18 percent of media inclusion was ace Remain contrasted and 82 percent genius Leave. It's hard to demonstrate convincingly that this steady drumbeat of features legitimately impacted voters' basic leadership. What is clear, in any case, is that it affected the national discussion and, specifically, assumed a plan setting job for supporters, which in the U.K. (as in the majority of Europe) are bound by severe fairness controls and are along these lines increasingly trusted by purchasers to give an objective methodology. Remain battle strategists were sure that the message of financial hazard would succeed – as it had in the Scottish freedom submission – yet they didn't factor in a profoundly threatening press whose mottos filled in as a reverberation chamber that supporters could barely stand up to. This reverberation chamber was especially obvious on the vaunted BBC, which, by a tragic fortuitous event, is inundated in dealings with the administration about the recharging of its 10-year contract, dependably a precarious and sensitive assignment. Therefore, its regularly confident writers have been fixated on "balance": Any contention that gets broadcast appointment is joined by a counter argument, anyway obviously ridiculous. This nonsensicalness was in plain view, for instance, amid a communicate on the exceptionally persuasive Radio 4 Today programme, which included a famous researcher on the enormous logical research dangers of Brexit. She was then "adjusted" by a minor and completely unrepresentative malignant growth expert who had recently remained as a contender for the counter the EU UK Independence Party. Generally speaking, the BBC's EU choice inclusion was significantly more slanted to pursue instead of lead. Movie executive Lord David Puttnam, the previous delegate director of Channel 4, a contending supporter, significantly depicted the BBC's news coverage amid the battle as "clogged up." In her post-referendum media roundup, the Guardian's Jane Martinson revealed that, within an hour of Leave's declaring victory, Sun editor Tony Gallagher told the Guardian: "So much for the waning power of the print media." There was a further twist a few days later, when, on one of the most dramatic days in British politics, prominent Leave campaigner Boris Johnson, long considered the most likely next Conservative leader, abandoned his leadership bid. A leaked email suggested that, among other obstacles to a successful bid, he didn't have the support of Murdoch or Daily Mail editor Paul Dacre. Even in the age of social and digital media, which so many commentators believe will democratize communications, old-fashioned media proprietors and editors still serve as political kingmakers in Britain. (Barnett, 2016)[47]

5.4.4 Importance of Media in UK

Modern diplomacy has developed over the last four hundred years, adapting to changes in governments, communication, and most recently, technology. In addition, the changing communication scene in the diplomatic realm has led to the global media occupying a more and more prominent role in international diplomacy and foreign policy negotiation. The impact of the media on information availability cannot be underestimated. Europeans consistently identify the media, primarily television and newspapers with increasing reliance on the internet, as their most important sources for information, with "more than sixty percent of the citizens across the EU member states naming television news and forty per cent naming daily newspapers as the most important sources for acquiring information about European affairs". The number and diversity of media outlets is also increasing. The past two decades have seen a shift from public broadcasting to commercial broadcasting of news in the Great Britain. Significantly, this has led to an increased pressure for ratings and viewership, which some contend has changed the nature and substance of television news reporting in the country. Particularly significant in the global impact of television journalism are two channels, CNN and BBC World, both "key 24-hour news networks watched in newsrooms, diplomatic enclaves and middle-class homes across the globe". BBC World, the British Broadcasting Corporation's 24-hour global news and information channel, which is available for viewing in more than 167 million homes in over 200 countries globally. Another documented result of the involvement of the global media in diplomacy has been the change in speed with which decisions must now be made. When communications are received, decisions must be soon forthcoming, or the world will see the players in the decision-making process as weak or undecided. However, policy makers would often do well if allowed more time to make important international decisions. They often no longer have that option. "In an age of satellite television and the internet, policy messages must be not only accurate, but fast. Silence is a vacuum that the media will fill with someone else's viewpoint" if policy makers or government actors do not participate. Further, foreign policy and negotiations must be constantly communicated in a way that the public can access, not just more knowledgeable diplomatic personnel. In today's world of global communication, policy makers must recognize that the policy cannot be explained clearly and understandably, too many different audiences, is not sustainable". As the public is directed in what to think about, they further use this criteria in making a number of evaluations, such as the effectiveness of their government and leaders, the appropriate course of action for their country, and the most pressing issues of the day.

5.4.5 Using the Media in Diplomacy

In addition to simply responding to the media's actions or coverage of events, governments and state-actors in the international arena have learned to use the media to further their own diplomatic agendas. Governments also use the media to advance their policies and views through limiting or granting access to various members of the media. For example, when Tony Blair travels to Brussels, certain members of the media are typically invited to accompany him and thereby granted increased access to his agenda and plans. This allows them to report stories other media outlets may not have access to, but at the same time is used by government officials to control or at least influence the stories being put forth. For example, leaks regarding Tony Blair's concern regarding Rupert Murdoch were leaked to the press, and eventually became part of a Channel 4 documentary.

5.4.6 Examples of Media Influence

Middle East Policy by UK: Mainstream media amplification: In the UK's "mainstream" media, many key British foreign policies are not covered at all. There are perilously few articles reporting the extent of UK support for Israel or the Sisi regime in Egypt. Even the war in Yemen has been little scrutinized; there is criticism of UK arms exports, but little if any mention of the air force maintaining Saudi warplanes and storing and issuing the bombs for their use. The Mail on Sunday's report on covert British action in Yemen is a revelation partly because such coverage is so infrequent. Although mainstream articles do reveal aspects of UK foreign policy, it is more typical for reporting and commentary to amplify the policies of the state or to spread disinformation. False assumptions pervade the media, such as that the UK policy in the Middle East is based on support for democracy and human rights. The 1953 Anglo-American coup in Iran was about maintaining the interests of oil firms –

in Britain's case, the Anglo-Iranian Oil Corporation, the forerunner of BP. Fifty years later, the 2003 invasion of Iraq was also mainly about oil, as was the 2011 war in Libya. The UK's support of Egypt's Sisi regime appears to be mainly about oil and gas interests in the country. The special relationship with Saudi Arabia seeks to promote BAE Systems and other large arms corporations. The extensive revolving door of personnel between government and corporations plays a key role in ensuring that elite interests are aligned. David Omand, the former GCHQ director, went on to work for the arms corporation Babcock; General David Richards, the former army chief of staff, was tapped to chair the UK advisory board of the US arms corporation DynCorp; and John Sawers, the former director of MI6, was appointed a non-executive director of BP, among other examples.

The Assange case and the UK's global defense of media freedom: Human rights advocates frequently point to the absence of consistency and rationality between states' expressed responsibilities, from one viewpoint, and their activities, on the other. And still, after all that, the strains encompassing the UK's ongoing way to deal with the objective of securing media opportunity all inclusive and its projection appear to be striking. Inside not exactly seven days, the UK government has gone from displaying its new battle to safeguard media opportunity – explicitly the arrangement of the Foreign Secretary's Special Envoy and a board of lawful specialists "to help nations to nullify obsolete and draconian laws and fortify lawful instruments to ensure writers", just as a worldwide gathering to be held in London on 10 and 11 July, co-facilitated with the Canadian government (on 5 April) – to confronting a melody of alerts from wide scope of human rights associations, experts and activists – including the American Civil Liberties Union, Human Rights Watch, the Committee to Protect Journalists, the Knight First Amendment Institute, the UN Special Rapporteur on opportunity of demeanour, David Kaye, and Pentagon Papers informant, Daniel Ellsberg – that the UK's conceivable removal of Julian Assange to the United States to confront, right now, a solitary charge of scheme "to submit PC interruption" would represent a risk the legal and real movement of columnists, particularly their correspondences with their sources, setting a "hazardous point of reference" for the future indictment of "inheritance" news media associations. Against the setting of disturbing patterns of physical assaults against columnists – which are every year counted by such associations as Committee to Protect Journalists, the International Press Institute and Reporters without Borders—the Foreign Office's crusade with its clear spotlight on journalistic wellbeing is to be invited. While a specific endless supply of articulation ventures had existed under the Foreign Secretary's antecedent, this most recent activity possibly offers a manner by which the UK can cut out its administration in a specific topical region of human rights, particularly when its job inside UN bodies dangers being weakened under the ghost of Brexit. As a remote approach activity, it can likewise be Recognised from the situation of UK experts towards the issue of removal.

The UK government has underlined principle of law-based contentions, rehashing that Assange's case "is presently a legitimate issue under the watchful eye of the courts" (Prime Minister, Theresa May) and "nobody is exempt from the rules that everyone else follows" (Foreign Secretary, Jeremy Hunt), and that "it is totally right that Assange will confront equity in the best possible manner in the UK" (Minister for Europe and the Americas, Sir Alan Duncan) and "we execute the legal procedure decently and reliably, with due regard for balance under the steady gaze of the law" (Home Secretary, Sajid Javid). Such encircling, in any case, makes light of the dynamic job that the UK government, not just the legal executive, will play in any removal procedure under the Extradition Act 2003. The full removal demand from the United States would should be made to and guaranteed by the Home Secretary before being submitted to the court. Regardless of whether the courts maintain the removal, the Home Secretary holds a watchfulness to reject it. In the event that there is a contending removal demand from Sweden if the examination concerning a claim of assault there is continued, the Home Secretary will likewise settle on which demand is heard first by the courts. Though UK pastors underscore the job of the legal executive for this situation, the UK's worldwide remaining on media opportunity holds tight the activities of UK's state experts evaluated inside and out. As Human Rights Watch's Executive Director wrote in the Guardian, "the main thing remaining between an Assange indictment and a noteworthy danger to worldwide media opportunity is Britain". What's more, though the UK government may wish to isolate the Foreign Office crusade from

Assange's removal case, the manner by which the last continues will doubtlessly influence the accomplishment of the previous. The UK's very own record on media opportunity, which has been put under more noteworthy examination through the overflowing of discourses against Assange's conceivable removal to the United States, will be considerably increasingly uncovered as the Foreign Office crusade advances, especially around the season of the July gathering. The capacity of the Foreign Office to viably advance crafted by the Foreign Office's legitimate board—which is planned to, in addition to other things, "[offer] counsel to governments", "[encourage] and [support] governments to help guarantee...universal commitments are implemented" and "[promote] best practice...to secure a lively free press"—will be especially tested if Assange is undoubtedly removed to the United States.

The likelihood of Assange's removal will typically be brought up in intergovernmental for an, eminently the Human Rights Council which next meets in two months time, by different states wishing to level a charge of pietism against the UK and the United States and furthermore to avoid consideration far from their very own more unfortunate, frequently desperate, opportunity of articulation records, in a way that is reminiscent of references made concerning the disclosures of mass reconnaissance by Edward Snowden. The danger of Assange's capture may likewise serve to push the UK further down opportunity of articulation rankings. Effectively noted as "one of the most exceedingly terrible positioned Western European nations, to a great extent because of a ponderous methodology towards the press, regularly for the sake of national security" a year ago, the UK has worryingly dropped eleven spots from 29/180 of every 2013 to 40/180 out of 2018 in Reporters Without Borders' World Press Freedom Index, in the middle of Trinidad and Tobago and Burkina Faso. The UK's administration on media opportunity relies upon the UK's own believability in the field. Shoring up the UK's remaining in the field requires three clear advances. In the first place, the UK ought to guarantee that the long-standing certifications of real journalistic works on, including ensuring the secrecy of sources and distributing released open intrigue data, are not disintegrated through Assange's arraignment in the United States. Second, it implies that the Foreign Office's worldwide crusade ought to be established in the current group of universal law on media opportunity – particularly concerning the wellbeing of writers, remarkably a progression of Human Rights Council and Security Council goals, coming full circle in Human Rights Council 39/6 of 27 September 2018 which offers an extensive worldwide lawful and approach system to handling the issue to date – just as existing worldwide activities – especially the UN Plan of Action on the Safety of Journalists and the Issue of Impunity and UNESCO's observing in the zone. Given there has been standardizing expansion and an expansion in systems on the issue of writer wellbeing (however the proposition for a Special Representative of the Secretary-General has still not been acknowledged), the Foreign Office's lawful board should deliver how to handle the "usage hole", an issue that distracts associations, for example, Article 19, yet which isn't just or even essentially a matter of lawful mastery, yet rather requires a more extensive, interdisciplinary comprehension of the territorial, national and nearby obstacles to use of legitimate benchmarks.

Third, it requires the UK setting a model by basically checking out its own residential and outside arrangements, too its pioneer heritage. Regarding residential strategy, free discourse associations have raised genuine worries about negative ramifications of the instituted enactment, quite the Investigatory Powers Act 2016 and the Counter-Terrorism and Border Security Act endless supply of journalistic sources, just as about the administrative system proposed in the Online Harms White Paper distributed on 8 April, which is clearing in its extension and might confine the capacity of news sources to post remarks on their sites. As the focal point of the Foreign Office crusade, the safeguard of media opportunity additionally exhibits an unmistakable good reason for reassessing the UK's exchanging associations with those states with heinous media opportunity records, including Saudi Arabia whose air strikes in Yemen have not forestalled UK arms deals to the nation, thus far at any rate. At last, the Foreign Office battle could pressurize numerous Commonwealth states to nullify "obsolete and draconian laws", which have their foundations in pilgrim arrangements and for which subsequently the UK bears a specific memorable duty. Laws on criminal criticism, lewdness and subversion, for example, still exist in numerous Commonwealth individuals, including India, Pakistan, Bangladesh and Malaysia, and are getting out for annulment. The Foreign Office battle could accordingly fill in as a trial of the UK's capacity to practice its influence among its Commonwealth accomplices specifically and on opportunity of articulation terms.

5.4.7 BBC Report on Muslim Village in Vitez

A good example is in the case of April 1993 when Martin Bell, a British news reporter working for the British Broadcasting Corporation (BBC), filed a report from a small Muslim village just north of Vitez. What made the report so remarkable was not its content, showing scenes from the massacre in the village, but simply the effect that the story had. This short report brought a war into the living rooms of millions of television viewers. This coverage did not move the problem up on the political agenda, at least not publicly. (Adan, 2017)[48]

5.4.8 British Intervention in Bosnia

Another key example is that of the British intervention in Bosnia which was arguably triggered by the television scenes of the mortaring of the bread queue in Sarajevo in May 1992, which were followed soon after by film of the Omarsk a mine concentration camp. This led to considerable pressure from the media to send troops to Bosnia. The continuing television coverage kept goading ministers into action; whether or not to send troops to Bosnia became the constant subject of debate in Britain and elsewhere. It was noted: It is hard to believe that, without the television picture on the screens in the United Kingdom, British Troops would ever have been dispatched to a part of Europe that could not, by any stretch of the imagination, beheld to be a vital national interest. The media impact on policy seems also to depend on several variables least of which is the amount of media coverage given to a particular issue.

Coverage of Iraq War 2003: The crew of the HMS Ark Royal, Britain's flagship naval vessel, demanded that the BBC be turned off on the ship because of what they saw as a clear anti-Coalition or "pro-Iraq" bias. One BBC correspondent had been embedded on the ship, but the crew said they had no complaints of his reporting specifically. The sailors on board the ship claimed that the BBC gave more credit to Iraqi reports than information coming from British or Allied sources, often questioning and refusing to believe reports coming from Coalition sources while reporting Iraqi claims of civilian casualties without independent verification. The ship's news feed was replaced with Sky News. Ironically, it later emerged from a study conducted by Professor Justin Lewis of the School of Journalism at Cardiff University that the BBC was the most pro-war of British networks, a finding confirmed in a separate study by the German newspaper Frankfurter AllgemeineZeitung.

5.4.9 Media in Chechnya

Since the beginning of the Second Chechen War in 1999, Russian government experts are claimed to have executed an arrangement to utilize lawful and untouchable techniques to confine media access to the contention area. The Russian government's control of all Russian TV slots and its utilization of oppressive standards, provocation, restriction, terrorizing and assaults on columnists, including the hijacking of Radio Liberty journalist Andrei Babitsky by the Russian military, totally denied the Russian open of the autonomous data on the contention. Neighborhood columnists in Chechnya face extreme provocation and block, while outside writers and news sources are forced into blue penciling their reports on the contention, making it about incomprehensible for writers to give adjusted inclusion of Chechnya. Since 2001, with the features ruled by updates on the Israeli-Arab struggle and the U.S. – drove War on Terrorism, the contention has been totally overlooked by the worldwide media. Hardly any Russian writers keep on covering the Chechen clash, and even less set out to reprimand the administration, rather picking self-control. In 2005, the Duma passed the law making the columnists having the option to approach and distribute data about fear based oppressor assaults just with authorization from those coordinating counter-psychological militant activities. On August 2, 2005, reacting to the airing of a meeting with Shamil Basayev, Moscow restricted writers of the American Broadcasting Company arrange from working in Russia. In 2006, the Duma endorsed the Law on Fighting Extremist Activity, widening the meaning of "radicalism" to incorporate media analysis of open authorities and accommodate detainment of as long as three years for writers and the suspension or conclusion of their distributions. The law was utilized that equivalent year to close down the Russian-Chechen Friendship

Society and indicted its official executive Stanislav Dmitrievsky of "fanatic" exercises. Likewise in 2006, Moscow columnist Boris Stomakhin was condemned to five years in jail on charges of "inducing ethnic contempt" in his reports about the contention in Chechnya. On 7 October 2006, Anna Politkovskaya, Russian writer and political lobbyist surely understood for her restriction to the Chechen clash and Russian experts, was shot dead in Moscow in a clear contracts slaughtering. In March 2007, a Levada Center survey asked Russians how they thought the circumstance in Chechnya was shrouded in the Russian media: 49 percent said they figured the inclusion does not give a reasonable feeling of what's going on, while 28 percent said it isn't target and "conceals" the issues that exist there. Just 11 percent said they were content with media inclusion of Chechnya. In September 2007, police and security powers in the neighboring republic of Ingushetia were issued requests to quit illuminating the media regarding any "episodes of a psychological oppressor nature." Essentially all the nearby Chechen media are presently under all out control of the expert Moscow Chechen legislature of Ramzan Kadyrov.

5.4.10 Conclusion

The new Conservative government, under huge pressure from the same press barons who undid Johnson, has stalled on implementing Leveson's recommendations, and the British press today therefore feels free to break its own industry code with as much frequency and impunity as before 2011. To deflect criticism, it has established a "new" regulator, the Independent Press Standards Organisation (IPSO), which is owned and run by the major publishers. As the referendum campaign demonstrated, IPSO has been ineffectual in holding its newspaper members to account. Those same commentators who preach the revolution of social media also like to cite new media like BuzzFeed, Vice News, and other online outlets as examples of greater plurality and more opportunities for journalists. These are all welcome additions, but so far they have been unable to compete with the legacy of traditional news brands, which are extending their online presence. According to some sources, the entertainment-focused Daily Mail website, which attracts upward of 200 million global visitors every month, is the most popular English-language site in the world. Perhaps that will gradually change.

Meanwhile, broadcast journalism still aspires to the highest standards of accuracy and impartiality, and another hope lies in detaching those broadcast newsrooms from their mind-numbing dependency on agenda-driven newspapers. (Barnett, 2016)[49] All of these changes, however, will be gradual and hardly constitute a journalistic revolution. Meanwhile, it is hard to avoid the conclusion that Britain's mainstream media failed us at a time of greatest need, with political consequences that will reverberate for decades. The developed countries such as British have a strong background on the applied and practice based research which is key in the media for purposes of credible and exact data. This should be adopted by the developing states as the applied and practice-based research is accompanied by knowledge transfer where media and communication industry co-operates with the media and communication policymakers. This could be a key ingredient in the influence of foreign policy as the information obtained is reliable and very valid for public consumption and foreign policy formulation.

5.5 Russian Foreign Policy and Social Media

5.5.1 Introduction

Collapse of the Soviet Union saw media's advent as a potent instrument and lever of influence in Russia. The role of media in promoting Russian foreign policy and exerting the influence of President Vladimir Putin has become increasingly visible since the conflict Ukraine and other domestic and international confrontations. Media is a key instrument of influence, culture, politics, and businesses are also important in broader Russian influence efforts abroad. Russia adopted its foreign policy based on goals and objectives as reflected in modern world's view. It evaluates the global situation and analyses the processes unfolding in the world and its regions. On its basis the foreign strategy of the country has been found in full recognition of the fundamentally new geopolitical situation in the world. Russia, with its growing competition in all spheres in polycentric world order especially in social, economic and moral values, adopted a new global model. Evidently, Russia is well placed to consolidate its role as one of the centers of the new multipolar system and actively impact the global situation with a view to ameliorating it, strengthening security and stability, putting in place favorable external conditions for the country's internal development to ensure sustainable economic growth and thus a higher quality of life for Russian citizens. Russia's independent foreign policy is liked by Asian, African, Latin American and European countries. Russia has consistently advocated an inclusive and positive agenda aimed not at restricting but rather amplifying ties between states. Russia stands ready to join efforts with all those who are equally willing to cooperate in line with the principles of equality, mutual respect, mutual benefit and norms of international law, as well as recognition of the central role of the United Nations in global affairs and as reflected in UN Security Council, the Group of 20, BRICS, SCO and CSTO. (Vera Zakem, 2018)[50] The Ukrainian crisis was a consequence of a policy of strengthening one's own security as manifested by successive waves of NATO expansion despite assurances to the contrary at the highest level and in violation of solemn declarations on the establishment of a system of equal and indivisible security in the European and Atlantic region. Russia's point is to keep working under these situations and to remain open to talks. There is no viable alternative to mutually beneficial and equal-footed cooperation between Russia and the EU, as our countries are closely intertwined by virtue of numerous geographic, economic, historical and human ties. Russian effort to create Eurasian Economic Union is making a tangible contribution to the development of wide-ranging cooperation in the region. Russians firmly believe that gradual steps towards creating a common economic and humanitarian space from Lisbon to Vladivostok based on the principles of equal and indivisible security will in shaping a new architecture on the European continent, and equal-footed harmonisation of the processes of European and Eurasian integration. Russia's foreign policy has in recent years become more assertive than it had been in the first two decades since independence. The Kremlin surprised many with its 2008 war in Georgia, its 2014 seizure of Crimea and intervention in eastern Ukraine, and its 2015 deployment of forces in the Syrian civil war, lies the theory that Russia should play a larger role in the world, one where Moscow is free to act according to its own interests without being beholden to others and where no issue of global significance can be resolved without Russian participation. While the post-Soviet region continues to be a focal point for Russian foreign policy, Moscow is also recalibrating its approach to the U.S., the European Union, and China, among others, as it defines its global interests. The viability of Russia's assertive approach, however, depends on many factors, not least the health of the Russian economy. (Areg Galstyan, 2017)[51]

5.5.2 Media and Authoritarian Regimes

Dictator routines much of the time utilize state-possessed media to outline and clarify their residential and remote arrangements, regularly referencing national markers and conjuring social personalities to legitimize their activities. State-supported media records of continuous occasions, in this way, are required to adjust to and be steady with government-endorsed story. Russian state-claimed media fundamentally expanded its inclusion of Georgia and Ukraine, in the months going before Russia's military intercessions. This expanded inclusion was regularly predicated with an expanded talk of conventional Russian geopolitical adversaries, for example, the US. State-possessed news sources give dictator routines an important asset that helps outline occasions and arrangement choices. Ongoing examination has assessed dictator routines' vital utilization of state-claimed media to control contradict or to impact general feeling amid political emergencies. Approach confining, be that as it may, is best on the off chance that it is predictable with the current originations of the express, its place inside the bigger political structure, and the pre-built up social characters. State-supported media records of recent developments for the most part are predictable with these prior stories. At the end of the day, dictators frequently outline their very own activities and the activities of remote states inside a lot of natural tropes, which can regularly be consolidated into portrayals, for example, regardless of whether the state is a superpower, rising force, provincial power, partner, adversary, or some mix. These tropes help contextualize, legitimize, and comprehend either the regime's, or an opponent state's, remote arrangement activities.

5.5.3 Media Effects and Political Behavior

There are several accounts of how individual process information provided be media outlets, such as Receive-Accept-Sample (RAS) and motivated reasoning. Each of these theories expect that individuals with low politically sophistication may change their attitudes when presented with a counter-attitudinal message, whereas politically sophisticated individuals mediate messages that counter their pre-existing beliefs. An alternative account, selective exposure, holds that individuals selectively choose media sources that fit with their pre-existing views. Individuals that select like-minded news are less likely to receive counter-messages that may change or mediate their attitudes, and when they do they are more likely to show hostility towards the media source. State-owned media alters information and affects political behavior. Countries with state-owned media substantially raise the costs of individuals to engage in selective exposure. A large population is susceptible to media influences. In the absence of counter-balancing information and limited options for selective exposure, large segments of the population can be influenced by a centralized and orchestrated account of policy or events.

5.5.4 State-owned Media

Autocratic regimes frequently use media to cement their own political power, even as the media environment has become more commercial and less centralized since the 1990s. Despite risks associated with undermining the state capacity to respond to environmental and economic crises by restricting credible information flows of bureaucratic performance to the central regime, autocratic regimes are incentivized to restrict media freedom in order to prevent the public from knowing of policy failures. In an effort to gain the benefits of information without the risk of fueling discontent, autocratic regimes frequently attempt to permit some media freedom, within a specific boundary, in order to minimize any collective action against the regime. Russian media presents government-scripted stories and pre-publication censorship. Autocratic media support regime goals, as well as provide a higher-quality product on state-owned and state-affiliated media to maintain viewership. Media self-censorship relates to the choice, distortion, and emphasis of stories covered. Coverage critical of Vladimir Putin, for instance, is not allowed on state-aligned. An advantage of self-censorship is mechanism to control non-state-affiliated media. These mechanisms produce media coverage that toes the party line. At the same time, state-owned media are able to take advantage of relatively high programming quality, and subsequent viewer interest, resulting from reporter creativity. Even non-political shows, but ostensibly entertainment programming, such as legal shows, can be used to push the government's agenda.

Independent, private-owned media, conversely, are often disadvantaged in financing and may have lower programming quality, on average, than state-owned media outlet. That state-media reflect their government's positions and policies is important because the public often has higher or equal levels of trust in state-owned rather than independent media. Trust, combined with the lack of well-resourced competition, means that state-owned media can effectively relay the government's policy positions to the public.

5.5.5 Foreign Policy and State-owned Media

State-owned media can be used to frame and justify a government's policy position. State-owned media can also be used by the government to solidify or coordinate policy with domestic elites. Mass media, and more recently social media, is used to coordinate the interests of central and local elites. Russia, in particular, has used mass media to central power and limit the authority of local politicians. The ability of a regime to project policies onto its population, however, is not absolute. Even with state-owned casting policies in a favorable light, a government faces some restrictions when presenting formation to the public. States, in other words, are constrained and framed by the messages and identities that they have previously invoked. To account for the constraints imposed by national identities and value systems, we adopt a foreign policy approach to analyzing state behavior towards its neighbors. Foreign policy approaches consider both international and domestic features that serve to structure and constrain the choices available to a government regime. Interactions with other states, state leaders adopt perceptions of themselves and assign identities to other states. Media reflect domestic elite preferences and their expectations of appropriate state behavior. Russian state-owned media serves as foreign friends and foes, as part of an effort to generate a well-curated and managed message for the public. Governments use these NRCs to reify their own influence and to manage how foreign events are perceived domestically. Thus, states have an incentive to maintain NRCs and frequently use them as a point of reference for making sense of and understanding unexpected events. Operating within a foreign policy theoretical framework, authoritarian regimes can raise the salience and context of specific issues or interactions with neighboring states within the broader understanding of a state's position within the international system. For instance, following the Maidan protests that resulted in the ouster of Ukraine's President Yanukovych, the Russian government de-scribed their intervention in Ukraine and support of militant forces in Donetsk and Luhansk within the broader context of a geopolitical struggle with the US, rather than simply as an attempt to maintain political control of a traditional ally. Efforts to unite and control domestic (and sometimes foreign) populations through normative influence via mass media is a critical component of state sovereignty, and is a cheaper alternative to state-building and political control than coercion.

While independent media tend to be event-rather than policy-driven, i.e. their coverage is driven by event-occurrence and salience, state-owned media outlets may be used to shape public response/perception, even before a state implements a policy. (Danylyuk, 2018)[52] State-controlled media may thus be used to re-assert identities that a government wants to emphasize. For instance, governments can justify intervention in neighboring state by invoking the role of great power, protector of a region or co-ethnics, or a regional or global balancer. Mass communication can also be used to co-opt potential partisans in neighboring states. As an example, following the 2013–2014 Maidan protests and subsequent departure of the pro-Russian President Yanukovych from Ukraine, Russian media repeatedly referred to a region in Ukraine – stretching from Donbass in the East, to Crimea and along the coast adjacent to the Black Sea in the South, to Transnistria in Moldova – as Novorossiya. In the aftermath of the Maidan uprising, Russia claimed that Novorossiya was historically a Russian territory – citing the conquests of Catherine the Great – and referred to the new government in Kiev as a fascist junta, attempting to invoke geographical and political divisions from World War II. Such references could potentially be used to provide justification for intervening in a neighbor in effort to protect co-ethnics, as well as attempt to assert a greater – Russian identify and generate support from those living in southern and eastern Ukraine who may view Russian news broadcasts advocating this perspective.

5.5.6 Russian Media and Foreign Policy

Governments are constrained in the manner in which they can portray both themselves and others depending on pre-existing NRCs.

Governments can manufacture support in the buildup to potential international conflicts by framing the coverage of the target. Thus, we expect to see an increase in the number of new stories about a target prior to military intervention. In the case of regional or rising powers, such as Russia, constructing support for potential conflict abroad can be relatively easy, if prior NRCs have emphasized an explicit sphere of influence or a security complex. Governments can simultaneously build nationalist sentiment and direct this energy against target states. Governments can direct state-owned media to cover issues and run stories on target states to raise the salience of these states and magnify grievances with them. To remain consistent with a state's NRCs, governments can invoke similarities between the target of their aggression and other enemies of the state, such as other traditional rival powers.

This can be done by stating that a target is in danger of potentially moving under the influence of a traditional rival. Doing so can help reduce domestic aversion to the use of force against co-ethnics. State-owned Russian media did precisely this in the months prior to intervening in Georgia and Ukraine by increasingly referencing traditional rivals, such as the US. Russian NRCs, under President Putin, have emphasized the roles of a regional power, an independent great power, and an aspirant global power. The creations of the Commonwealth of Independent States (CIS) and Eurasion Economic Union (EEU) have even been described as evidence of neo imperial or hegemonic role in the post-Soviet space on the part of Russia. In addition, since at least 2006, the Russian government has once again viewed the US as its primary geopolitical rival. Given these NRCs, one would expect Russia to have an interventionist foreign policy towards neighboring. Russia is directly or indirectly involved in a number of outstanding disputes: the status of Abkhazia and South Ossetia with Georgia, the annexation of Crimea with Ukraine, the status of Transnistria with Moldova, a border dispute with Estonia, and possession of the Southern Kurils with Japan. Russia has also expressed concern about the welfare of Russian-speaking populations in Estonia, Latvia, Lithuania, Moldova, and Ukraine. Russia has been invited to send troops to help defend a neighbor's territorial integrity in the cases of Tajikistan and Uzbekistan. Lastly, Russia has also been involved in managing the conflict in

Nagorno-Karabakh region between Armenia and Azerbaijan and, more recently, in Syria. To justify such an interventionist foreign policy, Russia has framed many of these disputes and actions as part of a larger conflict between itself and the US. NATO expansion, for example, has been argued to serve a destabilizing influence on Russia, especially as Russia is increasingly dissatisfied with its global status and faces economic difficulties. It is therefore unsurprising that Russia viewed and framed the conflict with Georgia within the broader context of US efforts to undermine Russia's great power status by its involvement in the colored revolutions and NATO expansion. (Vera Zakem, 2018)[53] Russian officials accused the US of aiding and orchestrating the Maidan protests, and used this claim to justify potential intervention in the crisis.

Ukrainian and Georgian cases experience interventions in the time series of Russian news coverage in the form of Russian military involvement. Russian interference in Ukraine began with the appearance of "little green men" on 27 February 2014. After initial denials, Russian President Putin admitted that the forces were, in fact, Russian troops. This military intervention culminated in the formal annexation of Crimea by Russia on 18 March 2014. Russian military "tourists" entered Eastern Ukraine in March 2014. In the case of Georgia, Russia sent military forces into South Ossetia and Abkhazia, two breakaway regions supported by Russia, on 8 August 2008 and 9 August 2008, respectively. From a methodological perspective, these interventions indicate that there are periods of stability in the relations of both the Ukrainian and Georgian governments and Russia, punctuated by significant animosity. The interventions may lead to variation in Russian media coverage of each neighboring state. Pertinent to observe that new stories involving both the target of Russian aggression, as well as its traditional rivals, by state-owned media prior to the onset of military intervention are increasing. In contrast, independent media is more events-driven and fluctuation in coverage should coincide more directly with events on the ground. Increases in state-owned media coverage should precede the Russian military interventions in Crimea on 27 February 2014 and Eastern Ukraine in March 2014.

5.5.7 Analyzing Russian Media

Focus is on Russian-language state-owned media outlets to analyze the Russian government's manipulation of news coverage aimed at maintaining consistency with pre-existing NRCs. By analyzing primary sources in their native language, the impact of Russian media coverage can be assessed more directly than if relied on secondary sources compiled by academics, or English-language state-owned media, such as Russia Today. Secondary sources may reflect ex post rationalizations or critiques in light of subsequent events, while English-language outlets may present an account intended for foreign, rather than domestic, audiences. A key word in the headlines of state-owned media, the more salient the government wants the topic to be to the public. Corpus of interest is the new headlines from Russian media websites. The frequency analysis of the proper names in the headlines of the Russian news channels is based on two sources. The first one is the key state-controlled Russia-24. Russia-24, formerly Vesti1 ("news" in Russian), is a state-owned news channel. Russia-24 promotes the official position of the Russian government and serves as one of the Kremlin's propaganda devices that serves to shape the public opinion. Though banned in Ukraine, Moldova, and Latvia, the network is popular among Russian-speaking minorities in several neighboring formerly Soviet republics. Observing counts of key words have consistently been sufficient to extract substantively meaningful features of texts. (Elena Labzina, 2017)[54] The second source is the independent private Russian channel Dozhd ("Rain" in Russian). As an independent media outlet, Dozhd is not privileged to private government information. Thus Dozhd provides purely events-driven news coverage and functions as a placebo to the state-owned news coverage in analysis.

5.5.8 Anatomy of Russian Media Influence

Following the addition of Crimea and the beginning of the Russo-Ukrainian War on the Donbas, the subject of Russian promulgation as a component of the Russian cross breed animosity against different nations has turned out to be especially well known. Logical and journalistic articles are expounded on Russian publicity; political and military pioneers notice it in their addresses; universal and national focuses and establishments are being set up to neutralize it. It is hard to differ with the way that lately, the Russian data effect on the number of inhabitants in different nations has turned out to be relative or much bigger than that did by the USSR amid the Cold War. In the meantime, even in master exchanges, there is an absence of comprehension of both the idea of this impact and its instruments. Eyewitnesses' consideration is for the most part centered around purported "counterfeit news" and on authority bits of gossip about Russian purposeful publicity, for example, RT (once Russia Today) and the Sputnik news office. Such a methodology enormously limits the field of perspective on the analysts, confining it to only a by and large falsehood, which spreads through Kremlin's outstanding media. Thus, the proposed countermeasures are decreased to the fast invalidation of wrong data and impediments to communicate official Russian broad communications in some nation.

It overlooks the way that the best impact ought to be acknowledged through channels that are not related with Russia. This is particularly valid for the effect on the gathering of people, which is contrary about Russia. Ukraine, unfortunately, did not become an exception with the West and was deprived of the strategy of countering Russian information warfare. In August 2014, six months after the occupation and annexation of the Ukrainian Crimea and on top of the Ukrainian-Russian military confrontation in eastern Ukraine, the government decided to ban 14 Russian TV channels for "propaganda of war." The decision was obviously belated and inadequate, since it concerned only channels registered in Russia, not those controlled by Russia, and restricted the activities of only those media that directly called for war with Ukraine. (Elena Labzina, 2017)[55] However, the Kremlin's ability to influence Ukrainians was not limited by these TV channels. Russia has built up its communication tools and influence long and vigorously not only for marginal pro-Russian audiences, but also for quite patriotic pro-Western citizens of Ukraine, giving it much more time and resources. It's hard to believe, but the most popular Ukrainian TV channel Inter, covering 97 percent of the entire territory, was founded in 1996 by Russian state television. Later, Inter was sold to Dmitry Firtash, a pro-Kremlin oligarch, who had close ties to Vladimir Putin, Gazprom, and the leader of Russian organized crime, SevaMogilevich. Now Firtash is in Vienna, where he expects to be extradited to the United States, where a criminal case has been launched against him. Another media group, UMH, which brings together more than 50 brands with leading positions on the radio (7 popular radio stations), the Internet and the press (including the Ukrainian franchise Forbes and Vogue), is still controlled by the family of ex-President Yanukovych, who is in exile in Moscow. The leadership of the group is carried out by a close associate of Viktor Yanukovych, a former MP from his party, Elena Bondarenko. Bondarenko publicly denies Russian aggression against Ukraine, called the shooting of participants of the anti-Russian Revolution of Dignity not tight enough and actively participates in the Russian campaign to worsen Ukrainian-Polish relations. Taking into account the situation of Yanukovych, whose fate depends directly on the Kremlin, it is difficult to believe that there is any independence of this group. Despite being constructed in advance channels of Russian communication and propaganda in the Ukraine, preparation for hybrid aggression required additional media capacity. On the eve of the war an active creation of new media began. In 2013, Multimedia Invest Group, which brings together 4 popular radio stations, 2 TV channels, an Internet portal, a magazine and a newspaper, was created in Ukraine. Media experts say that the group's protagonist is also part of Yanukovych's entourage. The newspaper, Vesti, which is part of this group, first came out in print in May 2014, in the midst of Russian aggression against Ukraine. The newspaper has repeatedly been accused of having its messages coincide with the main narratives of Russian propaganda which is reduced to the inevitability of an anti-government revolution in Ukraine and the collapse of the country being blamed solely on the West, NATO and the United States. (Danylyuk, 2018) Radio Vesti, despite being part of the same group began broadcasting in March 2014 and chose another position. The radio claimed to be impartial and underlined (sometimes excessively and grotesquely) Ukrainian patriotism and anti-Russian propaganda.

At the same time, the station repeatedly provided the opportunity to speak to representatives of pro-Russian terrorist organizations, Russian politicians, observers and it manipulated telephone polls. The list of Ukrainian media controlled by Russia or its local allies also includes the most popular information channels 112 and News One, as well as Channel 17. Despite the generally accepted view, social media and networks, at least in Ukraine, are also not deprived of influence from Russia. In 2015, the president of Ukraine, Petro Poroshenko, appealed to Mark Zuckerberg to create a separate Facebook office for the administration of the Ukrainian segment of the network, which, according to many experts, is administrated from Moscow, which leads to interference in the process of information exchange, including the removal of some Facebook posts. Zuckerberg refused to assist Poroshenko, denying the existence of the Russian office. This data is without a doubt worth looking at, however it is completely unquestionable that the primary huge private financial specialist in Facebook with a venture of $200 million was the Kremlin oligarch, Alisher Usmanov, who as of now controls the Mail.ru gathering, which incorporates Vkontakte and other famous administrations. With the developing number of news sources, the significance of general feeling pioneers who can translate data from various sources is developing.

Prevalent columnists, political specialists, TV and radio has generally moved toward becoming pioneers on the national dimension. What's more, Ukraine isn't a special case.

From 2010 to 2015, the most powerful pioneers of general feeling in Ukraine were prevalent TV and radio hosts, Evgeniy Kiselyov and Savik Shuster. In spite of the for the most part Recognised picture of equitable columnists and warriors for liberal qualities, there are sure focuses in the accounts of these people which gives an altogether inverse view. Specific consideration ought to be paid to Russian media administrators in Ukrainian media, the quantity of which has expanded essentially as of late. For instance, Mariya Stolyarova, an innovative maker of the most recent news on Inter TV channel, was ousted from Ukraine in February 2016. In Ukraine, the Russian resident Stolyarova touched base in 2014. Preceding that, she functioned as a military journalist for the Russian TV channel REN-TV, which is related with Vladimir Putin. As an agent of REN-TV, Stolyarova figured out how to cover the Ukrainian-Russian clash in the Donbass, where she didn't hide her compassion toward the Russian upheld separatists. While taking a shot at the Inter TV Channel, Stolyarova kept on organizing the exercises of other Russian reporters who worked in Ukraine, and partook in the parliamentary decisions that occurred in Ukraine in 2014 as a political and media expert. She counseled various government officials including the individuals who proclaimed expert Ukrainian and professional Western positions. (Areg

Galstyan, 2017) Realizing Russia's influence on Ukrainian media, Western powers are trying to promote the development of independent media in Ukraine, spending tens of millions of dollars annually. However, little progress has been made in this area. This is largely due to the fact that Russia successfully penetrates these new entities, neutralizing them or even uses them for its own goals.

New military doctrine adopted by Russia in December 2014 on the use of the protest potential of the population of the enemy state, it is difficult to underestimate the role of media resources in the modern war. To date, unfortunately, the West has not been able to develop an effective strategy to protect its own information space from Russian penetration, and, moreover, to develop effective instruments of its own influence. It is obvious that without the return to the Cold War information policy, as well as the introduction of sanctions on the creation and possession of Western media by subjects affiliated with Russia, the Kremlin will only increase its own capabilities, which will inevitably be used for political sabotage, discrediting national governments and bringing the power of Russian influence to Western countries.

5.5.9 Conclusion

Television is the most popular source of information for Russian citizens, followed by the internet, radio, and print media. The Russian government directly controls and operates state media and exercises considerable influence over private media through both formal and informal means while seeking greater control over media with larger audiences. Russia's rich business elite, commonly referred to as "oligarchs," owns most of Russia's media. President Vladimir Putin and his inner circle view domestic and international media as key instruments in promoting Russian state interests. Russia's media has three primary functions in contributing to Russian foreign policy: mobilizing and sustaining domestic political support for its foreign and security policies; presenting official perspectives and policies to foreign audiences; and influencing foreign audiences through disinformation and propaganda. The Presidential Administration plays a central role in aligning Russia's media strategy and messaging with the Kremlin's foreign policy objectives on a day-to-day basis. Putin selectively exercises personal leadership, known as "manual control" or ручноеуправление, when

Russia's political system, his personal legitimacy, or Russia's national security are at stake. Putin also often personally delivers key messages, something that can attract considerable domestic attention as well as large international audiences extending well beyond those accessible solely through Russia's state-controlled external media. Surrounding President Putin is his inner circle of key advisers who are classified as messengers, strategists, bureaucrats, and owners. In addition to mapping out Russia's internal media network and decision-making processes in the media, a baseline assessment of Russia's external influence has been developed. In addition to media, other key levers of influence are culture and society, business, and politics. In analyzing Russia's broader external influence, Russian media's decision-making and messaging has been explored.

- Vladimir Putin's "manual control" of Russia's messaging in high-stakes crisis situations. In absence it may complicate Russia's decision-making, including on messaging
- Putin's control in armed conflict zones over entire media
- Putin's aides manage Russia's day-to-day media/messaging activities, even during armed conflict
- Putin's involvement and visibility appears correlated to how high the stakes are for Russia in any given situation, with Putin playing more of a leading role in the grey zone conflict in Ukraine, for example, than in political interference in Montenegro
- Moscow's refusals to acknowledge some of its covert and overt conduct may have aims other than deception, such as preserving freedom of action, winning leverage through ambiguity, or allowing its adversaries to save face. (Vera Zakem, 2018)[56]

Media is a key tool and will continue to play a significant role in Russian foreign policy. Through state and independent media, Putin plays a central role in delivering the Kremlin's message and shaping its domestic and global media strategy.

1) The Presidential Administration and Putin's inner circle play a coordinating role in aligning Russian foreign policy and messaging and also implement key media influence decisions on Putin's behalf.

2) Since Putin's return to the presidency, Russia's government has significantly tightened its control over external messaging. Russia's leadership seeks closer alignment between messaging and policy so that state external media will more directly support national policy objectives.
3) Putin plays a central role in decision-making and messaging in the media. Putin is a highly experienced statesman and leader whose exercise of manual control and personal presentation of messages is critical to Russian foreign and domestic policy. While his inner circle and the Presidential Administration implement key media strategies and often carry out the message, the system is designed around having Putin at its center and any eventual transition in Russia could have important implications for Russia's media decision-making and messaging.
4) Putin and his inner circle have direct and indirect control or influence over Russia's media. The Russian government directly controls state media and directly and indirectly influences private media. The Presidential Administration is the most important formal institution in managing Russia's media and messaging.
5) While media is a critical element of influence, Putin and his administration also have power in the cultural, society, business, and political spheres in target countries. Thus media are ultimately only one instrument, albeit quite an important one, in a much larger toolkit designed to exert influence externally.

Authoritative regimes use state media in tandem for foreign interventions. State-owned media add context by linking target states to other, traditional enemies. Russian state-owned media does initiate coverage of targets in the months preceding military interventions. Russian state-owned media increased the number of headlines with Ukraine and Crimea prior to the onset of the March 2014 military invasion of Crimea. Russian state-owned media increased coverage of Georgia before the August 2008 military invasions in South Ossetia and Abkhazia. In both cases, state-owned media coverage intensified prior to the onset of actual fighting; this is in contrast to the events-driven coverage from independent media, which increased at the same time as military intervention. Further, there also evidence that Russian state-owned media is more likely to discuss target states as it invokes a traditional rival, the US. (Elena Labzina, 2017)[57]

Putin and his close aides direct state-owned media to manufacture support for its foreign military adventures, and frames these conflicts in a manner consistent with a pre-conceived national roles; namely, as part of a broader geopolitical struggle with the US.

5.6 Importance of P5 Countries

China, France, Russia, the United Kingdom, and the United States: the permanent members of United Nations Security Council (Big Five, or P5) are the five states which the UN Charter of 1945 gives a permanent seat on UN Security Council. These countries were all allies in World War II and are nuclear weapons states. 15 UN member states are on UNSC, 10 of which are elected. P5 have veto power, which helps them prevent adoption of any "substantive" draft Council resolution, regardless of its level of international support. Abundance of information with its reach of 80 per cent plus to the world populace, one cannot wish away the penetration media has especially, social and electronic media. The world has virtually become one village. Any happening in any part of the world can reach the farthest and remotest place is in real time. With the advent of artificial intelligence in the information technology age, it will play a lot of role in influencing world opinion. The P5 or permanent five members of the United Nations Security Council have the following advantages as compared to other developing/developed countries like the media, including social media and its outreach to the global populace. They have well-oiled and robust media. They always use them to their advantage with checks and balances present, including on social media. In this world of unipolarity it is always being challenged by other rival P5 countries and they always manipulate media to best of their advantage. P5 countries play and succeed in their endeavour whosoever knows media intelligently in swaying the world opinion. These P5 countries have the largest and biggest media outreach and they can sway the world opinion as they always use in real time manner, hence, the open market economy always tends to tow in line with these P5 countries. The UNSC meets regularly to assess threats to international security, including civil wars, natural disasters, arms control, and terrorism. Syria's civil war posed challenges to the Security Council as it has attempted to stabilize the region, curb the use of chemical weapons, and resolve a mounting humanitarian crisis. Similarly, Russia's frictions with the United States and European Union following its annexation of Crimea in early 2014 and North Korea's nuclear weapons programme have added tensions. (Staffer, 2018)

5.6.1 Veto Power

The veto power of the P5 enables them to prevent adoption of any "substantive" draft Council resolution, regardless of the level of international support for the draft. The veto does not apply to procedural votes, which is significant in that the P5 can vote against a "procedural" draft resolution, without necessarily blocking its adoption by the Council. The veto is exercised any "P5"—casts a "negative" vote on a "substantive" draft resolution. Abstention or absence from the vote does not prevent a draft resolution from being adopted. The P5 have used veto power to varying degrees. Russia used the veto most, blocking more than one hundred resolutions since the council's founding. The United States is the second most frequent user. China's use has increased in recent years. In 2014, China joined Russia in vetoing a resolution that would have referred belligerents in the Syrian civil war, including the individuals in the Bashar al-Assad regime, to the International Criminal Court. In 2017, China and Russia vetoed another resolution on Syria, which would have sanctioned entities involved in the production of chemical weapons. Russia vetoed several other resolutions on Syria later that year and in 2018. Most recently, in June, the United States vetoed a resolution condemning Israel for Palestinian civilian deaths during border protests in Gaza.

Since 2014, increased tensions between US and Russia are seen in the council, leading to concerns that the body may now be no longer able to defuse crisis. For example, in July 2015, Russia vetoed a resolution that would have created an international tribunal to prosecute the pro-Russia separatists in eastern Ukraine who are thought to have shot down a Malaysian Airlines passenger jet using a Russian-made missile. The Syrian conflict has proven to be particularly difficult to manage, given that Russia has used its veto power a dozen times to block resolutions aimed at holding the Assad regime accountable for atrocities documented by UN sources.

5.6.2 India and P5

For India, "no reform of UN is complete without the composition of the Security Council changing to reflect contemporary realities. This requires expansion in the membership of UNSC in both the permanent and non-permanent categories." The Indian quest for the Security Council permanent membership is "an essay in persuasion" lies at the heart of repeated Indian pleas for reforming the UN, the only existing universal organization of global governance, according to India's Prime Minister Manmohan Singh. UN founders wanted a "security specialist" Council whose purpose was maintenance of international peace and security. Its uniqueness lies in its pursuance of security-specific mandate and efficiency, it has a rigid representation system with an extraordinary decision-making power/procedures. In the 1945 San Francisco conference itself, India showed keen interest in Security Council's composition, especially basis of election of non-permanent members. Here, India strongly vouched for factors such as population, industrial potential, willingness and ability to contribute to international peace and security, and past performance, and quest for representation for various regions for states to be selected for the Security Council. India did not have to press for a vote on its amendment as the Sponsoring Powers accepted this suggestion and modified their original proposals. India has had seven terms for a two-year non-permanent member seat, the last being 2011-12, only behind Japan, Brazil and Argentina. Except for the first time, when India held the seat earmarked for the Commonwealth group, it has held the seat on every other occasion on behalf of the Asian group. India has been a member of the Council during 1950-51, 1967-68, 1972-73, 1977-78, 1984-85, 1991-92, and 2011-12 which can be called a "rehearsal for permanent membership". In the last term, India had the non-permanent seat with the largest votes in the General Assembly of the UN showing its popularity. Remember that in 1996, India had lost the elections to Japan by a wide margin for a non-permanent seat. The usual Indian preference in the UNSC has been to be a part of democratic majority adding to the adoption of reasonable resolutions and decisions.

Indian interests in Security Council started when Mahatma Gandhi felt India, then including Pakistan and Bangladesh, should be veto-wielding member of the Security Council. But the leadership precedence for independence and handling the tough, bloody partition followed by the India-Pakistan conflict on Kashmir moved their attention and interests away from the possible opportunity of a seat. Jawaharlal Nehru, India's first PM, did not take the offer to join the Security Council by both the superpowers, the US and the then Soviet Union in 1950 and in 1955 respectively, keeping in mind the emerging Cold war calculus and also refused to join at the expense of China. India, since its independence and even before that, has been active in all activities undertaken by UN and the various UN organs including the various discussions on the Agenda for Peace and the Agenda for Development, the Millennium Development Goals, and various UN summits, including most importantly on climate change. India also contributed most importantly by being instrumental in establishing the G77 of developing states at the UN, other than supporting the establishment of various bodies like the UNICEF on a permanent basis, the UNDP, the UNEP, and the restructuring of the economic and social fields of the UN and the UN Development Fund.

India also makes a strong case by highlighting its regular, significant contributions to the UN. In the arena of peacekeeping, India has remained the largest cumulative contributor of UN peacekeeping troops with around 180,000 troops since the 1950s. Most importantly, India has today almost twice the number of peacekeepers deployed on ground as do China, France, Russia, the United Kingdom and the United States combined. Being a "pen holder" as the permanent member of the Security Council, India would similarly assume the mantle of international peace and security decision-making. India thinks it can carry the necessary abilities, actual and potential, which entitles it to a permanent seat. India could get the leverage needed to expand its geo-political and geo-economic clout globally. It would be like an equalizer to China, its rival and an emerging hegemony in Asia and a rising strategic and security concern in its immediate neighborhood and beyond. India has always seen itself as a democratic alternative to the authoritarian China in a leadership role in Asia. India's millennia old civilizational existence also demands it to be at the top of international hierarchy of states.

5.6.3 India, Media and the P5

India and the United States of America recently faced a somewhat similar situation when it comes to media and the extent and use of social media. In 2016, the US presidential elections were held and the social media played a significant role in it. So significant is the role that there were talks that the elections were rigged and influence by pro-Russian people who wanted Donald Trump at the helm of affairs. Apart from such allegations, the social media and media was also used by the candidates themselves to further their campaign. It was one of the most used tool for campaigning during the 2016 presidential elections. However, the bad effect of it remains and has grown this seed of doubt among many that the elections were rigged and influenced. Hence, it appears that the presidential elections is in shadow of the media. India, too, had its crucial 2019 Lok Sabha elections scheduled in April and May 2019 and the use of social media and its influence on elections was a big questions in front of the people of the largest democracy. But, here is how India differentiated itself. The social media giants were forced to sit down at a table together along with the Indian government and devise methods to prevent fake news, rumours mongering and influence during the elections. The social media giants devised many rules to combat influencing during elections and the elections went off largely peaceful in India. Along with social media, the government and traditional forms of media like TV, newspapers, radios also did their bit in strengthening their gate keeping exercise and filtering out fake news and rumours. This helped India in maintaining a fair and peaceful election exercise devoid of any influence unlike in the US presidential elections. India and China too have similarities with both countries trying to prove their supremacy in the South Asian region. While one has the power of the veto, India is purely basing its claim to supremacy on economic, infrastructural development of the country and its neighbors. The difference however lies in the fact that China has state controlled media and no news which is anti-state is ever portrayed to the world. In India, diverse view about the government – pro and against – are telecast which are signs of a healthy democracy and a growing superpower. The media in China is almost non-existent and is equivalent to a government mouth piece. The 'free press' tag is only a dream in China while in India dissenting views are aired freeing in the country, making the signs of a great nation. In the further sections of the P5 countries, the role of media in these countries can be compared to the role of media in India, which is fair and unbiased. Various examples have been listed where the media forced the P5 countries to change their foreign policies.

REFERENCES

1. Adan, A.M. (2017), *Influence of the media on foreign policy of a state: Kenya and Britain, United States International University*, Thesis Report, Degree of Master of Arts (International Relations) United States International Univerisity, Africa.
2. Barnett, S. (2016), "The tragic downfall of the British media," Foreign Policy.com, July 8, 2016, Blog, https://foreignpolicy.com/2016/07/08/the-tragic-downfall-of-british- media-tabloids-brexit
3. Macshane, D. (2017), "Brexit's impact on Britain's foreign policy," *Carnegie Europe*, Blog, July 28, 2017, https://carnegieeurope.eu/strategiceurope/72665.
4. Williams, P. (2004), Who's Making UK Foreign Policy? *International Affairs (Royal Institute of International Affairs 1944-)*, https://onlinelibrary.wiley.com/doi/epdf/10.1111/j.1468-2346.2004.00425.x

CHAPTER VI

Influence of Social Media on Foreign Policy:

Case Studies Indo-US Nuclear Deal and Media

The 123 Agreement signed between the US and India is known as U.S.-India Civil Nuclear Agreement or Indo-US nuclear deal. The framework for this agreement was a July 18, 2005, joint statement by then PM Manmohan Singh and then U.S. President George W. Bush, under which India agreed to separate its civil and military nuclear facilities and to place all its civil nuclear facilities under International Atomic Energy Agency (IAEA) safeguards and, in exchange, the United States agreed to work toward *full* civil nuclear cooperation with India. This U.S.-India deal took more than three years to come to fruition as it had to go through several complex stages, including amendment of U.S. domestic law, especially the Atomic Energy Act of 1954, a civil-military nuclear *Separation Plan* in India, an India-IAEA safeguards (inspections) agreement and the grant of an exemption for India by the Nuclear Suppliers Group, an export-control cartel that had been formed mainly in response to India's first nuclear test in 1974. On August 18, 2008 the IAEA Board of Governors approved, and on February 2, 2009, India signed an India-specific safeguards agreement with the IAEA. After India brought this agreement into force, inspections began in a phased manner on the 35 civilian nuclear installations India has identified in its Separation Plan. The deal is seen as a watershed in U.S.-India relations and introduces a new aspect to international nonproliferation efforts. India and France inked a similar nuclear pact making France the first country to have such an agreement with India. In 2016, the countries agreed to build 6 US-designed reactors in India. There was an entirely different set of reporting and commentary – often very intense – for the 5 years, from the time the India–US nuclear accord was signed in 2005 and through the legislations passed in the US and India. The discussions and comment in the media were many in number and they were of different shades. The core of the discussions was on India's autonomy vis-a-vis the US post the deal. The accord was supposed to be about nuclear power, but it did have implications for India's nuclear weapons programme as well. On weapon-related matters, what was significant was the form most of the commentary took. The comment and analysis in the press either looked at the deal entirely in terms of what it would do to control (or liberate the constraints on) India's weapons programme or ignored the weapons aspect altogether. The media coverage in some ways reflected the wider political discussion. No major political party used the occasion to question the weapons programme, or for that matter India's nuclear power programme.

In a different dimension, the texture of media coverage and discussions changed significantly around 2005. With the celebration of the growth of the Indian economy (the "9% GDP growth" years of 2003–2008), came the projection of India as a major player on the world stage. Here references were often made to India's status as a nuclear weapons state. The importance of India's position as a weapons state came to be stressed as the nuclear weapons delivery systems expanded. The launch (2009), sea trials (2013) and formal induction (2016) of the INS Arihant, India's first nuclear powered submarine to be fitted with ballistic missiles, and the testing of longer range versions of ballistic missiles (5000 km Agni-V) were seen in the media as making India's deterrent effective vis-a-vis China. China, rather than Pakistan, became the focus of attention.

6.1 India-China Border Disputes

The border between India and China is not clearly demarcated throughout. Along certain stretches of its 3,488-km length, there is no mutually agreed Line of Actual Control (LAC). India, following Independence, believed it had inherited firm boundaries from the British, but this was contrary to China's view. China felt the British had left behind a disputed legacy on the boundary between the two newly formed republics. Nearly six decades have passed since then, but the border issue remains unresolved. It has turned into one of the most protracted border disputes in the world. Not a shot has been fired across the India-China border since 1962, but the Indian media's China "war" never quite ended. Border "skirmishes" and Chinese "intrusions" into Indian territory still dominate the coverage of China by Indian newspapers and television channels more than half a century on. But a change seems to be slowly taking place. The Indian media seem to be finally accepting that China does things other than stealthily intrude into Indian land or plot strikes across the border. The border issue remains a major concern, but war cries in the media are heard less and less. So finds a survey by a team of researchers at the Observer Research Foundation, an Indian think-tank that comprises retired diplomats, bureaucrats, other policymakers, academics and journalists. In their survey, the authors analyzed China-related editorials carried by five leading Indian newspapers – *The Times of India, The Hindu, The Indian Express, The Economic Times* and *The Financial Express* – between 2012 and 2014. The years chosen are significant, because they mark the rise to power of the two current leaders of China and India – Xi Jinping and Narendra Modi. Not surprisingly, the survey finds the border issue dominating the editorials. But what is new is an increasing plea for mutual trust and closer economic cooperation between the two long-estranged neighbours. Thus, an editorial in *The Economic Times* said on September 20, 2014, "...minus the passion that television anchors bring to bear on barren wasteland, the border is the least of our problems". "While the border still remains a very sensitive issue for India in particular, the newspapers do not allow it to hijack all other issues...The print media's interest in China is expanding to cover its domestic issues as well," says the report, titled "Understanding China".

Even on border issues, voices are sometimes getting more realistic than jingoistic. At the height of patriotic outbursts, the Indian media generally ignore the historical fact that the two countries do not have a mutually agreed border or that they differ even on the Line of Actual Control (LAC). The highlight of the 2014 editorials, the survey found, was the desire for a pragmatic resolution of the India-China border dispute by the then new Modi government. That may not have been achieved, but there was clearly a lull in the high-pitched media attention on border "incursions". The other issue that was found to have dominated the Indian media's perception in these years was the rise of China. The overall view is still cautious but there seems to be a growing acceptance in the Indian media of China's increasing economic clout and its role in global affairs. That sentiment was reflected in an editorial in *The Hindu* of November 29, 2014, which said China was "too important to be ignored, and it is unwise to believe it can be kept at bay".

6.2 Indo-Pakistan Relations: Post Mumbai Attack

In the case of Indo-Pak relations, media has always played a very important tool. India & Pakistan are one of the most traditional and historical rivals since the partition of subcontinent. In every race starting from military, technology, sports, diplomacy, arms race & even the cultural race by citizen which is carried through media, both India & Pakistan are head to head. India & Pakistan are the two nuclear armed historic rivals. Both the countries have a long history of armed conflict. Since the partition of sub-continent in 1947, both these countries have been facing each other in many types of conflicts starting from the massacre of independence itself, four major wars, river water issues, Siachen conflict, arms race, Kashmir issue & many other issues for that matter. With such a rich & historical rivalry, alongside with military, political leadership, science & technology field, economical race, the citizen & media of both countries have also been engaged in the rivalry and has played its role which indeed is very important. Armies of both the countries have gone through some major reorganization and modernization programmes which has brought the war to even higher standards of technology and tactics including nuclear battlefield. During past conflicts, mainstream media has been playing its role shaping the mindset of the people of both countries to develop hatred against each other but post internet revolution, social media has become one of the most important and dominant battlefield where the citizen of both countries are doing online warfare. Role of social media and citizen journalism cannot be ignored in case of Indo-Pak conflict. While studying the conflicts between both India and Pakistan, it is important to learn and find out how the social media plays its role and the impacts of citizen diplomacy and citizen journalism on the relations of both countries in conflicts like latest LoC tension on border, Mumbai Attacks, India's involvement in Baluchistan, etc. and how it makes the relationship between the two countries, good or bad. Thus, it can be sum up saying that in Indo-Pak relations, social media is playing a negative role and is dominated by war-mongering elements from both sides that use it for negative agenda-setting.

Just like the mainstream media, social media is also playing its critical role in the relations between India and Pakistan. In past, the mainstream media of both sides was state owned and acted as a mouthpiece of the state itself. Later privately owned mainstream media emerged but it was also being manipulated by stake holders for agenda setting purposes. Both sides blame the media of each other in escalating the tension and propagating propaganda against each other at the hands of war-mongering elements. Peace journalism focuses at finding the structural causes of conflict. Media coverage always shapes the course of events at the time of peace and war between the two parties. War coverage and war journalism is more dominant in the case of India-Pakistan journalism than the peace journalism. Most of the stories from the newspapers of both sides promote war journalism and the peace journalism is ignored. In most of the news from both sides, the other side is portrayed more of an enemy rather than a friend. As the mainstream media is playing a negative and war-mongering role in the two countries, social media is one step ahead of that. Whatever happens on mainstream media is reflected on social media in a more intense and escalated manner. In 2008 Mumbai attacks, Indian media played a very irresponsible role and even the supreme court of India declared that the media made the situation worse by unethical reporting and it should be regulated. In Mumbai attacks, the reporting was done in a way which caused problems the security forces carrying out the operations. It was officially declared in India by the court that media played a key role in helping the terrorists. Indian officials blamed media for showing classified footage and content which helped terrorist handlers across the border to get the latest news and inform it to the terrorists carrying out the attacks in Mumbai. Bench of Indian court also blamed media for letting the terrorist operatives on Pakistani sides know and inform to the operatives carrying out the operation that Ajmal Kasab has been caught and that a senior police official has been killed, along with other important developments of the attacks. Also it played a negative role in society and globally made the situation terrible.

Social media was one step ahead and while mainstream media was blaming Pakistan within some limits, social media openly waged a social media war with Pakistan in case of Mumbai attacks. Opinion leaders openly started blaming the state of Pakistan for carrying out Mumbai attacks and globally an impression was successfully established that the state of Pakistan is behind the Mumbai attacks. On the other side of the border, Pakistani social media fought back blaming Indian media openly on social media for the escalation of conflict bringing the two countries at the brink of war. In the relations of India and Pakistan, Kashmir has always been the central cause of conflict. Wars have been fought over Kashmir numerous times and both countries are still at war at the Line of Control. Former US President, Bill Clinton referred to the line of control as the most dangerous place on earth. India says that Kashmir is its integral part while Pakistanis say it is a disputed territory and the problem needs to be resolved. Kashmir is one of the longest going territorial conflicts in international history and has always caught the global attention. Even in the times of peace between the two countries, the LoC is at war. It is at war all the time and small exchanges of fire between the border forces of both countries are practiced in routine. The media used this tension to report in a war mongering way and portray it as a major war between the two countries. The reporting of LoC issue with full of sensationalism makes things worse. The social media in this case is again one step ahead of mainstream media. A small news of routine fire when enters the arena of social media, is portrayed as a major clash between the two armies causing a lot of damage, etc. The military of both countries always comes under pressure with such actions of the media and is sometimes compelled to fire or attack the enemy check posts at the Line of Control to satisfy the public hunger of revenge. With such sensational reporting, and its response on social media, political and military leadership is pushed to keep an aggressive stand on the enemy. Anti-Hindu sentiments in Pakistani society and anti-Pakistani sentiments in Indian society play their role on social media and become active by writing blogs and using Facebook and twitter to fire at the enemy. Hatred spreading videos are prepared on YouTube and shared through Facebook and twitter to promote the escalation. Even a small routine firing incident is often portrayed as a major clash. Many times the military public relations personnel from both sides have to issue a statement denying many fake news and rumors which gain popularity through social media. A major flaw in social media is that it is greatly used in spreading propaganda and rumors. Since the users are citizens, not practicing journalists, so whatever they hear is spread out and everyone spreads news in his/her own interpretation and there is nobody to check or regulate it. Having following in millions, when such baseless news and rumors are spread at national level, the consequences are serious and harmful if not fatal.

Former President of Pakistan Pervez Musharraf is known for handling Indian media with an aggressive manner being a military dictator. On many occasion he has blasted on Indian media and journalists. On one occasion he fired back at a question asked by Indian journalist by replying that what kind of democracy India is running by kicking out Pakistani players and artists and also by pointing out that if Indians want to talk about Kargil, they first have to respond on East Pakistan and Siachin. Famous Pakistani defense analyst Zaid Hamid is known for dealing with Indians in a very aggressive manner and he primarily uses social media. He has more than 35 thousand followers on twitter and almost 190 thousand fans on Facebook. With such a vast reach on social media, he openly blasts the Indians the way he wants. On the comparison, "Aman ki Asha" which is a peace initiative by the two media groups of India and Pakistan has only a combines fan following of just 15,000 fans from both India and Pakistan. With such comparison it is clearly evident that people from both sides of the border on social media are more interested in war and talk of war instead of peace. Zaid Hamid is openly holding Indian government and security agencies responsible for the Taliban uprising in Pakistan and Balochistan issue through social media. Such statements cause anger and rage in his followers on social media and there is a major part of Pakistani nationalist youth and citizens following him. Similarly Sheikh Rasheed, a Pakistani politician is very popular among the people because he openly criticizes India on media and has a great fan following on social media. Famous Indian defense analyst Bharat Verma is known for speaking against Pakistan and having anti-Pakistan/anti-Islam sentiment. Many compare him with Zaid Hamid on Pakistani side. Bharat Verma equally and aggressively responds and attacks Pakistan through mainstream and social media and is very popular in India for that.

Many channels of mainstream media invite him to have panel discussions with Pakistani analysts like Zaid Hamid and Gen. (R) Hameed Gul. Social media is also used by actors on both sides to create public knowledge and awareness. Secret documents when leaked on social media through wiki leaks become talk of the town.

6.3 Impact of Social Media on Global Politics

Media has changed from being a monologue to a dialogue – or even more, an open debate, with personal opinions featuring in mainstream media, opinions that are unfettered and uncensored, regulated only by norms of civic decency. In fact, the effect social media and real-time content have on voters isn't just an intellectual debate anymore, but a reality. A decade ago, a young senator named Barack Obama took his grassroots presidential campaign onto dozens of the then emerging wave of social media websites. Obama's team revolutionized the use of social media in an election they felt was unwinnable using traditional techniques. The campaign made use of advanced digital media features that capitalized on the networking, collaboration, and community-building potential of social media to create a political movement. The Obama campaign website was a full-service, multimedia center where voters not only could access information, they also could watch and share videos, view and distribute campaign ads, post comments, and blog. Supporters could donate, volunteer, and purchase campaign logo items, like tee shirts and caps. The campaign was active on Facebook, Twitter, and YouTube, as well as a range of other social media platforms that catered to particular constituencies, such as BlackPlanet, AsianAve, and Glee.

The campaign pioneered digital micro-targeting tactics. It used social media to collect data on people's political and consumer preferences, and created voter profiles to pursue specific groups, such as young professional voters, with customized messages. The new media trends established in the 2008 campaign have carried over to the realm of government and politics more generally. Social media have become a pervasive force in politics, altering the communication dynamics between political leaders, journalists, and the public. According to Adweek, politicians are stepping up their social media campaigns. It is estimated that politicians will allocate nine percent of their media budget to digital and social media in an effort to win over millennials. Every election, politician, issue and event is being talked about in the public and debated with a level of emotion that couldn't have ever been anticipated. Politicians have more opportunity today to control any narrative surrounding them than ever before. Campaigns have embraced their potential and so have political groups. Twitter specifically has changed the political landscape for many politicians. Twitter is typically used as a platform for self-expression and news management, providing local and national leaders with the opportunity to gauge sentiment in real-time at a rate that has never existed before. Donald Trump used Twitter heavily in his 2016 presidential campaign. "I like it because I can get also my point of view out there, and my point of view is very important to a lot of people that are looking at me," Trump said. The complexities of the new media system, however, are reflected in the diversity of available content. The information distributed via the vast communications network runs the gamut from fact-based, investigative reporting from professional journalists to brash fabrications. In the new media era, the boundaries that separate these disparate types of information have become increasingly muddled. Professional media editors have been replaced by social media and analytics editors whose primary motivation is to draw users to content regardless of its news value. Audience members have to work hard to distinguish fact from fiction, and to differentiate what matters from what is inconsequential. In addition, the economic incentives underpinning new media companies, such as Google, Facebook, and Twitter, are predicated on attracting large audiences that will draw advertising revenue. Political content is used to drive consumers to social media products, rather than to perform the public service function of informing the citizenry. Commercial pressures lead media organizations to feature incendiary stories that receive the most attention. In a nutshell, social media has redesigned structures and methods of modern political communication by transforming the way politicians interact with voters and with each other. But, the role of this marvel in increasing electoral participation and political engagement is neither clear nor simple.

Over time, global media has been manipulated to advance political agendas or national crises. The most recent example of global media propaganda that comes to mind is the Syrian Civil War. Images of the destruction due to the social revolution between the rebels and the leaders in Syria are used as a tool to create certain feelings towards the war. The BBC, for instance, uses social media and their own influence in news media to advance their political stance. The news source will continuously post images and stories about the victims or displaced peoples in order to "humanize" them and the war itself. They use the media as propaganda to encourage compassion around the globe. Today they are promoting an anti-Trump agenda through feature articles such as Meet the People Leaving Trump's America. More often than not, however, we experience propaganda in the media that is targeted to "de-humanize" global populations or conflicts. During the Second World War, for example, media was used for military propaganda to gain public support and subconsciously influence American citizens' mentality against the Japanese. Images such as these, ones that are extremely controversial and compelling, create a sense of emergency within the public sphere. This was and remains the ultimate purpose of propaganda through the media today, to create public discourse around a particular topic and encourage social action or reform. Like the BBC's coverage of the Syrian Civil War, media is used to manipulate the emotions and actions of the people. Most recently, we have begun to see this effect in the U.S. politics, specifically during the Presidential campaign. In consideration of the amount of information available versus the amount of information that is actually published, we can assume that today's media may be heavily interested in protecting the status quo. The hesitation within all news sources to put out the Russian dossiers implies a need to maintain the values of traditional media.

CHAPTER VII

Data Analysis, Data Interpretation and Presentation

To solicit the information about usage of social media and its tools it was decided to conduct a survey of social media usage by different groups of stakeholders. A list of stakeholders who use social media for various purposes was prepared and thirty stakeholders were selected for the pilot study. Social media is used by most of the students, teachers, researchers, media personnel, government officials and politicians etc. To test the structured questionnaire designed for this purpose, it was distributed among these stakeholders and they were requested to inform us if they faced any difficulty in understanding the questions. They had been given sufficient time to think and fill in the questionnaire. The researcher so far has not received any suggestions to modify the questionnaire. Hence, it was decided to distribute the questionnaire to all thirty stakeholders to conduct the pilot study. Nobody suggested any improvements to the questions asked to them. Questions were designed to keep in mind the objectives of the project. There were twenty-five questions included in the questionnaire. To know the views of various stakeholders who are using social media and social media tools, about the use of social media and its impact on Indian Foreign Policy, a structured questionnaire was developed and distributed to 550 participants which includes postgraduate students, research scholars, defense officers and faculty members etc. Out of which, we have received 483 responses from various groups of stakeholders.

7.1 Data Analysis of the Pilot Study Conducted

In the beginning, we conducted a pilot study to test the questionnaire which we have prepared for stakeholders and we have conducted the pilot study about the use of social media by students, researchers, faculty members etc. from the post graduate students of Department of Defense and Strategic Studies and research scholars of the department. For this purpose, we have developed a structured questionnaire to test these questions from these users. The analysis of these questionnaires is given in the first chapter of this project. First six questions are about the use of social media, social media tools, purpose of using social media tools, their participation and contributing views on India's Foreign policy through these tools and how they update their knowledge about Indian foreign policy.

7.2 Data Analysis of the Entire Respondent Group (483 Questionnaires)

After implementing the pilot study and confirming that all the questions set in the questionnaire are ready to be distributed to the stakeholders, we started giving out the questionnaires to the respondents. All the questions are designed as per the objectives set for this project. We have distributed 550 questionnaires to various categories of stakeholders which includes, post graduate students, research scholars, faculty members from Defense and Strategic studies department, Political Science department, International relations department from various Universities in the country, Army officers who are associated with Defense department and received 483 responses (87 per cent). Following universities are included in this study.

Departments of Defense studies from Universities in Maharashtra state and other Universities, i.e. Savitribai Phule Pune University, Pune; KBC North Maharashtra University, Jalgaon; Goa University, Panjim; Jawaharlal Nehru University, Delhi; Chinese Studies Centre, Delhi; Chandigarh University, Chandigarh; Gorakhpur University, Gorakhpur (UP) and Central University of Gujarat, Ahmedabad. Out of the 550 questionnaires distributed to stakeholders from various University departments, we have received 483 duly filled in questionnaires. Following table shows the statistics of the questionnaire distribution and responses received.

Table 1: Showing distribution of questionnaires and its percentage

University	*Department*	*Questionnaire distributed*	*Questionnaires Received (Response)*	*Percentage*
SPPU, Pune	DDSS	80	73	91
SPPU, Pune	Other departments	250	234	93.6
JNU, Delhi	International Relations	55	45	81.81
Goa University, Panji		60	46	76.66
Chinese Studies Centre, Delhi	Chinese Studies Centre	25	16	64
Chandigarh University	DDSS	10	03	30
Gorakhpur University, Gorakhpur	DDSS	45	32	71.11
Central University of Gujarat, Ahmedabad	Centre for Security Studies	25	16	54
KBC North Maharashtra University, Jalgaon		25	18	72
Total		575	483	84

At the beginning of the questionnaire, personal information of the stakeholders was asked which includes, name, designation, qualifications, working experience, email and contact number etc.

Q. 1

Table 2: Use of social media networking

	Personal level	*Student*	*Research scholar*	*Teacher*	*Media person*	*Political purpose*	*Govt. official*	*General*
Participants	275	272	83	46	28	40	42	177
Percentage	29	28	09	05	03	04	04	18

Chart 1: Use of Social media by various stakeholders

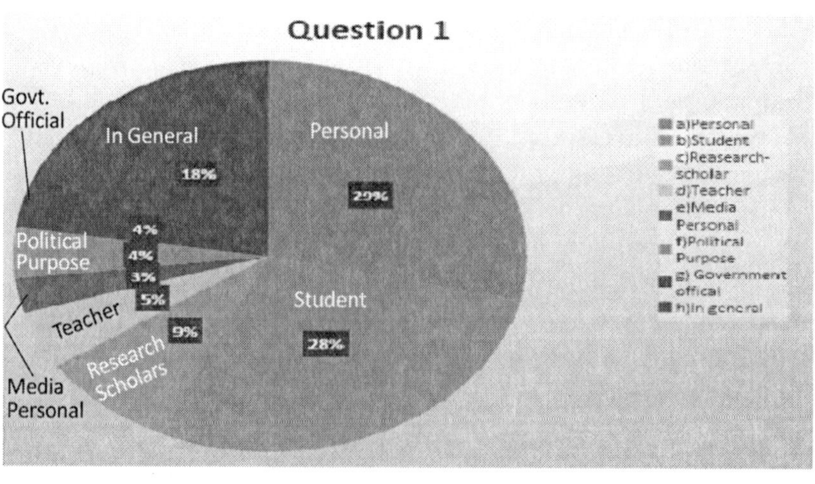

This question was asked to the stakeholders that whether they use social media networking. Out of 483 stakeholders use social network for various level. Eight options were provided to the stakeholders. 275 (29 per cent) stakeholders use social networking for their personal use whereas 272 participants (28 per cent) use it at the student level for searching information for their study. 83 (9 per cent) research scholars use social networking for searching research level information for their research topic, 46 (4 per cent) participants use social networking for teaching purposes, they will seek the information on various teaching topics which they need for teaching purposes, whereas 28 (5 per cent) participants use to find information about media level information, what media provided information on various areas, current news in detail etc. 40 (3 per cent) participants use social networking for political purposes to find political information through social networking sites. 42 (4 per cent) participants said that they use social networking sites as a government official, searching for information about official authentic information by the government. 177 (18 per cent) participants said that they use social networking for general purposes. It appears from the above statistics that 29 per cent stakeholders are using social networking for their personal level use, followed by 28 per cent stakeholders, who use social media networking as a student for their studies.

Q.2 It was asked to the participants which social media tools they used.

Names of the social media tools are provided to them: Facebook, YouTube, Twitter, LinkedIn, Blog, Slideshare, Instagram, Snapchat, MySpace and Flicker. Out of the 483 participants, 34 per cent participants use Youtube as the biggest social media tool. The details of social media tools and its use by the participants is mentioned in the following table.

Table 3: Showing use of social media tools

Social media tools	*No of participants using social media tools*	*Percentage*
Twitter		12
Facebook		31
MySpace		00
LinkedIn		9
Blog		6
Flicker		1
Youtube		34
Slideshare		4
Snapchat		3
Instagram		3

Chart 2: Use of Social media tools

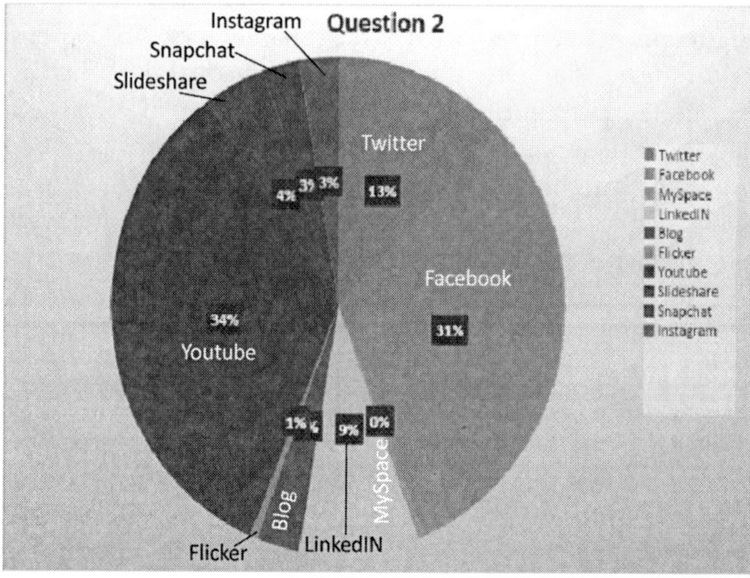

It shows from the above table that YouTube social media tool is used by the majority of the participants (34 per cent) because participants get videos which they required for their use, also they can upload the videos which they have prepared on the specific area or topic, YouTube videos are available on any topic which are required by persons, even educational videos are also available whereas Facebook is another social media tool used by 31 per cent participants in which participants can communicate with their friends. Nobody uses MySpace as a social media tool nowadays.

WhatsApp is another social media tool which is used by the majority of the people to communicate with their friends, colleagues and also chatting, sending videos, messages, and communicate over the phone free of cost.

Q. 3 This question was asked to know the purpose of using social media tools and five options were provided to participants who were requested them to tick mark the option. (A – Personal. B – to obtain knowledge and information in various subject areas. C – to upkeep information and knowledge. D – Personal study and research. E – personal interest in the Indian Foreign Policy)

Chart 3: Showing purpose of using social media tools

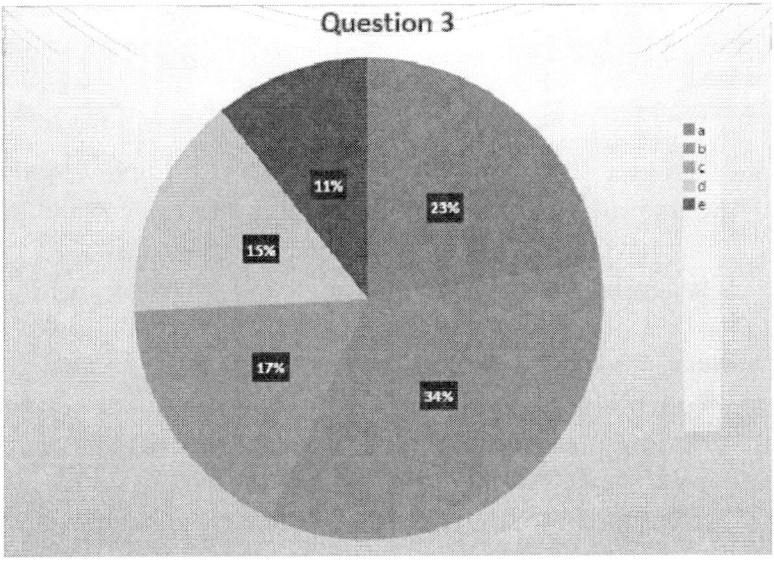

Out of 483 participants, 238 (23 per cent) participants said they use social media tools for their personal use whereas 358 (34 per cent) participants use these tools to obtain knowledge and information in various subject areas which they required for their study and interest. 182 (17 per cent) participants mentioned that they use these tools to upkeep the information and knowledge, 158 (15 per cent) participants use social media tools for their personal study and research purpose. 112 (11 per cent) participants use these tools for their personal interest in India's foreign policy. It is revealed that a majority of the participants, (34 per cent) use social media tools to obtain knowledge and information in various subject areas in which they are interested, followed by 23 per cent of participants who use social media with the purpose of using it for their personal interest.

Q.4 Further this question was asked whether they use these social media tools for contributing their views on various nationwide problems or policy making of the government. There are 165 (34 per cent) participants giving a positive response to this and said that they contribute their views on the nationwide problems or occasional problems through these social media tools whereas 267 participants (55 per cent) replied that they are not contributing their views through social media tools. 51 participants (10 per cent) did not reply to this question. Some of the participants provided supporting remarks with their answer. When the matters covering national security, welfare of the society, social security issues and women empowerment were discussed, one participant contributed his views on these topics through social media tools. Some of the views of the participants are as follows:

- Policy regarding youth and Indian culture, skill development programme introduced by the central government and state government, then a participant contributed his views.
- Whenever there is any information which is wrong or misleading the people, then the participant tried to correct it and also show interest in Indian culture.
- Creating awareness by sharing authentic and trusted news regarding any social mishap, ex-accident, riots, natural calamity among people through social media tool.
- Contribute views on education system in India and Jammu Kashmir issues.
- Being a civil services aspirant, I have a habit of studying and making opinion on the various policies of the government of India and other countries which affect India and contribute my views through Facebook post.
- Use social media tools to contribute views for social upliftment or cost related issues.
- Put comments on particular event or government decision on foreign policy.
- With regards to various schemes which are incorporated for women and senior citizens and children's for their security and bright future.
- In connection to social problems like atrocity etc. cases happening in the society, participant contributed his views on political stands taken by government and other policies, criticise and appropriate comments were put on social media platform.
- Contribute views and express opinion and alert people about fake news.
- Some times against religious racism or caste discrimination, explaining fake news or any stuff which is hindering on social media.

- Use social media as a tool to understand the views of panel like Rajya Sabha TV and other news channel debates which helps me to understand the concept in detail.
- My government website of Government of India, web portal used to give feedback and opinions on government policy to create pressure and ensure development good public policy.
- Provide views related to education system, especially about primary education and do some serious policies for 1 to 5 standard education.
- Contributing views on corruption and reservation through social media platform.
- Contributing my ideas on India's external problems like farmers suicide, naxalism etc.

Q. 5 This question was asked to know how many participants expressed their views on India's Foreign policy through social media tools. There are 82 (16.97 per cent) participants who replied that they have expressed their view on Indian foreign policy, whereas 359 (74.33 per cent) participants said that they never express their views on foreign policy, 42 (8.69 per cent) participants did not reply to this question. It means that a majority of the participants do not express their views on Indian foreign policy through social media tools, the reasons for which may be varied., There are a few reasons identified from the participants that social media is not the place to discuss such sensible issues without knowing the factual information. Many times our Prime Minister and Foreign Minister visit other countries to represent India and discuss the relationship of two countries, social media is not a place to comment on our officials critically. Following are some of the comments raised by participants in their questionnaire regarding.

- Our Foreign policy department does not require suggestions and we have scholars from the Indian Foreign Service cadre who are well educated enough to solve the issues of small countries like Maldives, Sri Lanka.
- Social media has a major effect on the policy making in India's neighborhood countries to spread positive or negative messages to the nation.
- India's proactive policy on Doklam, India's policy on terrorism

has raised major debate among the people.

- Social media's participation on foreign policy is not feasible, it only discuss internal issues, however the discussion on social media put some pressure on makers of the policy.

Q. 6 To know how frequently participants are visiting the website of Ministry of External Affairs, Government of India to get recent updates on Indian foreign policy. Following table shows the frequency of visits to the website of the Ministry of External Affairs to know the updates on Indian foreign policy.

Table 4: Shows frequency of visit to the Website of Ministry of External Affairs to know updates on India's foreign policy

How frequently visit the Website of Ministry of External Affairs	*No. of participants visit*
Daily	22
Weekly	52
Monthly	52
Occasionally	137
Never	49
No reply to this question	171

From the above table, it shows 137 participants visit the website of the Ministry of External Affairs, Government of India, occasionally. Some of the participants visit the website daily, weekly and monthly, but the majority of the participants 220 never visited the website or they have not replied to this question. Those who visit the website frequently as per their convenience replied that they get the updated information about the decisions taken by the government on security, culture, International trade, export and import.

Q. 7 This question was asked to know the opinions of the participants about various incidents that happened in the country and whether these incidents play a decisive role in framing the foreign policy and if the answer is yes, then it was further requested to specify any incident where the government has taken decision to decide foreign policy based on social media. Out of 483 participants, 266 participants (55 per cent) said that due to the incidents happened in the country, it made the government change or modify their foreign policy. Whereas 126 participants (26 per cent) expressed that there is no effect of the incidents happened in the country to frame the foreign policy. There were 91 participants (18.84 per cent) who did not provide any response to this question. Participants has given few examples of the incidents where government has taken decisions to decide policy or modify the foreign policy and they are as follows:

- 26/11 terrorist attack on Taj Hotel, Mumbai when terrorists came from Pakistan.
- Terrorist attack on the parliament.
- Illegal migration of Rohingya Muslims who migrated from Myanmar to India in such case Central Govt. has taken a firm decision.
- Continuous attack by terrorists in Jammu and Kashmir area and in such incidents Government of India changed its policy and did not to talk with Pakistan.
- Bangladesh Refugee.
- Uri and Pathankot attack incidents by terrorists.
- Kulbhushan Jadhav case.
- Formation of public opinion on Major national events like Commonwealth games.
- Recent banking fraud by Nirav Modi, and Mehul Chokshi and Vijay Mallaya.
- Indian Bangladesh border issues.
- Prime Minister speech from Red fort regarding Baluchistan.
- In recent period, demand of reservation to Maratha Community in Maharashtra.
- Teesta water dispute with Bangladesh.
- Government play sensitive role in H1-B visa policy with USA.
- Buying Chinese goods in India, Government take certain measures against this policy.
- JNU sedition case: Kanhaiya Kumar and Umar Khalid charge sheet filed by Govt.
- Surgical strike made by Indian Army in Pakistan.
- Demonetization and GST implementation.
- Nirbhaya rape case in Delhi, issue raised regarding security of girls.
- In spite of being a known nuclear power India has always refused to be a part of NP, however recent events have pushed

India to reconsider its stand and now it is seeking membership of a member of nuclear pact and regimes.

- Khalistan issues, in which separate demand of Khalistan by few people.
- Issues of Naxalism, International player like China play very important role to induce naxalism in India by providing secret weaponry help and funds making it inflammatory.

Q. 8 The participants were further asked about their views on if there is a change in the Central Government, does it inevitably change the foreign policy of the current government. Five options were provided which are: slightly changed as per the situation, completely changed in certain cases, completely revised, never changed and any other. The analysis of this question showed in the following table.

Table 5: Showing views when central govt. changes, it change their policies

Options	*No. of Participants*	*Percentage*
A) Slight changes as per situation	323	68
B) Completely changes in certain cases	111	23
C) Completely revised	17	3
D) Never changed	18	4
E) Any other	13	2
Total	483	100

Chart 4: Opinions of the stakeholders when Central Government changes, it change their policies

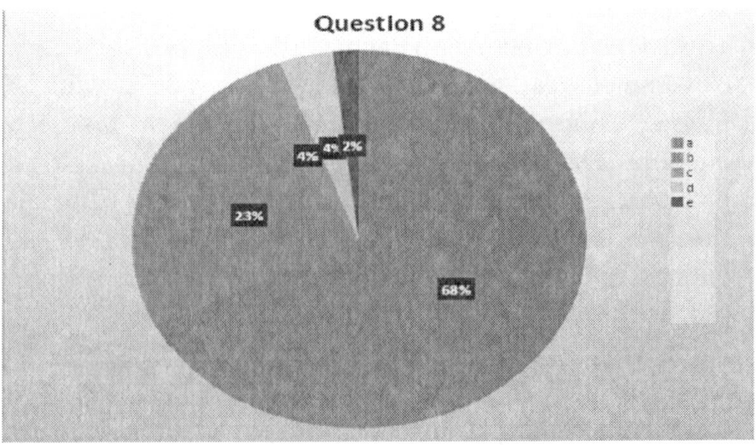

From the above table it reveals that there are 323 participants (66.87 per cent) who are of the opinion that the government slightly changes their policies as per the situations followed by 111 participants (22.98 per cent) participants who replied that the new government completely changes their policies in certain cases whereas very few participants 3.71 per cent opined that the new government completely changed their policies in certain cases.

Changing complete policy in certain cases is possible because it depends on the present situation, pressure from people in the country and critical comments from the opposition parties in the country and forces from media. In India deciding the foreign policy, the process is complex, certain factors are involved in deciding the policy for Nation. In a democratic country, like India amendment in certain policies is also a complex process. Central Government is finally responsible for all matters to the foreign policy.

Q. 9 This question was asked to seek the opinions of the usage of social media tools and its influence and effects on our Indian foreign policy. Out of 483 participants, there are 379 participants (78 per cent) participants who expressed their opinion that the use of social media tools is very important and could influence on India's foreign policy, whereas 64 participants (13 per cent) expressed that there could not be any influence of the use of social media tools on India's foreign policy. While justifying to support their opinions, some participants have submitted their views, they are as follows:

- The information which is available on social media tool like Youtube is sensitive, hence it affects our security
- Due to social media influence, many ties like India's National security policy was influenced and shifted from passive to active.
- With the help of social media tools, the government will be able to get some better views of public in terms of Indian national security.
- Propaganda through social media tools can affect our national security.
- Social media is an independent watchdog and can be used by anyone and has also large audience with live syndrome. It does

not have any security code and there could be internal leakage of vital information.

- Up to a certain extent it does influence a certain section of the society, however, since the size of the country distribution is huge, no major cases have come to light.
- It does influence Indian national security as the social media is an important tool which shares the opinion of all and at the time government has to take into consideration these issues e.g. spread of terrorism (ISIS) through social media.
- The young minds who are at an impressionable age can get influenced other way the presentation of the message on social media is important and negatives need to be rebutted effectively.
- Influence may be partially, as social media tools have a very wide reach and at a time there may be instructions in sharing of opinion of a section of the public.
- Through Social media tools, wrong messages are spread in the country, it some how creates the mob killing crimes due to misunderstanding, which also creates the target killing situation by mob killing e.g. In the village of Maharashtra state, three persons were killed by a mob in 2018 due to misunderstanding.
- Recently there were incidents of mass lynching in various parts of the country, though it was fake news, innocent people died. Sometimes social media is used by terrorist organizations, in order to influence the people by making videos or releasing violent information.
- It can bridge the gap between policy makers and public with better understanding of decision making and rational behind it.
- Social media can be used for various purposes but it also misused by people, many fake news has been spread through various medium, specially through WhatsApp, now a days this will affect our national security.
- Cases like questioning army surgical strike information or posting negative propaganda against army forces on social media affects morale of soldiers.
- Due to social media, we have came closer globally, it can

definitely have an influence and effect on India's national security.

- More data is available on internet which is accessed by people like complaints and cases people can be brainwashed through social media.
- Recently many Indians had joined the war in Syria and this is a serious problem and the government must take action against such social media accounts.
- Social media provides a platform for both persons who are nationalist and activists. We should check the activity of the latter by the cyber crime department.
- Most of the people on media have a habit of posting everything on social media regarding love potting, minute details as protests, personal views about policies, religious views of majority people may make some countries feel uncomfortable and expose people's faith about their government.
- Social media has a profound effect on almost everything and at a time it can hinder things similarly it can influence as well as affect India's national security as an attacker may get loads of information on various things working internal ideas, living conditions etc. this can be used to single out target groups.
- Today caste politics and religious incidents or symbiolic identity politics continuously helps in generating hate among people of one caste to another or one religion to another.
- Social media helps in building opinions, construct and consolidate citizens views on particular issues. This information can further be used in shaping nation and security policy. The present government policy on deploying army forces in conflict prominent areas in Jammu and Kashmir has caught greater citizen opinion.
- There are many cases in which specially Indian officials from defense forces were caught involved in sharing important information of defense which influence Chinese and Pakistan.
- Unchecked social media tools can be a real security threat, most transnational criminal networks co-ordinate with their sympathisers, agents, finance them and accomplish through

social network platform, hence security measures must be put in place to avoid filtration in Indian database.

Q.10 Indian National Security and India's Foreign Policy, these two aspects are very important aspects in Indian democracy. In India all communities, religions, castes are living since long ago but when the problem arises about our security, all the people, all political parties forget their disputes with each other and come together to face the problem collectively. Since the study is related to social media and its influence on Indian National security and India's Foreign Policy, Opinions from the students, teachers, researchers and army officers are very much important in this study. To seek the opinions of the stakeholders from the above categories, out of 483 participants in this study, 287 participants (59 per cent) opined that social media positively influenced on our national security and foreign policy. Whereas 112 (23 per cent) participants opined that social media tools does not have any influence on our national security and foreign policy. To support the positive responses given by the participants, they have provided few information, incidents happened in which social media influence is evident. Few information is as follows:

- Psychological framework is changed by the social media and also its use and misuse affecting the verdict/decision making of policy makers
- It impact domestic and international mindset. The performance of the government and administration is judged by the narrative hogging in social media.
- No one has been able to control and monitor social media as yet, many information which is available on surface website needs to be analyzed and due attention be given and timely correct the system and policy before any wrong incident happens.
- There are many Think tanks like I.C.W.A., O.R.F. and V.I.F. publishing Hindi articles on Twitter and Facebook which is very useful for the awareness about security to the people when ordinary person will be aware about security, they will react on the government policies which may be harmful to India's security

- Social media does influence India's National security and Foreign policy, the opposition on social media affects diplomatic relations, softening of relations with Pakistan due to terrorism has an impact in shaping these national security and foreign policy.
- Indian youths are self-motivated towards nation building when there is any question/problems arising with our security, all youths or all peoples of the country are united and express their opinions through social media tools.
- Social media plays a major role in national security and foreign policy if some incident happened between two countries and it will spread by media and it has a large impact on united nation policy making.
- People can pose serious questions to the government being behind the screen rather facing the government and such influence make an impact the government to take major step.
- The present government is using social media tools like Twitter, Facebook etc. to give information about government programmes and its policy. Everyone share views on Twitter and Facebook. For example, Max e-governance, digital India.
- The question of to what extent social media produces the opinion of general public is unanswered, but it does in many ways. The government also uses social media as a propaganda tool to sway the opinion of the masses.
- It is a witness as the government is moving towards digitization and using various social media platforms thus social media does have a role in shaping our security and policy.
- Rise of paid media is possible only because social media can help manipulate the all incidents regarding security and policy.
- The domestic politics can influence foreign policies, in similar fashion social media targets both government and non-government actors across the borders which eventually has an impact on Indian foreign policy.
- Impact is there definitely on national security as there have been cases of confidential data leaks, video leaks and also current scenario of rumors to lynching leading to social tension

- Social media influence is not complete, but it is showing small influence in Rohingya issues, Assam riots of 2012 and exodus of students from Bangalore and Hyderabad.
- Currently the cases of mob lynching is a good example of wrong use of social media for the internal security but as far as foreign policy concerned it has less impact.
- Some institutes which are so called social or religious are creating radicalism by creating fake messages and some higher authorities are spreading fake stories during their speeches and people without confirming those things are believing in those, which is so bad for the society.
- One impact could be "digital currency" i.e. Crypto currency use. Its use has been increasing national foreign security issues and the government has to take note of this when dealing with cyber vulnerable countries.
- Social media which puts things into citizens perspective in good or bad manner and citizens reacts on it like now days Assamees NRC issues. We don't know real things, but media is the only right way to collect reliable data.
- Recently happened cases of gang rapes, this is shameful to the people of the country, however the news we heard in India that women are not safe in India then of course the impact of national security arises.
- The present government has tried to influence the social media. There are allegations that the ruling party has opened numerous fake accounts in various social media platforms and through they are trying to influence the media.
- In troubled northern regions like Jammu and Kashmir that expose insurgency and militant rebellion. Social media is used to fan, spread propaganda on the brutal crackdown and this affects India's national security as there is always backlash from civil society organizations and international community that condemn the government's act. India's foreign policy is framed with priorities given to curbing threats imposed by social media for instance the ending tensions between India over Pakistan occupied Kashmir coordination between rebellion groups in Punjab is believed to have support of Indian Muslim in Canada,

same to Tamil Nadu. That is believed to get support from Sri Lanka and most coordination are through social networks platform. So India, in framing tourism policy relations with China, Pakistan, Canada or Sri Lanka, takes into consideration these emerging trends which are mostly propagated through social media.

- Through social media, there are so many communal groups activated in India, e.g. Cow slaughtering and Gau mata and foreign terrorist group connecting with Indian young generation through social media like ISIS.
- Use of social media as a tool by terrorist organization for ideological realization and recruitment. Government of India in order to steer public opinion, media act as an important tool for contemporary foreign policy makers of specially liberal states.

Q. 11 Present Government is more active on social media as compared to other political parties, however to know the opinions of the stakeholders on this issue, they were asked if the present government is more active in using social media than the previous government. Out of 483 participants, 403 participants (83 per cent) responded that the present government is more active in using social media, however very less participants 32 (6 per cent) opined that the present government is not active on social media. It was also asked to the participants that the areas in which government are actively using social media. Following are the answers from respondents which are areas on which present government is active through social media.

- Man ki Baat programme of Prime Minister of India through radio and TV and messages are provided through social media.
- Swachh Bharat Abhiyan Programme of the central government.
- Ganga cleaning programme.
- Smart cities programme in which majority of the cities are identified to improve infrastructures of these cities and propaganda is done through social media.
- Digital India programme in which present government is promoting and insisting the people to use digital transactions for banks and shopping.

- Education sector where social media is being used to spread the messages to the public.
- Interaction with NRI's and projection of Indian policies and change in policies affecting FDI's projecting strong leadership and consistency, projecting growth and sharing of information.
- Bullet train programme, developing Indian Railway facilities, online reservation, use of internet during travel, improvement in present infrastructure are propagated through social media tools like Twitter, facebook.
- Sending public awareness advertisements through social media as well as TV, newspaper media, etc.
- Make in India programme which helps industries and developing new industries as well existing industries.
- Jan Dhan Yojana programme by the central government in which poor people can open their account in any nationalized bank with minimum amount of Rs.10/-
- Under Digital India programme, Government has initiated BHIM app, Digilocker programme in which any Indian citizen can open account and upload and store his important papers with security and download any time. NAMO App.
- Present government implemented issuing Aadhar cards to each citizen of India and Aadhar card is connected to many accounts to check the personal details of person with security.
- Electricity to each village in India programme.
- Social welfare schemes like medical insurance for poor people and their family. Rs.5 lakh insurance, crop insurance for the farmers etc.
- Assembly elections and Lok Sabha elections propaganda through social media.
- Jammu Kashmir issues, Section 370, special status of the state.
- Visa issues for all people made simple.
- Prime Minister visits to various countries and its detailed information is propagated through social media.
- Beti Bachayo Abhiyan, E-governance, subsidized gas cylinder to all and poor people.

Q.12 Do you think that powerful nations like the U.S., UK, China, Russia, France etc, are active on social media to influence the Foreign Policies? **Yes** or **No**

There are few powerful countries in the world like US, UK, China, Russia and France which are considered developed countries, however, India is a developing country. Majority of the developing countries as mentioned above are using social media for various purposes. Social media sites like Facebook and Twitter are more popular and increasingly part of the lives of the people in United State.

US

According to Pew (2012) center study, it was found that about half of the U.S. population uses social media which includes 80 percent of the people from 18-29 years old. Social media structure which is considered general provide unlimited access to information and equal, protected participation (Loader and Mercea, 2011). Internet facilities are accessible to every person, anyone can distribute information and make both participation in information acquisition free from outside influence (Fuchs, 2012)

UK

According to Table 6, 44 million people using social media may be from their computer, laptop etc. Active mobile users of social media are 38 Million. Sharing of information through social media is also more. However, research says that young Britons are unhappy and lack confidence in themselves and their future.

Table 6: In United Kingdom, following table showing the active users of social media in January 2018

	Total No. of users in Millions	*Share of population Percentage*
Active social media users	44	66
Active mobile social mediausers	38	57

Source: Statista, 2019, The Statista Portal, https://www.statista.com/statistics/507405/uk-active-social-media-and-mobile-social-media-users/

CHINA

In China, there are three hottest social media platforms they are WeChat, QQ and Weibo. WeChat is used for messaging and nearly 500 million active users are using this app in China. According to the EMarketer report half of the country's smart mobile phone users are using the app in 2017. According to Huileng Tan from CNBC 730 million active social media users estimated globally, however the large numbers of users in China using social media platform.

FRANCE

According to Cint, the result of the survey conducted on the distribution of social media use in France in 2017, 35.04 percent users used Facebook, overall number of Facebook users in France is expected to reach 33.88 million people by 2022. The Penetration rate of social media services was highest among 18-24 year old young boys. 94 percent of the respondents of this age group reported that they are using social media services. Globally Facebook is the most popular social media platform with 2.234 billion active users followed by Whatsapp is second 1.5 billion active users ahead from YouTube.

RUSSIA

According to the statistics from Statistica web portal, user of social media users in Russia were 60.5 million in 2013, 75 million in 2017 and 79.2 millions in 2019. It indicates that the use of social media is increasing year by year in Russia. In order to seek the opinions from the stakeholders that whether these powerful countries mentioned above are active on using social media to influence foreign policies of their country. From the data collected through questionnaire, out of 483 participants, 294 participants (61 per cent) positively says that these countries are using social media for various purposes, whereas 93 participants (19 per cent) do not agree with this. 96 participants (20 per cent) did not reply to this question.

Q. 13. In spite of China playing an important role in International power politics, do you think that it is actively involved on social media? **Yes** or **No**

If yes, please support your answer.

China is a developed country from Asia and is playing an important role in international power politics and helping Pakistan at various new projects. This question was asked to know the opinions of the participants that even though China is playing an important role in international power politics, whether China is not actively involved on social media. Out of 483 participants, 177 participants (36.64 per cent) said that China is actively involved on social media whereas 181 participants (37 per cent) said that it is not. It seems from the responses that marginal respondents say China is not actively involved on social media. As per the report of eMarketer, there are three popular applications, they are WeChat, QQ and Weibo are most popular applications used by the users in China. There are 500 million active users in China of WeChat app in 2017. QQ application was launched 18 years ago even though it was the largest social app in China, recently it was rebranded to focus on entertainment among China's youth. Weibo app is called China's twitter. There are 340 million active users of Twitter with the key reason that this growth was the evolution of the service into a multimedia blogging platform with similar features of Twitter, Pinterest and Tumbir combined. Younger Chinese more aware of negative impact of social media. WeChat remains the most popular social app, while Weibo makes a come-back with younger users.

According to Kantar Report on social media found that Chinese respondents are generally happy with changes brought by social media. Social media give score impact on their lives is 79.8 but as compared with other age groups, people born in 1990s showed more caution against negative impact of social media. China has disrupted censorship drive on Whatsapp. It has been accessible through virtual private networks (VPNs) only, but some of them are blocked.

The opinions expressed by the participants are as follows:

- There is direct control of the Chinese government on social media that is why people are unable to express their views on social media.
- To some extent Chinese government is active on social media, it regulates censors and uses it for the party's interest.
- Chinese government policy is not that open to the world, they

are very cautious.

- China does not get involved itself on social media because many social media sites are banned in China, they have adopted aggressive foreign policy.
- China is most emerging country after USA, China try to create dominance not on Asia but over the world. Today it is not possible to be powerful nation without social media.
- China has its own social media networking, their social media platforms are a little bit different from other countries.
- China has its own influence in the Asia to build one belt road initiate via string of pearls policy to connect every part to whole.
- Chinese social media is active but it is clearly dominated by their security agencies.
- Chinese companies are making a global reach as per recent activities.
- China has restricted many social media tools like facebook, etc.

Q. 14. There are many strategic think tanks which are working in India independently. The major think tanks are as follows:

- Asian Development Research Institute, Headquarter at Patna
- Centre for Asian Strategic Studies, New Delhi, India
- Centre for Policy Research, New Delhi
- Indian Council of World Affairs, New Delhi (ICWA)
- Institute for Defense Studies and Analyses, New Delhi
- Institute of Peace and Conflict Studies, New Delhi
- National Maritime Foundation, New Delhi
- Observer Research Foundation, Mumbai, Chennai and Kolkata
- South Asia Analysis Group
- Strategic Foresight Group, Mumbai
- The Takshashila Institution, Bangalore
- United Service Institution, New Delhi
- Vivekananda International Foundation, New Delhi

It was asked to the participants if they agree that strategic think tanks influence foreign policies through social media. Out of 483 participants, 227 participants (47 per cent) opined that they agree with the statement, however 146 participants (30 per cent) participants do not agree with this statement, whereas 110 participants (23 per cent) did not reply to this question.

Some of the important views provided by participants are given here:

- As the riots happened between any of the religion or caste, it directly circulated through social media tools, networking sites or news and it influences the foreign policy.
- Ruling party has their own think tanks who provide information to the ruling party which influence our policy.
- Data available on social media provides an insight into the opinions of the public with regards to the situation without actually taking into account the level of competence of the respondents.
- Because of the bureaucrats as political houses are at a loss when it comes to heavy subject like foreign policy. Hence, the role of these academic think tank is important, sometimes they are a part of the advisory board of the nation.
- Strategic think tanks derive opinions from various state of society and analyse them and forward them to the government agencies or policy makers for consideration.
- Strategic think tanks do influence foreign policies but most of the time they are not too open on social media and maintain distance from it.
- Almost all the think tanks have their Facebook or Instagram, Linkedin, Twitter account which regularly publish events/ academic articles that shape/reshape the perception of the people involved in foreign policy making.
- Strategic think tanks give in-depth analysis as they are the best source, articles delivered by the scholars of think tank helps in opinion forming.
- Strategic think tanks used to shape minds of people as well as policymakers for any critical decision they gives advice to government. E.g. IDSA helps govt. in foreign policy making.
- The people in think tank are great minds and have lots of experience than the people on social media.
- They are an important stakeholder while taking decision on

foreign policy in the nation's interest and national interest is directly connected with the people, since people of the country have a connection with social media, logically think tanks influence foreign policy through social media.

- Think tanks provide their publications, research work online. As a result the information is able to reach a good number of people and this shapes public opinion, for decision making for people and in turn dictates how foreign policy is formed.

Q. 15. Recently there is political competition in India because Lok Sabha elections will be held in 2019, hence all political parties are now ready propagate their agenda to the public through social media, TV channels, Newspapers etc. New media are forms of communication and facilitate the production, exchange of political contents, and information on social media platform within the available network and establish interaction and collaboration among them. New media have a very wide range of implications for democratic governance and political practices. They have altered the ways in which government institutions operated and political leaders communicate amongst each other, they are using social media system and transformed the political media system and redefine the role of journalists. They have redefined the various ways of elections contested and observe how citizens engaged in politics. Ideally, the media is playing several essential roles in a democratic society. Their primary purpose is to inform the public, providing citizens with the information needed to make thoughtful decisions about leadership and policy. The media act as watchdogs for checking government actions and comment on these actions and propagate among the public. They set the agenda for public discussion of current issues, and provide a forum for political expression. They also facilitate community building by helping people to find common causes, identify civic groups, and work toward solutions to societal problems. This question was asked to know the opinions of the stakeholders about if social media reflects the political competition on India's foreign policy and what are the limitations of social media data for research scholars. Out of 483 participants, only 81 (17 per cent) participants opined positively and 106 (22 per cent) participants express negatively. Few opinions of the participants are given here:

- There is no limitation for social media research scholars can use the data for their research work who is doing research on foreign policy.

- Without verifying the data available on social media is not good and meaningful for interpretations and conclusion, however, researcher has to verify the data available on social media.
- It may reveal various working policies and ethics of politics. All information is open to the environment which may be properly analyzed for research.
- Data available on social media provides an insight into the opinion of the public with regards to the situation without actually taking into account the level of competence of the respondents.
- Contents available on social media are not always authenticated, their periodicity and corrections are always question mark.
- India being a democratic country, the social media with his wide outreach can be used to obtained real-time feedback on the issues.
- Social media need to be carefully analyzed before being considered. Any kind of competition to established with institutional ID that has significant levels of control over individual minds of reflection of individual beyond this important authority of social media and get always authentic information available on social media with interest.
- Social media reflect meaningful political competition over India's foreign policy, media reveals matters related to casteism, community, religions, regional and social problems and issues.
- The followers on Facebook, twitter, we can see the popularity of Barak Obama, Narendra Modi, Angela Morkel etc. It certainly reflect the political campaign. There are certain limitations of social media that are fake news and cyber security.
- Information on social media can be twisted faked etc. so it can not reflect meaningful political competition for research scholar, this is not truly platform to access information.
- Social media partly reflect meaning political competition because sometime emotion sentiments matter more than logic brain washing.

- Each stakeholders has its interest in Indian foreign policy so social media give chance to everybody to propagate their views but there are chances of propagation of wrong information which affecting negative.
- Social media remains relevant in keeping up with political development by citizens contribution, their opinions on various events development and issues and government on a number of instances provide platform which are online on how best the public feel about given issue before government make policies.

From the above opinions of the stakeholders, it is clear that social media is providing platform for political competition for everybody, however while propagating the issues, social problems, discussions over foreign policy etc. through social media, the information, data available on social media is to be verified by the researcher.

Q. 16. Do you think that social media has an impact on the foreign policy? Yes or No. If you think so, please give details

Foreign policy of any country is an important issue for every layman of the country. Foreign policies are decided by mostly governments of that country. In case of India, we have democracy, hence we have procedure by act to decide our foreign policy. According to the constitution of India, foreign policy is to be discussed in Lok Sabha and Rajya Sabha and passed by a majority of votes.

It was asked to the participant that whether social media has an impact on foreign policy in India, with response to this question, out of 483 participants, 238 (49 per cent) participants are of the opinion that social media has an impact on foreign policy, however, 143 (29 per cent) participants are of the opinion that there is no impact of social media on foreign policy. 102 (21 per cent) participants did not respond to this question.

While expressing the opinions of the participants in this survey, some of the major views of the participants are discussed here:

- Social media is a platform where everyone keeps his her views/ opinions on any issues or any activity which shows its impact on that issue, whether it may be foreign policy or any other national issues.

- Due to social media, information is now easily accessible or available, and it helps people connect which has considerable importance in foreign policy.
- Various issues can be public agenda and this can affect public opinion on foreign policy and have a major impact in shaping public opinion.
- It is not necessary that all the details are given to the media, there are certain policies which are confidential with regards to security of nation.
- Basically, young people are more actively involved in social media and project their views that has direct impact on the formation of foreign policy.
- At least social media acts as a platform to represent various opinions of experts and problems in the country and how citizens are responding to it, which could all together have an impact on foreign policy.
- If some bad things happened in the country and if wrong information is spread on all social media platforms, it can degrade the image of the country and also affect the foreign policy like religious riots, caste conflicts etc and can change the mind of an opposite country about us.
- Social media can act as a wheel e.g. Arab Spring, which utilized Facebook as a platform to bring masses together. This forced Arab countries to shift their foreign policy.
- Social media is an active feedback area where members of the public can offer their approval or dissenting views on a given policy and government can take into account their considerations while framing policy.
- Government has been increasing the use of social media to share their foreign policy priorities in an effort to receive feedback, engage in diplomacy and attend to influence on outcome.

Q. 17. According to Manas Chatterjee the greatest and most imminent threat of all is the threat of terrorism which started on 9/11. This threatens economic, social, and political security of all people in all countries. Although co-operative efforts with a strong world government can handle other threats, security from terrorism cannot be assured.

Due to the technological advancement, the living conditions of many people (but not the majority) have been greatly improved. But we need to devise policies that deal with these serious problems in order to secure not only military security (including security against terrorist threats), but also economic, social and cultural life of people

There are two main doctrines about the relation between war and national economy. The first considered that economy based doctrine of the market which is a cause of war. The second one established doctrine that market and economic knowledge are essential for the realization of peace.

To know the opinions of the participants they were asked what criteria they think leads an editor to include items concerning war, peace or any other foreign policy events in the news or any media. We further asked them whether journalist follows rules in making such decisions or do they act spontaneously. Participants expressed their opinions, few are quoted here.

- There should be strict rules to be followed by editors but as per my view they don't follow rules. As per law they are free to express their views but when it comes to country, the rules should not be the same for war-peace related news.
- The media have their own agenda, barring a few media houses, most are having their leanings and criteria for editors is to create sensation securing their interest. It does appear that they follow rules.
- Items concerning war, peace and foreign policy are of interest to the entire public security of nation is and everybody's concern.
- Editors, journalists must complete information, their views with knowledge they have and background knowledge to cover any event truthfully, meaningfully and effectively.
- Most journalists are more interested in the TRP rating and are often in a hurry to submit news without doing in depth analysis without depth knowledge of the background and issues.
- The events whose effects are long lasting, might be related to our society, government which may cause trouble within and around our nation and they are the events which are written in

papers, editorials.

- Media is the fourth pillar of India. It plays significant role in decision making. It creates a firm public opinion being a democracy and politicians have to act according to the journalists.
- Sometime rules and regulations have been broken by journalists, they give priority to fake news or politically favorable news which increase their TRPs. It can spread wrong message among people.
- One would always see it as spontaneous event or social media are really interested in foreign policy for instance every year India attends UN general meet nothing much get highlighted but last year the reply given to Pakistan became sensational news.
- Media or editors are guided by their funding agency, they can manipulate news according to their own purpose but when it comes to image of India or national integrity, it don't think, they bargain.
- It is both constructive and destructive intention propaganda and driven by personal or commercial profit of news channels, some journalists might follow the rules but mostly act spontaneously.
- It depends on the gravity of issues and it can be the criterion sometimes at the other times, it is done to gain more news and followers, thus, journalists follow rules.
- Editors are usually academicians journalists or even politicians and they have some specialization or experience in their field and they come up with their personal opinions on an issue. Sometimes they are useful for the government, sometimes not.
- They have the freedom to write their own views but giving the optimal views is understandable, there is no point in giving views before policy makers and influence people to think about their views.
- It again depends on journalists to journalist, sometimes it is necessary to reveal data so that everyone would be aware but sometimes just for the TRP, spontaneously false data makes it way.
- Any decision that the government is taking as policy is going to

affect people of the nation so they try to unfold the various things in front people who might not have knowledge about that issue.

- To keep the society informed, war, people and other foreign policies events are issues of public concern and any event touching on them must be disseminated to the public to avoid anxiety, tension and propaganda.

From the above views of the participants, it is true that journalists and editors are following certain rules, however, they are propagating the news which they presume important from their own views to increase the sale of their newspapers or to increase TRP rating. It is obviously necessary for the journalists and editors that they verify the reality of the news or understand the issues which relates the nation's integrity or security and study in-depth and then informed the public the reality.

Q. 18. "The Foreign Policy of a nation is always made and implemented with an eye on the situation in various regions of the world. A situational change in West Asia or South-East Asia or Africa necessitates a change or modification of the foreign policies of many nations." The cultural heritage and the history of a nation are again important and valuable factors of its Foreign Policy. The norms and traditions that characterize the life of the people of a state are highly influential factors of its foreign policy. During the process of interpreting and formulating the objectives of national interest, the decision makers are always governed by their cultural links, historical traditions and experiences.

This question was asked to the participants that whether religion, minorities, class, caste and poverty are some of the factors which affect foreign policy of India. Out of 483 participants, 258 participants (53 per cent) are the opinion that the above factors are affecting India's foreign policy whereas 148 participants (31 per cent) said no that these factors are not affecting India's foreign policy. There are 77 participants (16 per cent) who did not reply to this question.

There are various factors of India's foreign policy, they are, Geographical factor, economic development, political traditions, philosophical factor, historical factor, cultural factor, National interest, military strength, ideological basis, domestic milieu and international milieu. Participants have also given some factors that affect India's foreign policy, they are, Hindu –Muslim conflict and poverty in the country. Some of the factors which participants has identified and provided answers to are:

- Minorities clashes in India.
- Nation's interest which decides foreign policy from time to time as and when interest changes.
- Indo-Sri Lankan tension about fishermen and maritime boundaries and other domestic factors.
- Social and cultural problems like reservations in government services to some backward classes.
- India take into consideration its religion, economic status of its citizens and other social value that exists. On trade front, India may not agree to enter into foreign relation agreement on trading that may undermine its religion, sanctity.

From the above points, it reveals in certain factors India's foreign policy is affected however it is a prime responsibility of the State and Central government to develop the life and condition of the poor people in the country in such a fashion that they should think that the government is doing sincere work for them. Hence, the present BJP government has a slogan "sabka sath sabka vikas "and accordingly government is planning various schemes for the people in India.

Social media should try to project the cultural traditions of Jammu and Kashmir, north east and make them feel that they are citizens of this nation. Government is trying to its best level to upgrade the life of all people in India by providing various opportunities, schemes etc.

Q. 19. What role do the internal security challenges in Kashmir, the North East or insurgencies like the Naxalites play in framing India's Foreign Policy? What role does social media play in it?

So far as internal security is concerned; it is the biggest challenge today in India. Citizens feel insecure in Jammu and Kashmir and definitely there are challenges before the internal security department. Government is making sustainable efforts to control the situation and to overcome the problems. Internal security overview reflects a positive trend to overcome earlier challenges of the country, however the rising incidents of terrorism cross the length and breadth of the country is a serious threat to our internal security.

In addition, there have been some major serial blasts in the recent past, resulting into colossal loss of lives and property. The Naxalism has been growing in strength and has grown spatially, spreading its tentacles to as many as thirteen States and close to 200 districts. Its consolidation remains the most potent threat to peace and order in the country

The social fault-lines of caste, religion, gender, ethnicity, region and language has always been a cause of concern for the internal security in India and continue to seriously challenge the same. The dilatory and ineffective judicial system with inefficient, politicized and unprofessional police system has not helped the matters either.

The intention to ask this question to the participants was if they are well aware about our security challenges both internal and external. Most of the participants have expressed their opinions/views on this, few of them are as follows:

- Social media plays an important role in Nakshalwadi area in which affected people are fighting against government for their problems and social media exposed these problems so that it reaches to the people.
- Social media collecting information and data from Naxalite area and this information have been reaching the public through social media.
- Internal situation is the guiding factor in formulation of foreign policy, suiting to the nation. Social media helps in formulation of opinions of people which affect the government decision.
- Social media is being used an advisory tool for gathering support and reaching out to the public to stop anti-national activities.
- Security challenges in the Kashmir creates tension between Indo-Pak relation. In north east invasion of China creates tension between India-China which adversely affect the economy of both nations.
- India's foreign policy is directed by internal matters, they are perception management in the world view, keeping these conflicts low profile and human resources being upheld. Social media highlights the nationalities and fight for national issues.
- Particularly in Kashmir valley where social media is destabilized,

terrorist Burhan Wani encounter episode is important lesson in showing how social media helps increase anti national sentiments in the Valley till date.

- Any kind of insurgencies, government is seen to blame the neighboring countries instead of having a dialogue between those who have quails, for example Naxalism, people are not happy with the government so they are against the government but instead of having a conversation, the govt has tagged them as terrorist. Even Kashmir youths are dropping out from schools to join militant organisations. Government should try to find out the reasons and solutions rather blaming Pakistan.
- I don't think social media plays an important role other than sharing information publicly but when internal security crisis happens, international organizations seek message from the government whether it is human rights violation in Jammu and Kashmir or North east.
- Due to Naxalites, more emphasis is given on internal security and social media can sometime hamper the peace and harmony between the different religions of India.
- To supply the information regarding government decisions to welfare of naxal areas and policy to be implemented in their area should be able to reach these people so that they know what the government has done for them.
- The role of foreign players in these issues create challenges in dealing with these issues, social media can be used to create awareness among people about seriousness of these issues and also security arrangement.
- In all the issues mentioned in this question, social media provides us a platform to be aware what is going on, while at the same time, allow us to debate and find out alternatives, the government becomes aware of what citizens want and thereby takes necessary suitable action.
- Social media is very dangerous. The articles hosted by people of a particular ideology can cause internal security issues from the insurgency to riots.
- Kashmir and North east or insurgencies like the Naxalites play

a role in forming India's global politics and has an impact on Kashmir issues as well.

- Internal security challenges in Jammu and Kashmir, North east states have much to do with cross border, social media has failed to create public awareness on these issues.
- Foreign policy has also relation with domestic politics and domestic politics is influenced by various issues such as Naxalism, Terrorism. In order to maintain relations with neighboring countries such as China, Myanmar, the governments keep in mind the importance of North-East region. Social media comes up with the issues happening in their region but again it has to be carefully looked to it.
- Peaceful solution helps but things like repression or atrocities on people creates bad impression, allegations on army of rapes, autocracies, AFSPA in Kashmir and NE is concerning.
- Government is trying to bring the people from Kashmir and the NE into the mainstream, but they do not accept the development programmes in their territory, they engaged in programmes in their territory in spreading hate stories against India via social media.
- There is an external threat when internal security gets challenged by their own people, Pakistan sponsored terrorism in J&K, China sponsored naxalism in North East to make India's foreign policy narrow or weak.
- Social media helps in contingency situation like Kashmir by spreading fake news and rumors and issues like fake human rights violation issues which could increase international pressure on India to frame its policies according to different conventions which might not suit India.
- These internal issues are always challenges in dealing with countries. Kashmir issue keeps firing atmosphere between India and Pakistan. In dealing with China and Myanmar, North east insurgencies have key factor. Naxalism has a role in dealing with leftist countries or communist country. These issues are always on the table with neighboring countries. Social media has an active role in Kashmir to gather masses and bring mob violence.

- India's foreign policy heavily depends on the internal security challenges in many of the states where there is presence of insurgent movement. A stable and peaceful domestic atmosphere is very necessary for successful foreign policy.
- The Kashmir problem has always been a concern internal security since time of partition. The North-east region still neglected by the government of India which leads to internal civil hearts. The role of media one can say is to just provide problems which are going on and not the solution as they do not have knowledge to share content.
- There are major security threat indications and the Indian government while framing foreign policy looks into the root causes of insurgency in Kashmir, North-east and Naxalites Insurgency in Kashmir could be attributed to religion connotation, historical injustice, and undue perceived influence from Pakistan. So when government frames foreign policy to curb Kashmir issue, it will opt for border tight security control between India and Pakistan. Issues on insurgency in North east, the government may attribute smuggling of weapons into Indian territory from the region and in turn, reduce foreign interaction with foreign countries. India wants to extradite foreign money launders and drug smugglers as they pose a threat to the national security of India, especially in the north east. Policy of non-cooperation and India's refusal to be a part of China on both one road, one belt initiative and giveaway Pakistan occupied Kashmir region has created tension as India is not ready to compromise national security.

Q. 20. Can scholars of International relations and conflict use social media data to illuminate questions of Foreign Policy and in particular does the structure on social media reflect off-line behavior?

The rise of the ISIS, the Russian annexation of Crimea, and the election of Donald Trump are not only three very important geopolitical events, they all are directly connected to the varying impact of social media on conflict. Social media is "a form of electronic communication and networking sites that allows users to follow and share content (text, pictures, video, etc.) and ideas within an online community". ISIS used/

is using social media to target enemies and recruit followers. Russia uses cyber warfare and misinformation. Trump used/uses Twitter as a campaign (and now governing) tool. It is no questioning that social media matters. The extent of the influence of social media on conflict and political struggle and the mechanisms at play still need to be captured more systematically. On the level of collective action, the review of literature suggests there is strong evidence that social media can raise awareness and importance of protest and facilitates groups getting "their story" out. Communication is assisted by social media through the exchange of information, the exposure of wrongdoing by elites, and mobilization and coordination of protest. Connections between activists are made easier, coordination and communication are less costly. Moreover, potential allies and activists can be targeted and recruited—a point primarily examined in the context of political violence and radicalization (e.g. ISIS), but also in the context of nonviolent social movements (e.g. the 2017 Women's March). Less focus has been placed on how elites/leaders use social media. This is surprising, given that leaders and governments are heavily active on social media to campaign, to gather support for their issues at home and abroad, and to influence and/or bypass traditional media.

Majority of the participants replied positively that international relations and conflict are always there and social media is always helping people know the situation and status of relations between two countries. If they are interested in detailed information about the conflict, they will get it so that they can come to some conclusion. The scholars who are studying international relations and conflict studies use social media to answer the questions of the Indian foreign policy. Some of the opinions of the participants are given herewith:

- Social media has penetrated deep into our daily lives therefore to use data available on social media is not that exceptional.
- Scholars can not use social media data for studying issues because most of the posts are created by the people of a particular ideology.
- Scholars are researchers and they are updated with social media tools like YouTube, Facebook.
- With the rising use of social media, it can be put to various

purposes by scholars. Even today the online view of foreign policy discussions seems to be confined to a few sections and offline ignorance is generally replicated on social media.

- I don't think that serious thinkers or policy makers would use social media data for any constructive work structure on social media and there is no true reflection online about behavior.
- Except for those who are highly interested and largely keep interest in foreign policy only those would understand the ground realities, a common man who is on social media will read or follow only those things which he finds interesting or is viral. Many a times social media is used as a means for political parties or rightist groups to spread hatred, violence and one would find likes for violence there.
- Social media data is not authenticated unless published or available from an official source hence it can not be used but the effect is offline behavior can be seen.
- Most of the news channels use Twitter quotes and Facebook quotes to drive their points. It is gradually finding more acceptance.
- Scholars have their analytical ability and they might be helping government to satisfy people, however, social media structure does not reflect offline behavior at least in the case of common man.
- Foreign policy is always multidimensional, social media is a tool to bring people's view on the table and democracy is always participation of people not only in internal sphere but also in external sphere.

In the view of the above points raised by the participants in this survey, it is clear that scholars are always of an analytical mindset and they always search for the truth and authenticated information from various sources. There are various opinions of the scholars in which few scholars are of the opinion that social media data is used to create firm opinions of the people whereas few scholars opined that it is not.

Q. 21. Frequency of the use of social media tools to understand Indian Foreign Policy

Chart 5: Frequency of the use of social media tools to understand Indian Foreign Policy

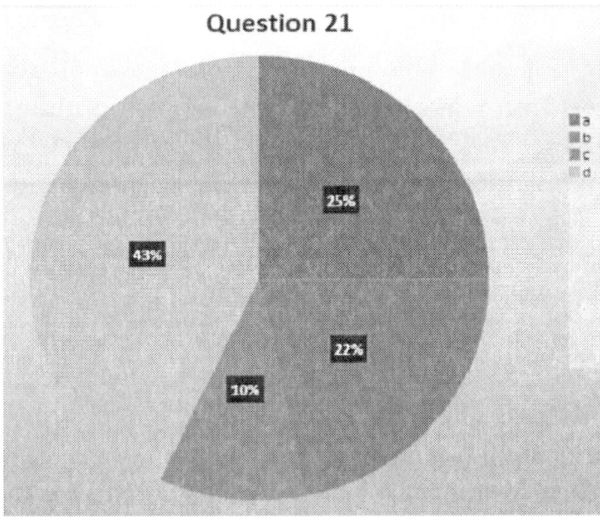

It was asked to the participants that how frequently they use social media tools to understand India's foreign policy. Four options were provided to them to answer this question. 25 per cent participants use social media daily to understand foreign policy information and updates, 22 per cent participants were using social media weekly for updates and indepth study, 10 per cent participants were using social media monthly to check the foreign policy information through their networks whereas a large number of participants i.e. 43 per cent participants use social media occasionally as and when they need the information about India's foreign policy.

From the above analysis it is revealed that majority of the participants are using social media occasionally to update their information and knowledge related to India's foreign policy, this percentage is more as compared to the daily use participants whereas only 10 percent participants are using social media once in a month which means that as and when they have time to update their knowledge for foreign policy they use social media. Reasons for using social media more or less varies because majority of the participants are post-graduate students from various universities and another reason could be that they have small topic in their syllabus about India's foreign policy or foreign policies of other countries. It also depends on the interest of the person who is not at all interested to know the current situation of our foreign policy or international relations with other countries. It is seen that most of the newspapers and TV channels providing information about our foreign relations to other countries when our Prime Minister is visiting various countries to maintain our relations with others.

Q. 22. How can social media be related with the India's National Security issues? Give your views / opinions.

Media's role in internal security can be analyzed in a triangular shape like news, views and issues. How the media presents national security issues to the public with popularity, propaganda or publicity can help either in strengthening or weakening of the basics of internal security. In the world scenario it has to strike a balance between people's right to know on one side and national security and social ethics on the other.

If we look at the perspective of issues, media can play a very important role in improving internal security as it plays the role of information provider, information disseminator and information transfer. It can mould the perception of both people and government which can lead to re-formulation of policies if they are wrong and can prevent negative outcomes which could have arisen and leads to discussion among people.

Through the background of reporting and free hand reporting, media can warn the governments about the issues which can become a security threat in future, like it can inform about the growing discontent in a particular area or group of people.

Social media can play of role of awareness creation among the public. It can disseminate information about the various programmes and policies that government has launched for vulnerable section and areas which are weak and thus create a feeling of belongingness and thus create a mass based shield against internal security threats. It can educate the people about the long term benefits of various initiatives taken by the government and create an environment among the public. It can act a morale builder of the public by showcasing the gains which country has made in different spheres, economic, social, technological etc. and thus creating a sense of pride among people, This sense of pride along the people helps in creating sense of nationalism, brotherhood if gains are equitably distributed. It can help in countering propaganda and act as a tool to play information war. For example, it can counter the propaganda by Maoists, North-East insurgent groups by providing right facts and figures.

It can help in creating social united public as a whole by showing such programmes which shows inter-group cordial relations, rich history of peaceful coexistence etc. It can help in bringing accountability among government institutions by highlighting lapses, atrocities committed by them or other lacunas in their operations. It helps in making institutions ready for any emergency situation as and when occurs.

Some of the important views expressed by the participants are listed herewith for discussion:

- Social media tools could provide information and knowledge to larger public who would take informed choices related to national security issues.
- Social media may be harmful for security issues as the dividing forces spread their vicious thoughts through it although it can be used for the benefit of the public.
- Do not think that social media can be related with India's national security issues though it does provide an idea but since national security happens to be a sensitive issue, it should be kept secret for social media.
- Social media can update the development as well as leak some classified documents which has huge impact on national security issues.
- In other words social media can also be called as device of public opinion when government frames foreign policy, public opinions are important in this respect.
- Strong relations between nations is build as information is spread quicker. However, social media like Facebook, Whatsapp may also spread wrong information among public through social media.

- Caste conflicts spreading false videos, morphed photos, religiously attacking videos information are circulated without questioning which leads to problems.
- Malicious content provided by individuals should be checked on social media.
- Sharing of information and important numbers on social media can lead to others getting hold of it through fake accounts. Violent hate videos of other nations are used for communal violence/excitement domestically.
- In the today's world, social media is playing a major role in all aspects as they have evolved as an institution where every citizen is connected directly and data leakes could be related to India's national security.
- The students and research scholars or people whose ideas or opinions on such issues can be showcased on social media however serious issues like national security issues are serious issues, social media is not the perfect platform this.
- Rumor, fabricated news, facts can create different opinion than the real one. Social media can deliver the controversial information like private information which can be utilized to create problems.
- There are people in masses who keep exploiting the current internal clashes and politics in India over social media and thus it can cause harm to the national security issues.
- Social media is double-edge sword. On one hand it can help solve national security issues but on the other hand it creates challenges. We have to be careful in dealing with social media while addressing national security issues.
- Social media is a medium to spread the voice of common people by providing views that war is not always a solution but national security can be maintained with force and dialogue.
- Social media is a threat to national security as it can lead to breach of privacy, radicalization, sparking of communal tension.
- Social media is a useful platform that Indian government used to sensitize public on issues that affect national security. Social media is also used by government to track cybercrime cases and

activities.

- Social media does not play a major role in my observation as people are not well read at large scale, only few are well aware of the issues, other just follow.
- Social media can play a good role in India's national security issues when it collects proper and authentic information and data regarding critical thinking. This should be spread to the people.
- Social media can be extensively used for country to propagate non-state actors. Government may reach masses through social media to make them aware of various programmes and steps to be taken for development of society.
- More people are unemployed in India but they are active on social media, they influence other people's conflict that can be used for political purposes.
- Social media can create chaos among common people. Many times photos, videos are fake, created for a particular purpose. In multilingual country like India, any small mistake on social media can cause trouble.
- The person using social media such as Facebook, his real identity is not used in such applications and hence, it is difficult to identify a terrorist or group.

From the above comments or opinions of the participants, it is revealed that social media is useful as well as harmful to society when it provides authentic information for the public, it is good but when fake or false information provided by social media through its various platforms creates confusion among people, it affects our national security issues.

Q. 23. Are you aware of Indo-US strategic partnership in the nuclear deal? **Yes** or **No**

Which social media tools are most effective for this strategic partnership? Please select from the below mentioned choices / options:

a) through electronic media
b) print media
c) news channels

d) social media
e) published literature

Before discussing the answers to this question, first we should know what is Indo-US nuclear deal and what are the challenges of this deal. Following points will clear the basics of Indo-US nuclear deal:

- The U.S.–India Civil Nuclear Agreement or Indo-US nuclear deal or the 123 Agreement was signed between US and India in 2005.
- Under the agreement, India agreed to separate its civilian and military nuclear activities.
- It also agreed to open up the civilian part to inspection by the International Atomic Energy Agency (IAEA).
- In return, the US offered to resume full nuclear trade i.e selling of reactors, Transfer of Technology, Uranium sale with India.
- The deal went through several complex stages including:
  i) amendment of US domestic law (Atomic Energy Act of 1954)
  ii) civil-military nuclear Separation Plan in India
  iii) India-IAEA safeguards agreement
- During the then US President Obama's visit, India-US civil nuclear deal was announced.
- This finalized the agreement between India and the US on supplier liability and tracking requirements.
- It enabled American companies to build nuclear power reactors in India.
- In 2016, during Indian PM's visit to US, 6 nuclear reactors were decided to be built in India by the American firm Westinghouse.
- Despite bilateral agreements, there is no sign yet of any contract between an American company and the Indian authorities.

7.3 WHAT ARE THE CHALLENGES?

- The U.S. sending the Westinghouse officials to India will reopen negotiations on the deal.
- Before deciding on a go ahead with the commercial contract, the Indian government should consider the following:
- **Liability** – Westinghouse went into major cost overruns leading to a financial crisis.

- It had to halt two of its reactors projects in the U.S, by when the construction was already 5 years over schedule.
- Amidst this, the Westinghouse's new buyers have already diluted the arrangement in India.
- They will not construct the nuclear power project in India, and will only supply reactors and components.
- Even if the India-U.S. techno-commercial contract gets finalized in 2019, it would take nearly another 10 years to construct a reactor.
- Given this, in case of a Fukushima-type nuclear accident in India, the liability that U.S. companies would carry is highly uncertain.
- **Trump effect** – Trump's US presidency has taken a sharp turn away from renewable energy.
- There are increased calls for mining, exporting and encouraging oil, gas, coal and shale trade into its foreign outreach.
- Notably, India recently, made orders for both oil and gas shipped from America.
- India may stand to loose Obama era support in financing renewable energy projects and facilitating India-U.S. nuclear deals.
- Also, the US has pulled out of the Paris climate change accord, coming as a shock for India.
- Notably, Obama administration had promised to help India reduce its dependence on fossil fuels on India's entry into Paris accord.
- **India's requirements** – India's own requirements from the India-U.S. civil nuclear deal have changed considerably.
- The Cabinet recently approved the 7,000 MW construction plan for 10 Indian-made pressurized heavy water reactors (PHWRs).
- With existing constructions and the current capacity of 6,780 MW, India hopes to have 14,600 MW of nuclear power by 2024.
- Besides the nuclear power plants, the Department of Atomic Energy is advocating PHWRs in more inland sites.
- This includes sites in Rajasthan, Haryana, Karnataka and Madhya Pradesh.
- It comes in the backdrop of concerns on too many nuclear projects in the southern coastline lying along tsunami and earthquake fault lines.

- India has also found much more comfort in its existing agreement with Russia's Atoms troyexport.
- This began with the Intergovernmental Agreement for Kudankulam 1 and 2 in 1988.
- **Cost** – Another issue relates to the cost that India is prepared to pay for nuclear energy through foreign collaborations.
- Indo-French negotiations for six 1,650 MW European Pressurized Reactors (EPRs) in Maharashtra's Jaitapur is delaying.
- This is notably over the differences between Department of Atomic Energy and the French company Areva (now handed over to EDF Energy company, UK).
- It pertains to arriving at the cost per unit.
- **Besides** – India must consider the shifts in the world nuclear industry before getting into negotiations with new companies.
- Many nuclear companies globally are facing with major losses over their nuclear businesses.
- As the pressure to lower nuclear power tariffs increases, nuclear safety requirements have become more stringent.
- More countries now see nuclear power as a "base-load" option.
- It is only preferred as a back-up option for unstable, but infinitely less costly and eco-friendly, solar and hydroelectric power options.
- All these signal that nuclear power is losing its primacy in the energy mix, which India must be aware of.

It was asked to the participants if they are aware about Indo-US partnership and nuclear deal. Out of 483 participants, 210 participants (43 per cent) said they are aware of the Indo-US deal whereas 43 participants (9 per cent) participants said no, they are not aware about this deal, there are 230 participants who did not reply to this question. It was revealed that the percentage of not answering this question is more (48 per cent) and the reason for their lack of awareness may be varied. Further it was asked to them which social media tools are most effective for this strategic partnership and they have been provided five options to answer. The analysis of these options is provided in the following table:

Table 7: Preferences of social media tools and its percentage

Social media tools	*No. of participants prefer options*	*Percentage*
a) Through electronic media	168	21
b) Print media	185	23
c) News Channels	215	26
d) Social media	124	15
e) Published literature	126	15

Chart 6: Showing percentage of using social media tools of various medias

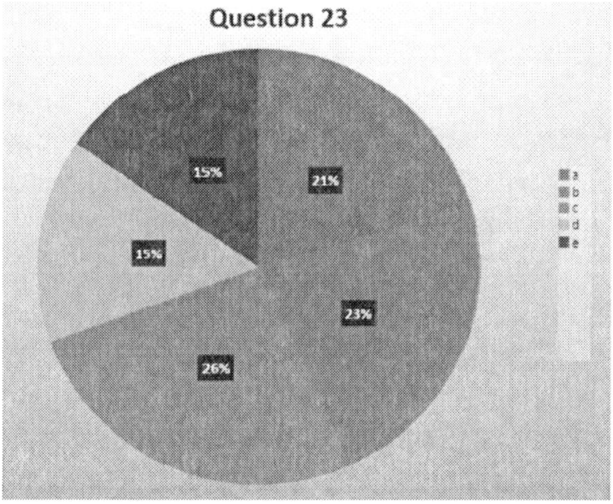

It revealed from the above table that 26 per cent participants know about the Indo-US nuclear deal through news channels which is the highest percentage, whereas 15 per cent participants know about the Indo-US nuclear deal from the published literature and social media tools, these may be books, journal articles, and social media tools are Twitter and Facebook and WhatsApp which is the lowest percentage. Electronic media and print media percentage are almost equal i.e. 21 per cent and 23 per cent. Electronic media includes e-books, online journal databases, web sites etc. Print media includes Newspapers and specific pamphlets published on this topic.

Q. 24. Are you aware of Indo-China border dispute? **Yes** or **No**

According to you, can social media raise this issue to Policy Makers, so as to have an influence on India's Foreign Policy?

In India majority of the people know about Indo-China border dispute, however to know whether participants in this project are aware about Indo-China border dispute, this question was asked to them as to how much information they about Indo-China border dispute. Out of 483 participants, 337 participants (70 per cent) participants said they know about Indo-China border dispute whereas 69 participants (14 per cent) did not know about this dispute and 77 participants did not answer this question as they may not be aware or they do not want to answer this question.

It was further asked to them whether social media can raise this issue to policy makers and the influence of social media on India's foreign policy. Some of the important views/ opinions of the participants are listed below:

- Without any positive approach of China, the dispute will be unsolved, it should require positive approach of both the countries. Social media can raise this issue to policy makers of both countries.
- The residents nearby the disputed border like Arunachal Pradesh and others are affected by this dispute, the opinions of the people from these states can be formed through social media.
- We need to take a balanced view and concentrate on the public on this subject so that some solutions can be suggested by public which is accepted by both countries.
- Social media must project actual facts about this issue, whether it is political issue or an issue between the two countries and government and put the reaction on social media.
- Social media can raise the temperature of the masses with nationality, love for the nation, patriotism etc. Doklam issue can be resolved diplomatically.
- Some limitations are required for social media because social media can make viral wrong messages regarding these matters and it can create a critical situation for border dispute.
- The opinions over social media must be filtered as now a days any Tom, Dick and Harry has their own opinion, so policy maker must try to filter data and exclude those opinions which are

against ethics.

- Chinese media may portray something entirely different.
- Indo-China border disputes have been hotly debated across electronic and social media however none of the governments has the final authority over foreign policy formulation not even the parliament.
- Social media can raise this issue to policy makers as we have witnessed in last few years that government is involving itself in direct democracy through social media for issues relating to MEA or BSF's soldier maltreatment issue.
- International dispute is solved by executive department of India because this provision is according to constitution.
- India's foreign policy to China is much wiser than in 1962 during war as we recently seen Doklam issue and how smoothly it was handled.
- Social media can put in place personal view in presentation which is not good for both countries. Government views are more important than social media view.

It is revealed from the above opinions and views from the participants that social media is very powerful tool among the people to create their views about Indo-China border dispute. As a researcher I would like to suggest that Social institute like Tata Institute of social Sciences, Mumbai, should conduct a survey on the border dispute issues from the people which are living nearby the dispute border and recommend to the government some solutions which they found in the survey result. This survey will help both the countries and if both the countries agree on some common solutions, this issue can be solved by both countries on the basis of factual data collected by TISS. Both the governments will have to make their foreign policy on this issue.

Q. 25. This question was asked to the participants about their awareness for India Pakistan conflict during Kargil war, Parliament attack and Mumbai attack and other similar issues.

Majority of the participants are aware about the India and Pakistan conflict because print media, books, articles are having the information about conflict, many researchers also write research papers on this and social media is propagating the issues from time to time. There are five options which were provided to the participants regarding how they know the information through these options. The analysis of these options are as follows:

> Out of 483 participants, 19 per cent participants get the information from electronic media available to them like TV channels, e-newspapers, Radio stations etc, 23 per cent participants were getting the information about India and Pakistan conflict on various issues through print media like newspapers, books, research articles etc.
>
> 34 per cent participants are receiving information about India and Pakistan conflict from News channels from TV. There are news channels in India which are delivering information constantly i.e., 24 hours to the public, it will provide information as well as videos of the events and the news. There are 13 per cent participants who receive information from social media tools like Twitter, Whatsapp, Facebook and last option, which is published literature, 11 per cent participants receive information from published literature, like books, daily news papers, research articles, experts who wrote on various print media etc.

Chart 7: Showing awareness for India Pakistan conflict during Kargil war

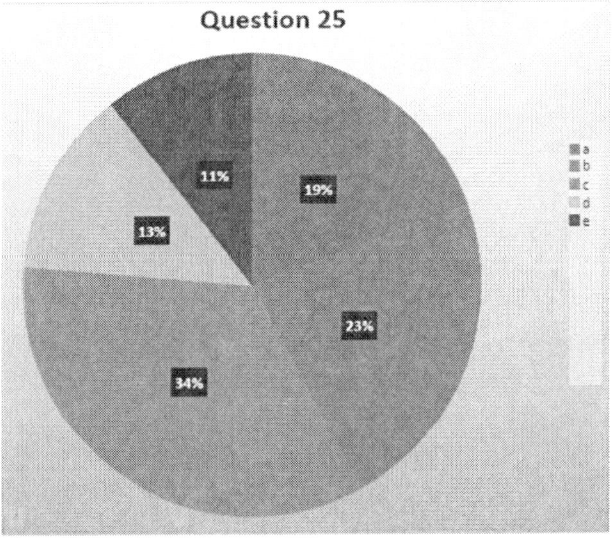

It reveals from the above analysis that majority of the participants i.e. (34 per cent) are getting the information about India and Pakistan conflict from News channels which is the highest percentage in this survey. Whereas lowest percentage i.e. 11 per cent from published literature. It means News Channels media is more effective than published literature because news channels shows live videos which have more impact on public minds whereas published literature you can see pictures and read the information which is collected by the writer of the article or book.

REFERENCES

1. Pew Research Center, "Social Networking Popular Across Globe," December 12, 2012, http://www.pewglobal.org/2012/12/12/social- networking-popular-across-globe/ (accessed on October 6, 2016).
2. Loader, B. D., and Dan Mercea. 2011. "Networking Democracy? Social Media Innovations and Participatory Politics," *Information, Communication and Society* 14(6):757–69
3. Fuchs, Christian (2012), "The Political Economy of Privacy on Facebook," *Television and New Media* 13(2): 139–59.
4. Statista (2019), The Statista portal https://www.statista.com/statistics/507405/uk- active-social-media-and-mobile-social-media-users/ accessed on 19/01/2019
5. *The Guardian*, https://www.theguardian.com/society/2018/apr/09/social-media-has- poisoned-us-young-brits-on-why-they-are-unhappy accessed on 19/01/2019
6. Kantar China Social Media Impact Report 2017, https://cn- en.kantar.com/media/social/2017/kantar-china-social-media-impact-report-2017/ (accessed on 20/01/2019).
7. Chatterjee, Manas and Jacques Fontanel Ed. *War, peace and Security*, Emerald Group Publishing Limited, UK, 2008.
8. Ravinder (2014), "Analysis of the Basic Factors of Indian Foreign Policy," *International Research Journal of Commerce Arts and Science*, Vol. 5, Issue 12, 2014, pp. 142-152

CHAPTER VIII

Twitter Data Analysis

8.1. WHAT IS TWITTER DATA?

In this chapter, we are analyzing the twitter data which we have collected from the twitter account of important personalities related to our topic of research. Before analysis it is better to understand what is Twitter data. Twitter data is the information collected by the user or person on the topic or access point from the twitter account. The person has a twitter account, can tweet his views or the official information if the person assigned office bearer through the twitter account. Twitter data can be collected from a single tweet. With this information, you can know demographics, total clicks on your profile or how many people saw your Tweet. This is just the tip of the iceberg, but understanding the data allows you to know how it's used and the patterns of your content.

8.2 TWITTER ANALYTICS

Twitter's built-in analytics tool provides access to additional data beyond shares, likes and Retweets. Over the past few years, Twitter continues to improve its analytic features for advertisers, marketers and the general public.

8.3 TOOLS FOR TWITTER

There are many tools for analysis of Twitter data, few tools are given here for information, however, we have analyze Twitter data by our own method which is explained in this chapter. Following are the tools:

8.4 KLEAR

Klear is a social media analytics and intelligence platform that provides social data services for brands, agencies and enterprises. Klear serves more than 2 million monthly visitors in three core areas: Social media monitoring, Influencer marketing and competitive intelligence.

8.5 BUFFER

Buffer is a software application for the web and mobile, designed to manage accounts in social networks, by providing the means for a user to schedule posts to Twitter, Facebook, Instagram, and LinkedIn, as well as analyze their results and engage with their community.

8.6 KLOUT

Klout was a website and mobile app that used social media analytics to rate its users according to online social influence via the "Klout Score", which was a numerical value between 1 and 100. Wikipedia

8.7 MANAGEFLITTER

ManageFlitter is a web-based application that assists Twitter users gain insight into their Twitter account. ManageFlitter provides a set of tools that allows Twitter users to effectively curate, prune and grow their Twitter account. Twitter is an application and tool for sharing official information by official person or individual and his opinion and reply to the tweets of others. In this project we have decided to collect the data from twitter of official persons who has been assigned the task to tweet important information of the government. We have tried to collect the data of five personalities from different countries who are important in deciding the foreign policy matters of that country. We have identified five countries i.e. India, US, UK, Russia and France. The methodology adopted for this purpose is as follows:

8.8 METHODOLOGY ADOPTED FOR TWITTER DATA SEARCHING

Many official people have a twitter account to communicate official information and views with the public. Government officials are having their official accounts from which they tweet official information and their official opinions and comments on the subject of tweet. Following are the steps of methodology used by us to search twitter data on India's Foreign Policy and national security topics. There are many fake accounts on twitter, hence to identify the official account on twitter, we have used the following steps

- Identified official twitter account of the office bearer who has been assigned the task to tweet on behalf of the government. Accordingly we have identified Indian office bearers such as Narendra Modi (Prime Minister, India), PMO, Rajnath Singh (Home Minister, India), former Raksha Mantri, Nirmala Sitaraman, former foreign minister Sushama Swaraj, Raveesh Kumar.
- Used advanced search tool which is provided by twitter to find out the official tweet of the office bearer on India's foreign policy.
- The office bearer tweets to the people to whom they send tweet, we have searched the tweet data from these people.
- There is a provision of hashtag in twitter, by using a special hash tag, we have searched the information on India's foreign policy, national security of India etc. through hash tags. If we click on the hash tag icon all related tweets can be seen on the screen, if a twitter account is official, a tick mark sign appears before the account on the screen. It means that it is the official account.
- There is also a provision to search by words in twitter. The provision is "Any of these words" hence, we search the tweet information related to our project topic i.e. India's foreign policy."
- After getting official account of the person to whom the task has been assigned by government official e.g. Raveesh Kumar.

- **Account Name – Raveesh Kumar**
  User id — MEAIndia (Ministry of External Affairs)

Table 8: Narendra Modi's Twitter Data Report
Total Tweets: 23.1 K
Profile Name: Narendra Modi

Sr. No.	*Contents of tweet*	*Date of Tweet*	*Likes*	*Retweets*	*Reply Received*
1	I thought – all Himalayan states and Bhutan – can we not do a special sports meet on a regular basis. Sportsman spirit brings happiness: PM	6/15/2014	481	338	67
2	A lot of things connect India and USA and one such thing is democracy: PM	9/29/2014	460	249	52
3	The much anticipated India-US StartUp Konnect programme has begun. PM will join shortly.	9/27/2015	297	164	8
4	In the heart of every Indian and Afghan, there is boundless love for each other: PM @narendramodi in the Parliament of Afghanistan	12/24/2015	2245	808	77
5	The two PMs at signing of the Joint Declaration on a Strategic Partnership between India and Singapore.	9/23/2015	780	266	38
6	I welcome Germany's strong support for India's membership of the international export control regimes: PM	10/5/2015	512	233	14
7	Petrapole-Benapole is a key land border crossing for India-Bangladesh trade. Over 50% of India-Bangladesh trade passes through Petrapol	7/21/2016	1194	325	41
8	Ties between India and Netherlands are very old. Our bilateral relations are very strong: PM @narendramodi	6/27/2017	2695	584	70
9	Prime Minister@narendramodi had a productive meeting with Mr. Nursultan Nazarbayev, the President of Kazakhstan, on the sidelines of the SCO Summi	6/10/2018	6432	923	200
10	Remembering Mahatma Gandhi and his message of peace, harmony and non-violence. PM@narendramodi and Emeritus Senior Minister Mr. Goh Chok Tong unveil a plaque marking the site where the immersion of the ashes of Mahatma Gandhi took place at the Clifford Pier in Singapore	6/1/2018	10322	1410	477

Sr. No.	Contents of tweet	Date of Tweet	Likes	Retweets	Reply Received
11	PM@narendramodi will be interacting with students from Nanyang Technological University in Singapore. Before the interaction, various MoUs are being inked which will boost collaboration with NTU and enhance research and innovation among students of India.	6/1/2018	1489	319	77
12	Tun Dr. Mahathir Mohamad and PM @narendramodi discussed ways to boost economic and cultural relations between India and Malaysia. @chedetofficial	5/30/2018	3546	604	121
13	PM @narendramodi landed in Kuala Lumpur. He would be meeting Tun Dr. Mahathir Mohamad and discussing aspects relating to India-Malaysia cooperation.	5/30/2018	5919	831	189
14	Enhancing the India-Indonesia partnership...President @jokowi and PM @narendramodi hold talks in Jakarta	5/29/2018	3491	581	142
15	PM @narendramodi paid tributes to the martyrs of Indonesia's freedom struggle at the Kalibata National Heroes Cemetery in Jakarta	5/29/2018	5867	925	179
16	President Putin and PM@narendramodi discussed ways to boost economic as well as cultural ties between Russia and India	5/22/2018	2576	566	299
17	New energy in India-Russia ties will benefit our citizen	5/22/2018	1944	415	126
18	Every Indian is proud of the governance of Shri Atal Bihari Vajpayee. As PM, Atal Ji took numerous steps to improve India-Russia cooperati	5/22/2018	2329	522	102
19	Friendship between India and Russia is special	5/22/2018	2639	500	144
20	Mr. Pushpa Kamal Dahal 'Prachanda', Chairman of Communist Party of Nepal – MC and PM @narendramodi had a wonderful meeting earlier today. They discussed various aspects relating to India-Nepal relations.	5/12/2018	2405	450	80
21	Nepal is at the core of India's 'Neighbourhood First' policy.	5/11/2018	1173	234	36
22	President Bidhya Devi Bhandari and PM @narendramodi held talks in	5/11/2018	2678	412	109

Sr. No.	Contents of tweet	Date of Tweet	Likes	Retweets	Reply Received
	Kathmandu. They discussed various aspects of India-Nepal ties.				
23	Mr. Nanda Bahadur Pun, the Vice President of Nepal and PM @narendramodi had a fruitful meeting today. They deliberated on ways to further cement India-Nepal cooperation.	5/11/2018	1758	391	71
24	The people of Kathmandu welcome PM @narendramodi. This Nepal visit of the Prime Minister will give a strong impetus to India-Nepal friendship.	5/11/2018	3495	821	139
25	Furthering India-China cooperation... Prime Minister @narendramodi and President Xi Jinping meet in Wuhan	4/27/2018	9080	1355	524
26	PM @narendramodi and Chancellor Merkel meet in Berlin. The two leaders are discussing ways to further strengthen India-Germany cooperation.	4/20/2018	8913	1324	380
27	The Indian diaspora in the UK brings our countries closer. The diaspora is playing a commendable role in furthering the India-UK friendship: PM @narendramodi during the talks with PM @theresa_may	4/18/2018	1303	357	47
28	PM @narendramodi and His Majesty King Carl XVI Gustaf met in Stockholm. They had a great interaction on ways to boost India-Sweden friendship.	4/17/2018	6003	915	235
29	One of the things I wanted to do in London was to pay homage to Bhagwan Basaveshwara: PM@narendramodi	4/18/2018	1884	473	87
30	I am here on the Jayanti of Bhagwan Basaveshwara. During my last visit, I had the honour of unveiling his bust in the UK. Centuries ago, Bhagwan Basaveshwara worked towards social empowerment: PM@narendramodi	4/18/2018	3499	765	142
31	To trade, innovate and invest, come to India. We are waiting for you: PM @narendramodi to the Indian diaspora in Sweden	4/17/2018	2193	471	123
32	Talking trade and business ties...top CEOs interact with Prime Ministers @narendramodi and Stefan Löfven.	4/17/2018	1764	436	116

Sr. No.	Contents of tweet	Date of Tweet	Likes	Retweets	Reply Received
	Sweden remains a valued partner for the @makeinindia initiative. PM highlighted the various investment opportunities in India.				
33	Dasho Tshering Wangchuk, Chief Advisor of the Interim Government of Bhutan and PM @narendramodi had a wonderful meeting. Their discussions will add great vigour to India-Bhutan relation	8/31/2018	3032	497	169
34	President Win Myint of Myanmar and PM @narendramodi met on the sidelines on the BIMSTEC Summit in Kathmandu. They had productive discussions on accelerating cooperation between India and Myanmar.	8/31/2018	4093	655	143
35	The Prime Minister of Thailand, Mr. Prayuth Chan-ocha and PM @narendramodi held productive talks in Kathmandu. Their discussions focussed on strengthening bilateral cooperation between India and Thailand.	8/30/2018	3838	648	119
36	Furthering India-China friendship. PM @narendramodi and President Xi Jinping hold talks on the sidelines of the BRICS Summit in South Africa	7/26/2018	6184	915	161
37	PM@narendramodi is in touch with MEA and other top officials regarding the wellbeing of Indian pilgrims stranded in Nepal. He has asked officials to extend all possible assistance to those affected. The Indian embassy in Nepal is working on the ground and assisting the pilgrims.	7/3/2018	6145	1149	236
	Total		124658	22831	5340

Source: https://twitter.com/PMOIndia (Accessed on 1st February 2019)

Mr. Narendra Modi, Prime Minister of India is a key person in making foreign policy of India. The process of making foreign policy or changing existing policy is to be discussed in both the houses of the Indian Parliament. The above-mentioned twitter data was collected from Narendra Modi's twitter account. The total number of tweets made by Narendra Modi are **231k**. However, we found 37 tweets related to India's foreign policy topic. There are 124658 likes received for all these tweets on India's foreign policy made by Prime Minister Narendra Modi and he made 22831 Retweets and received reply to 5340 tweets from the people who showed interest in foreign policy.

From the above 37 tweets made by PM Narendra Modi, which we have retrieved under India's foreign policy from his twitter account, it is revealed that he tweets on several areas and discusses topics with various important persons from different countries. The important areas of his tweets are summarised in the following areas:

- Sports spirit brings happiness between India and Bhutan
- Discussion with President and PM onIndia about Democracy similarity between these countries
- Startup programme in India and US
- India and Afghanistan boundless love each other
- Petrapole-Benapole is key land crossing between India and Bangladesh
- Various MOUs signed by PM between Nanyang Technological University, Singapore regarding collaboration in research and innovations
- Ties between India and Netherland
- Mahathir Mohd. And PM discussed economic and cultural relations and cooperation between India and Malaysia
- Friendship of Russia and India, Putin and PM discussed economic and cultural boost
- India and Nepal cooperation
- India–China meeting with Jinping and PM

Table 9: Nirmala Sitaraman Twitter Data report

Total Tweets: 15.4 K
Profile Name: Nirmala Sitaraman

Sr. No.	*Contents of tweet*	*Date of Tweet*	*Likes*	*Retweets*	*Reply Received*
1	#India&#Germany agree to establish Exchange Programme for Indian & German Startups. Thank	5/31/2017	275	117	10
2	Today, an interaction with German startups in Berlin to facilitate innovation & Startup cooperation between India & Germany.@startupindia	5/28/2017	351	111	20

Sr. No.	Contents of tweet	Date of Tweet	Likes	Retweets	Reply Received
3	Received at Hawaii by by Lt. General Bryan P. Fenton, Deputy Commander @INDOPACOM at Joint Base Pearl Harbor-Hickam. It is America's oldest and largest military combatant command. This year, in May, U.S. Pacific Command was renamed U.S. Indo-Pacific Command	12/6/2018	967	209	24
4	Furthering Indo-Russian defence and strategic ties; Smt@nsitharaman and Sergei Shoigu, Hon'ble Minister of Defence of the Russian Federation in the 18th IRIGC-MTC meetin	12/13/2018	370	81	11
5	Have had detailed discussions (twice) with a delegation of the families of those missing from 1971 war. Secretary @KSBSectt is working on inter ministerial coordination. Years ago families also visited jails in Pakistan. Efforts continue. @DefenceMinIndia @adgpi@SpokespersonMoD	12/17/2018	52	35	10
	Total		2015	553	75

Source: https://twitter.com/nsitharaman (Accessed on 27th December 2018)

Mrs. Nirmala Sitaraman, former Defense Minister of India now she is Finance Minister of India in 2019. She became Defense Minister from 3 September 2017. The total number of tweets made by Mrs. Sitaraman was 15.4 k out of which there are only 5 tweets are related to foreign policy. There are 2015 likes for her tweets. She did 553 Retweets during her period of Defense Minister of India and she received 75 replies for her tweets.

From the above tweets made by Nirmala Sitaraman on foreign policy of India, it is revealed that she made only 5 tweets which are related to foreign policy. The areas of her tweets are summarized on the following topics/areas:

- India and Germany exchange programme for startup
- U.S. Pacific Command was renamed U.S. Indo-Pacific Command
- India and Russia defense and strategic ties
- Discussions with the delegations from Pakistan about missing people from India from 1971

Table 10: Raksha Mantri Twitter Data Report

Profile Name: Raksha Mantri
Total Tweets: 3987

Sr. No.	Contents of tweet	Date of Tweet	Likes	Retweets	Reply Received
1	47 yrs ago on this day today, our Armed Forces not just made Pakistan surrender, but also established India as one of the strongest military powers in the world.-**#VijayDiwas** is the day to remember the valour & sacrifice of the brave soldiers who made this happen. **#VijayDiwas2018**	12/15/2018	235	89	13
2	Furthering Indo-Russian defence and strategic ties; Smt @nsitharaman and Sergei Shoigu, Hon'ble Minister of Defence of the Russian Federation in the 18th IRIGC-MTC meeting	12/13/2018	370	181	11
3	US Congressional delegation called on Smt **@nsitharaman** & discussed the range of issues pertaining to India-US defence cooperation. Both sides reaffirmed their desire to further develop defence partnership. **@USAmbIndia**	5/28/2018	458	143	9
4	Continuing its tradition of delivering ahead of schedule, GSL has delivered the most advanced ship of Sri Lanka Navy 25 days before the delivery date! GSL will display its made in India products at **@DefexpoI** which make it the biggest warship exporter of India! **@nsitharaman**	3/24/2018	725	214	27
5	"It is important that the spirit of cooperation between India-Vietnam extends to non-governmental private sector. I invite Indiansector participants to come and engage her seriously." – Smt **@nsitharaman** in Hanoi	6/13/2018	171	67	6
6	Strengthening India-Cambodia ties Smt@nsitharaman in a bilateral meeting with Deputy Prime Minister & Defence Minister of Cambodia H.E. Samdech Pichey Sena Tea Banh in Phnom Penh	6/10/2018	437	130	7
7	In order to reinforce defence cooperation between India and Russia with a focus on military technical cooperation, Smt @nsitharaman meets H E Army General	4/3/2018	1150	255	20

Sr. No.	Contents of tweet	Date of Tweet	Likes	Retweets	Reply Received
	Sergei Shoigu, Minister of Defence, Russia in Mosco				
8	Smt @nsitharaman in a bilateral meeting with Mr. Abdellatif Loudiyi, Hon'ble Minister of Defence, Morocco to boost defence and strategic ties between the two nation	9/25/2018	582	118	19
9	Honouring the courage and valour of the Indian soldiers who received martyrdom on the battlefield. Smt @nsitharaman visits and pays homage at the Indian Forces Monument at the Jakarta war cemetery, Indonesia	10/23/2018	624	141	11
	Total		4752	1358	123

Source: https://twitter.com/DefenceMinIndia (Accessed on 1st Feb 2019)

From the twitter account of Raksha Mantri, there are 3897 tweets were made from March 2018 to 15th December 2018. Out of which we found only 9 tweets which are concerned with India's foreign policy and national security. There are 4752 likes received to the 9 tweets made from this account and 1358 Retweets made from this account by Raksha Mantri. There are 123 reply received to all the nine tweets from various persons. The major areas /topic of the tweets are given below:

- India as one of the strongest military powers in the world.
- Indo-Russian defense and strategic ties
- India-US defense cooperation
- India-Sri Lanka relationship
- Cooperation between India-Vietnam extends to non-governmental private sector
- Strengthening India-Cambodia ties
- Reinforce defence cooperation between India and Russia for technical cooperation
- Boost defense and strategic ties between the two nation Morocco and India
- Homage at the Indian Forces Monument at the Jakarta war cemetery, Indonesia

Table 11: Sushama Swaraj Twitter Data Report

Profile Name: Sushma Swaraj
Total Tweets: 6326

Sr. No	*Contents of tweet*	*Date of Tweet*	*Likes*	*Retweets*	*Reply Received*
1	Leaving for Bangkok for Vishwa Sanskrit Sammelan and Indo–Thailand Joint Commission meeting.	6/26/2015	679	404	198
2	Indian Embassy in Turkey has given Emergency travel documents to your parents and they are flying back tonight. @nepratik	5/30/2015	633	358	170
3	Four Indians abducted in Libya – I am happy we have been able to secure the release of Lakshmikant and Vijay Kumar. Trying for other two.	7/31/2015	1699	1572	463
4	I had a good meeting with Foreign Minister of Iran HE @JZarif today. I raised the issue of nine Indian sailors detained in Iran.	8/14/2015	662	400	48
5	Unfortunate fire incident in Jizan Hospital, Saudi Arabia with many casualties. Our Consulate reports from Jeddah that all Indians are safe.	12/24/2015	568	216	58
6	@TiwariNd Our High Commission in Nigeria reports that Indian sailors are safe. We are trying for their release from pirates.	12/20/2015	29	19	3
7	Indian High Commission is there to help all Indian nationals in London. Please note Tel. Nos: 020 8629 5950 & 0207632 3035.	3/22/2017	6164	1954	261
8	I am happy to inform that we have secured the return of Capt. Atul Sharma, Sudhir Kumar, Balvinder Singh and Viyas Yadav to India. I appreciate the efforts of Shri B.N. Reddy Indian High Commissioner in Nigeria. We thank Nigerian authorities for their help. @india_nigeria	12/29/2017	17513	2521	607
9	There is a request for medical visa for two children from Pakistan – Anamta Farrukh (6 yrs) and Sahir (7 yrs). We have given them Visa for their treatment in India and pray for their early recovery. @IndiainPakistan	12/21/2017	10803	1094	954
10	I have asked Indian High Commission in Islamabad to issue medical visa to Maqbool Ahmad Qureshi – a Pakistan national for his	12/22/2017	1852	262	537

Sr. No	Contents of tweet	Date of Tweet	Likes	Retweets	Reply Received
	treatment in India. **@IndiainPakistan** https://twitter.com/umerawan007/status/943111814119870464 ...				
11	I have got the report from Indian High Commission in Islamabad. We are granting Visa for your treatment in India. @IndiainPakistan	12/19/2017	1248	140	65
12	Pakistan has agreed to facilitate the visit of mother and wife of Kulbhushan Jadhav and assured us of their safety, security and freedom of movement in Pakistan. /5	12/8/2017	5855	977	276
13	I have just spoken to Pradeep Rawat Indian Ambassador in Jakarta **@IndianEmbJkt** We have set up a facilitation centre at the airport and are providing assistance to the stranded Indian nationals there. I am in constant touch with our mission. **@cgibali**	11/27/2017	1392	295	69
14	MV Emerald Star with 26 Indians sank on 13 October 2017. While 16 Indians were rescued, remaining 10 could not be found. There was extensive search by Japan and Philippines which was joined by Indian Navy. /1	11/18/2017	1556	276	48
15	Paramjit Kaur is returning home tomorrow. I appreciate the efforts of Indian Embassy in Saudi Arabia.	11/3/2017	2293	433	174
16	Evangelin – Your country Russia is our time tested friend. My officials in Chennai will provide you all help.	10/10/2017	9282	2633	744
17	Indian High Commission official is escorting the mother and mortal of remains of the deceased son from Malaysia to Chennai. My heartfelt condolences to the bereaved family.	1/11/2018	1491	252	126
18	There is a blast in Indian restaurant Bombay Bhel in Mississauga, Ontario, Canada. I am in constant touch with our Consul General in Toronto and Indian High Commissioner in Canada. Our missions will work round the clock. The Emergency No. is: +1-647-668-4108. Please RT	5/24/2018	13417	7839	398
19	Here is the latest update from Canada. The 12 persons who were taken to hospital have been discharged. The other 3 persons who were critically injured are stable. According	5/25/2018	4093	432	131

Sr. No	*Contents of tweet*	*Date of Tweet*	*Likes*	*Retweets*	*Reply Received*
	to Police, at this stage there is no evidence to term this incident as a terrorist attack or hate crime.				
20	Police verification is not required for children. I have asked the @CPVIndia to give her the passport without police verification and take strict action against the concerned officer.	6/15/2018	2597	433	221
21	We have secured the release of three Indian nationals Sushil Kumar, Pankaj Kumar and Ajay Kumar – all from Himachal Pradesh who were abducted in Nigeria. I appreciate the efforts of Shri B.N. Reddy Indian High Commissioner in Nigeria. @jairamthakurbjp	4/11/2018	4894	1289	310
22	I am happy to inform that 21 Indian fishermen from Tamil Nadu who were stranded at Nakhitaghi (Iran) have been released with the efforts of Indian Embassy in Iran and our Consulate at Bandar Abbas. We are repatriating them to Chennai in batches starting from 3rd august 2018.	7/31/2018	23543	3685	871
23	I have just spoken to the Indian Ambassador in Switzerland Mr. Siby George. He has updated me on the situation. Our First Secretary and his wife were with the family during the day. Indian Embassy is providing them all possible help and assistance. @IndiainSwiss.	8/25/2018	1651	213	65
24	We are repatriating Rohit Pal and Rishab Gupta crew members of MV Maharishi Vamdeva from Fujairah. They suffered heat stroke because there was no air conditioning/ light in the ship. @CGIDubai provided provisions to crew members and is repatriating other members of the crew.	8/7/2018	1512	202	68
25	I am happy to inform that India has been elected to the United Nations Human Rights Council with highest number of votes. We have secured 188 votes out of 193.	10/12/2018	78326	16899	5100
	Total		193752	44798	11965

Source: https://twitter.com/SushmaSwaraj (Accessed on 1st Feb 2019)

Sushama Swaraj, former Minister of External Affairs, India. During her tenure as Minister she made 6326 tweets out of which we found 25 tweets which are concerned with India's Foreign Policy. For these 25 tweets she received 193752 likes from the followers and others, however, she retweets 44798 in number from her twitter account on the areas related to foreign policy and related topics. She also received reply on this twitter account from her followers which are 11965 in numbers. From the above statistics it revealed that she is the most popular minister and very active in solving the problems of people and also active in foreign policy of India. From the above tweets made by Mrs. Sushama Swaraj we have analyzed the areas in which she made tweets, these areas/topics are as follows:

- Indian Embassy in Turkey has given Emergency travel documents to your parents
- Indians abducted in Libya
- Our Consulate reports from Jeddah that all Indians are safe in Saudi Arabia
- Indian High Commission is there to help all Indian nationals in London
- Secured the return of Capt. Atul Sharma, Sudhir Kumar, Balvinder Singh and Viyas Yadav to India. I appreciate the efforts of Shri B.N. Reddy from Nigeria
- Medical visa request
- Blast in Indian restaurant Bombay Bhel in Mississauga, Ontario, Canada, provided help
- Release of three Indian nationals Sushil Kumar, Pankaj Kumar and Ajay Kumar – all from Himachal Pradesh who were abducted in Nigeria
- Indian fishermen from Tamil Nadu who were stranded at Nakhitaghi (Iran) have been released with the efforts of Indian Embassy in Iran

From the above tweet areas, it is revealed that Mrs. Sushama Swaraj helped many people who requested her in incidents which happened in other countries with the support from the Indian embassy in these countries.

Table 12: MikePompeo Twitter Data Report

Profile Name: Mike Pompeo
Total Tweets: 916

Sr. No.	*Contents of tweet*	*Date of Tweet*	*Likes*	*Retweets*	*Reply Received*
1	U.S. welcomes -**#Canada**'s decision to strongly condemn **#Iran** for ongoing sponsorship of terror & to add **#IRGC** to Canada's list of terrorist entities. Iranians are standing up to the corrupt regime's abuses. We support them & call on other nations to hold Iran's leaders accountable.	6/15/2018	18812	5837	453
2	We condemn the #Iran regime's execution of Mohammad Salas, a member of the long-persecuted Iranian Gonabadi Sufi Dervish community. We call on our partners & allies to join us in condemning his brutal & unjust execution. Iranian people deserve respect for human rights & freedoms.	6/18/2018	13100	4774	752
3	#Iran's support for Houthis in Yemen not only enables attacks on Saudi Arabia & UAE, but also risks increasing Yemen's already massive humanitarian crisis. Ayatollah Khamenei must be held accountable for destabilizing Gulf's security & prolonging suffering of the Yemeni people.	6/28/2018	7392	3419	878
4	Thanks to President Xi for hosting me. US and #China are firmly committed to the complete denuclearization of the Korean Peninsula, and facilitating a lasting and stable peace in the region	6/14/2018	7089	2119	250
5	I enjoyed speaking with the Chinese and American press, and answering questions along with State Councilor and Foreign Minister Wang. I welcomed the frank exchange of ideas.	6/14/2018	2930	729	118
6	5,000 Iranians arrested in January's protests. 30 women jailed for protesting the hijab. Hundreds of Sufi dervishes, dozens of environmentalists, 400 Ahwazis, 30 Isfahan farmers – all imprisoned by #Iran's criminal regime. Iranian people deserve respect for their human rights.	6/21/2018	9896	4823	1300
7	**@USUN** Amb. Haley has spent more than a year trying to reform **#UNHRC**. She has asserted US leadership on everything from	6/19/2018	8230	2172	546

Sr. No.	*Contents of tweet*	*Date of Tweet*	*Likes*	*Retweets*	*Reply Received*
	#Assad's chem weapons use to **#DPRK** to **#Iran**'s malign activity—all while putting U.S. interests first. She is the right leader to drive our efforts at the @UN.				
8	Delighted to host **@KingAbdullahII** at **@StateDept** yesterday. U.S. and **#Jordan** have a strong strategic partnership. Both countries are committed to defeating ISIS and supporting lasting and comprehensive peace between Israel and the Palestinians.	6/23/2018	5678	1391	244
9	Great to be in **#China** on my first trip as Secretary of State. Good to see Ambassador Branstad & members of the **@USA_China_Talk** team, and to meet with President Xi, State Councilor Yang and Foreign Minister Wang.	6/14/2018	2214	590	69
10	Enjoyed chatting with **@hughhewitt**. Discussed **#China**: it presents an opportunity & challenge; **#DPRK**: denuclearization is the path to a brighter future; **#Iran**: Iranians should be able to speak their mind, their human rights respected. Read the interview: https://go.usa.gov/xUxR2	6/25/2018	1649	498	126
11	U.S. has consistently pressed for reform of **#HumanRightsCouncil**. While HRC acted on some important human rights issues, its bias against **#Israel**& flawed membership destroy its credibility. Every year it passes many resolutions on Israel, but adopted only 1 on **#Iran**& 1 on **#DPRK**.	6/20/2018	3309	1178	245
12	For years **#Iran** pursued a secret effort to develop nuclear weapons. **#IranDeal** did not deter Iran's nuclear ambitions. U.S. seeks an arrangement that permanently prevents Iran from being able to develop or acquire nuclear weapons, or the ballistic missiles to deliver them.	6/28/2018	2207	834	219
13	As we commemorate the 50th anniversary of the Nuclear Non-Proliferation Treaty we must renew our efforts to reduce the dangers posed by nuclear proliferation, including confronting immediate challenges from **#DPRK** and **#Iran**.	6/28/2018	2384	747	123

Sr. No.	*Contents of tweet*	*Date of Tweet*	*Likes*	*Retweets*	*Reply Received*
14	**@khamenei_ir** fancies himself the leader of the Islamic world, but his regime has been totally silent as China – the top buyer of **#Iran**'s oil – has persecuted and detained hundreds of thousands of its Muslim citizens. #رژیم_ریاکار	9/13/2018	11662	4779	1300
15	We'll ensure those with a fire of faith in their hearts can exercise their God-given right to express it. From Iranian Christians & Uighur Muslims to detainees in North Korea & Turkey, we won't rest until believers are free to live their faith without fear of persecution. #VVS18	9/21/2018	9777	3265	851
16	Our thoughts and prayers are with the people of **#Indonesia** following the Sept. 28 earthquake and tsunami that struck Central Sulawesi. **@usembassyjkt** is closely monitoring the situation and we stand ready to assist as needed.	9/29/2018	2989	730	197
17	Happy to see **#Iraq** Parliament Speaker Mohammad Halbousi visiting our good friend **#Kuwait** on his first foreign trip. Good to reach out to Iraq's Arab friends and neighbours.	9/23/2018	3278	653	150
18	It was my honor to chair today's UN Security Council meeting on **#DPRK**. We reaffirmed that the world cannot accept a nuclear-armed North Korea and emphasized the importance of maintaining and enforcing international sanctions until final, fully-verified denuclearization. **#UNGA**	9/27/2018	1736	489	96
19	I commend PM Edi Rama's expulsion of two Iranian agents who plotted terrorist attacks in **#Albania**. European nations have thwarted three Iranian plots this year alone. The world must stand together to sanction **#Iran**'s regime until it changes its destructive behaviour.	19/12/2018	11549	4233	723
20	Just days after **#Hamas** indiscriminately fired thousands of missiles at **#Israel**'s citizens, **@UN** could not muster a resolution condemning this band of terrorists. This is yet another disgraceful act of bias toward the Jewish State.	12/6/2018	25309	9910	1500

Sr. No.	*Contents of tweet*	*Date of Tweet*	*Likes*	*Retweets*	*Reply Received*
21	Honored to join **@POTUS** for his working dinner with **#China**'s President Xi. We talked about the need for free, fair and reciprocal trade, and our commitment to the final, fully-verified denuclearization of **#DPRK**.	12/1/2018	11640	3090	359
22	The U.S. today declares it has found Russia in material breach of the treaty and will suspend our obligations as a remedy effective in 60 days unless Russia returns to full and verifiable compliance.	12/4/2018	5002	2208	167
23	On this **#HumanRightsDay**, spare a moment to remember the innocent Americans held hostage by **#Iran**, and their families. The regime must release Bob Levinson and all other U.S. hostages immediately. **#FreeIranHostages@HelpBobLevinson**	12/10/18	7612	3470	645
24	As **#Yemen** consultations with **@OSE_Yemen** progress in Sweden, the U.S. urges all parties to continue engaging to achieve concrete, positive outcomes for the people of Yemen.	12/10/18	1303	347	167
25	Great to be in studio today with **@foxandfriends**. We discussed the tragic attack in **#Strasbourg**, our work with **#Mexico** on border security, countering Russian, Iranian and Chinese aggression, and ensuring American foreign policy serves the American people.	12/10/18	2560	544	381
26	Glad to host **@Canada** FM **@cafreeland** & Defense Minister **@HarjitSajjan** with **@DeptofDefense#SecDef** Mattis at the **@StateDept** today. We discussed all the issues the U.S. and Canada work on together: **#DPRK**, **@NATO**, **#Ukrainc**, Syria, and Iraq – plus our own shared economic prosperity.	12/12/18	1648	419	264
27	Congratulations to **#Belgium** for choosing to fly with the 5th generation American-made fighter jet **@thef35** ! They'll fly alongside close **#NATO** Allies & longtime partners. We want a US-Belgium relationship where our our prosperity and security grow together.	12/4/2018	1386	368	78
28	Thanks to France, Germany, and the UK for joining the U.S. in raising concerns about	12/12/18	1513	555	112

Sr. No.	*Contents of tweet*	*Date of Tweet*	*Likes*	*Retweets*	*Reply Received*
	the Iranian regime's reckless missile activity. **#Iran** is in open defiance of **#UNSCR** 2231. That's indisputable.				
29	Our nations have a choice: bury our head in the sand or take commonsense action in response to Russia's flagrant disregard of **#INF**. **#Russia** has violated since 2000's, while US remained in scrupulous INF compliance.	12/4/2018	653	310	54
	Total		184507	64481	12367

Source: https://twitter.com/SecPompeo (Accessed on 1st Feb 2019)

Mike Pompeo is an American politician and attorney who, since April 2018, has served as the 70th United States Secretary of State. He is a former United States Army officer and was director of the Central Intelligence Agency from January 2017 until April 2018. President Donald Trump nominated Pompeo as secretary of state in March 2018. During his tenure as Secretary he made 916 tweets related to foreign policy. There are 184507 likes received for the tweets and he made 64481 Retweets for the period June 2018 to December 2018. During the six month period he received replies from 12367 followers and others. It is revealed that during the six month period, the response to his tweets is great. While analyzing his tweets we found the following areas on which he tweets. Areas of his tweets are given below:

- Iranians are standing up to the corrupt regime's abuses.
- Iranian people deserve respect for human rights & freedoms.
- Khamenei must be held accountable for destabilizing Gulf's security & prolonging suffering of the Yemeni people.
- Iranian people deserve respect for their human rights.
- US and Jordan have a strong strategic partnership.
- Human right issues from Iran on Israel.
- Iran efforts to develop nuclear weapons.
- Muslims to detainees in North Korea & Turkey.
- **Indonesia** following the Sept. 28 earthquake and tsunami that struck Central Sulawesi.
- World cannot accept a nuclear-armed North Korea.
- **Hamas** indiscriminately fired thousands of missiles at **#Israel**'s citizens.

- Need for free, fair and reciprocal trade between US and China.
- **Yemen** progress in Sweden.
- **Mexico** on border security, countering Russian, Iranian and Chinese aggression, and ensuring American foreign policy serves the American people.
- The issues the U.S. and Canada work on together.
- US-Belgium relationship on prosperity and security.
- Iranian regime's reckless missile activity.

From the above areas of his tweets it is revealed that he talks about US security and Iran issues on nuclear weapons. He also tweets about the relationship of the US to other countries.

Table 13: Theresa May Twitter Data Report

Profile Name: Theresa May
Total Tweets: 1634

Sr. No.	*Contents of tweet*	*Date of Tweet*	*Likes*	*Retweets*	*Reply Received*
1	Today's Brexit deal delivers: – No hard border in Northern Ireland – Secures a good financial deal for British taxpayers meaning more money for our priorities like housing, schools, and the NHS – Secured the rights of EU citizens living here, and UK citizens living in the EU	12/8/2017	1837	793	907
2	This deal is an enormous boost for the UK economy. I have always been clear that as we leave the EU we have an opportunity to build on our close relationships with allies like Australia. This is a perfect illustration that the Government is doing exactly that.	6/29/2018	3636	1069	1300
3	I've been in Bulgaria meeting EU and Western Balkan leaders, including @EmmanuelMacron and Chancellor Merkel. Next year the UK leaves the EU, but we are not leaving Europe. We'll continue to work with our allies to protect our collective security and champion our shared values.	5/17/2018	1270	312	609
	Total		6743	2174	2816

Source: https://twitter.com/theresa_may (Accessed on 1st Feb 2019)

Theresa Mary May is a British politician serving as Prime Minister of the United Kingdom since 2016. She was Home Secretary from 2010 to 2016 and Leader of the Conservative Party from 2016 until 2019. She made 1634 tweets, out of which we found only 3 tweets on foreign policy and relations of other countries. She received 6743 likes for the tweets she made on foreign policy and she made 2174 Retweets. She also received 2816 reply from her followers. We observed that her major areas of tweets are Brexit deals, UK economy, close relationship with Australia and Protect UK collective security.

Table 14: Gavin Williamson Twitter Data Report

Profile Name: Gavin Williamson
Total Tweets: 1548

Sr. No	*Contents of tweet*	*Date of Tweet*	*Likes*	*Retweets*	*Reply Received*
1	We cannot let the use of chemical weapons go unchallenged. Alongside our US and French allies we made a decisive, targeted, and legal strike to degrade and deter the Syrian regime's use of these abhorrent weapons that inflict horrific suffering on innocent civilians.	4/14/2018	300	128	69
2	It was a pleasure to be in Warsaw today to thank our troops who are keeping Britain and Europe safe – and also to pay our respects to Poland's fallen heroes who fought with us to protect our freedoms	6/21/2018	216	62	33
3	On Anzac Day we remember the sacrifice and courage of men and women from Australia and New Zealand. Our three countries still have the closest of partnerships. Lest we forget.	4/25/2018	154	53	6
4	I'd like to say a huge thank you to **@HMSSutherland** Their visit to Australia gave Britain's bid a massive boost to help secure the £20bn global combat ship deal. Well done to **@BAESystemsAus** **@DefenceHQ** **@tradegovuk** **@foreignoffice** and all involved	6/28/2018	350	90	12
5	We welcome the support from **@JensStoltenberg** and our **@NATO** allies to UK, US, and French action in Syria. It sends a clear message that the despicable use of chemical weapons will not go unchallenged.	4/14/2018	107	64	20

Sr. No	*Contents of tweet*	*Date of Tweet*	*Likes*	*Retweets*	*Reply Received*
6	I want to thank all the brave men and women of the @RoyalAirForce who were involved in identifying and tracking Russian Blackjack bombers and scrambling British typhoon jets in response. Keeping our skies safe 24/7 is just one of the many roles at which the RAF excels!	9/20/2018	###	398	131
7	Britain and its allies are firmly committed to Ukraine sovereignty as it faces down blatant Russian aggression.	9/21/2018	188	50	33
8	Pleased to announce we will be supporting #Ukraine by extending our military training operation there until 2020. I look forward to working closely with Ukraine and strengthening the important relationship between our two countries.	9/21/2018	217	120	33
9	An excellent **#AUKMIN2018** in Edinburgh with **@MarisePayne@JulieBishopMP** and **@Jeremy_Hunt** – strengthening our international and defence ties with greater commitment and renewed vigour. Our historic relationships has entered a new era based on our shared values and beliefs.	7/20/2018	52	13	8
10	It's great to welcome **@MarisePayne** to **#Scotland** today and see our T26 frigate programme taking shape in Govan – now £1bn has been spent with industry as UK shipbuilding experiences a renaissance. Brilliant chance to celebrate our close defence partnership **#Australia#UK**	7/19/2018	51	17	6
11	**@theresa_may** announced we are deploying a further 440 troops to Afghanistan. This is crucial to bringing stability to Afghanistan but also vital to preventing terrorism at home in the UK. We've had productive discussions today **@NATO** about the future of the alliance.	7/11/2018	54	19	10
12	As long as Ukraine faces Russian hostilities, it will find a steadfast partner in the United Kingdom. By continuing to work together, whether through training programmes or military exercises, we help Ukraine to stand up for our shared values. #Defence	11/21/2018	211	91	134

Sr. No	Contents of tweet	Date of Tweet	Likes	Retweets	Reply Received
13	It has been a pleasure to work alongside Jim Mattis to keep our two nations safe. He is a great friend and leaves with the UK-US security relationship as strong as it has ever been. I look forward to working with his successor as we continue to ensure international security.	12/21/2018	378	74	37
14	I was delighted to spend time in Oman and I thank the Royal Omani Army, Navy and Air Force for their gracious hospitality. #SaifSareea embodies the close relationship between Omani and British forces and I look forward to strengthening the important bond between our two nations.	11/4/2018	219	44	9
15	I am very much looking forward to working closely with the **#USA** to tackle shared threats. The UK has been with the US through thick and thin – we share values and stand together in global leadership. **@UKinUSA**	#####	47	7	17
16	It was a pleasure to spend time with my US counterpart Jim Mattis at the Reagan National Defense Forum in California this weekend. We discussed the special relationship between the **#UK** and the **#USA** and the enduring partnership our countries share **@UKinUSA**	#####	44	7	10
17	I was delighted to meet with Stepan Poltorak and we will continue to strengthen our defence partnership with Ukraine. I've seen on the frontline the effects of the conflict in the East, which reinforced my support for Ukraine's sovereignty, independence and territorial integrity.	#####	56	28	7
18	The statement I signed today with Ursula von der Leyen strengthens UK-German ties and bolsters the defence of two key NATO partners. This is an alliance we both hold dear. **#NATO#defence**	#####	116	34	16
19	My thoughts are with those affected by the devastating earthquake and tsunami in #Indonesia. Our Defence experts are speaking to the Indonesian Government. If needed we have assets on standby for immediate deployment to aid all those affected.	#####	87	16	4
	Total		4387	1315	595

Source: https://twitter.com/GavinWilliamson (Accessed on 1st Feb 2019)

Gavin Alexander Williamson CBE MP is a British Conservative politician who served as Secretary of State for Defense from 2017 to 2019, and has served as Member of Parliament for South Staffordshire since 2010. He made 1548 tweets on various issues and topics however we found only 19 tweets related to foreign policy, foreign relations etc. The period of his tweets is from April 2018 to Sept. 2018. During this period, he received 4387 likes on the tweets made on foreign policy and defense areas. He did 1315 Retweets and received 595 replies from his followers. He is having a total of 45.4 K followers till June 2019. The major areas of his tweets are listed below:

- Use of chemical weapons go unchallenged.
- Partnership of Australia, UK and New Zealand
- UK, US, and French action in Syria.
- Supporting #Ukraine by extending our military training operation there until 2020
- Strengthening our international and defense ties
- Celebrate our close defense partnership of Australia and UK
- UK-US security relationship as strong as it has ever been.
- Close relationship between Omani and British forces
- Share values and stand together in global leadership
- Support for Ukraine's sovereignty, independence and territorial integrity.
- UK-German ties and bolsters the defense of two key NATO partners.
- Indonesia earthquake and Tsunami.

Table 15: Jeremy Hunt Twitter Data Report

Profile Name: Jeremy Hunt
Total Tweets: 4252

Sr. No.	*Contents of tweet*	*Date of Tweet*	*Likes*	*Retweets*	*Reply Received*
1	Seems extraordinary that Google is considering censoring its content to get into China but won't cooperate with UK, US and other 5 eyes countries in removing child abuse content. They used to be so proud of being values-driven...	8/30/2018	1313	467	117
2	One of my first experiences as Foreign Sec	9/9/2018	1598	526	235

Sr. No.	Contents of tweet	Date of Tweet	Likes	Retweets	Reply Received
	was seeing Israel support the UK & others in getting the brave White Helmets out of Syria. Thank you. And to all Jewish people around the world we will NEVER allow the cancer of anti-semitism to return to Europe. Very happy #RoshHashanah				
3	Looks like Iranian legal system is impervious to the simple fact at the heart of this: an innocent woman is desperate to be reunited with her family. Spoke to Foreign Minister Zarif on Fri but that clearly wasn't enough. The fight goes on #FreeNazanin	8/26/2018	1271	562	205
4	The last time Russian military claimed to be on holiday was when they invaded Ukraine in 2014. Time to stop the fake TV shows – the world has found Russia out on this	9/13/2018	718	378	124
5	I'm at #UNGA in New York this week for talks with leaders on Burma, Syria, Yemen and Russia. If you've got questions about these issues, please send them in a tweet and I will do my best to answer you whilst I am here	9/24/2018	353	156	169
6	Russia feels threatened by Europe – but they are wrong. If they start following the rules everyone else does they will get the respect they crave – but if they choose their current path they will only isolate themselves even more	9/27/2018	280	66	109
7	If the regime in Syria repeats its horrible use of chemical weapons then our response will be strong and united. Discussed with @SecPompeo this afternoon how we uphold the global ban and avoid an entirely manmade disaster #EyesonIdlib	9/11/2018	298	125	182
8	Just met Iranian Foreign Minister Javad Zarif at #UNGA. I pressed for swift resolution on all our dual national consular cases, including Nazanin. NOT acceptable to detain innocent people arbitrarily at the cost of enormous human anguish	9/25/2018	401	128	56
9	Rule #1 as a new Foreign Sec: when reflecting in English with the Chinese on a conversation you had with them in Japanese about your Chinese wife, don't get any of	7/30/2018	3540	552	504

Sr. No.	*Contents of tweet*	*Date of Tweet*	*Likes*	*Retweets*	*Reply Received*
	those mixed up! Apologies to the long-suffering Mrs H...!				
10	Fantastic news that we – UK and friends – have secured evacuation of White Helmets and their families – thank you Israel and Jordan for acting so quickly on our request. The WH are the bravest of the brave and in a desperate situation this is at least one ray of hope	7/22/2018	2369	762	1300
11	With Archbishop of Canterbury **@JustinWelby** in front of Christmas tree decorated with messages to free Nazanin before her 40th birthday on 26th December. Time for Iran to do the right thing and free Nazanin and other innocent people wrongly imprisoned in Iran. **#FreeNazanin**	12/20/2018	380	164	45
12	The case of the two Reuters journalists imprisoned for exposing the Rohingya crisis sends a chilling message. Journalism must never be a crime, as I discussed with Amal Clooney who is doing a great job representing Wa Lone and Kyaw Soe Oo	12/13/2018	200	74	32
13	Dialogue is key to achieving peace in Yemen. At the talks in Sweden today I met with the Government of Yemen and the Houthi delegations to stress the need for all sides to continue to work towards a political solution	12/13/2018	88	33	20
14	Tough action in response to Russia's reckless behaviour – including in Salisbury – is absolutely vital. We welcome additional US sanctions and we will continue to work closely with partners to protect our collective security and the rules based int'l order	12/19/2018	105	41	33
15	Delighted to announce that UK will open new Embassy in **#Maldives**. Over 100,000 British people visit every year & this will help our countries to work together even more closely. Proud to continue the biggest expansion of **@foreignoffice**'s diplomatic network for a generation	12/4/2018	737	271	95
16	Deeply concerned by Iran's test firing of a medium range ballistic missile. Provocative, threatening and inconsistent with UNSCR 2231. Our support for JCPoA in no way	12/1/2018	409	207	223

Sr. No.	*Contents of tweet*	*Date of Tweet*	*Likes*	*Retweets*	*Reply Received*
	lessens our concern at Iran's destabilising missile programme and determination that it should cease				
17	The UK utterly condemns Russia's use of force against Ukrainian vessels entering the Sea of Azov. Once again, we see Russian CONTEMPT for international norms and Ukrainian sovereignty. Russia must release detained Ukrainian sailors and guarantee free passage through Kerch Straits	11/26/2018	1279	620	201
18	Fantastic news about Matthew Hedges. Although we didn't agree with charges we are grateful to UAE govt for resolving issue speedily. But also a bittersweet moment as we remember Nazanin & other innocent ppl detained in Iran. Justice won't be truly done until they too are safely home.	11/26/2018	3898	936	439
19	British-Iranian dual nationals wrongly imprisoned must be freed. I've pressed hard on this today – innocent people should not be turned into diplomatic pawns	11/19/2018	458	155	82
20	#UNSC meeting on Burma heard allegations of war crimes and genocide. Until there is accountability, no Rohingya will feel safe to return. So UNSC should consider all options including ICC referral or an ad-hoc tribunal if Burmese govt fail to deliver justice	10/25/2018	95	65	28
21	A very warm welcome to His Majesty King Willem-Alexander and Queen Máxima of the Netherlands to the UK for today's **#NetherlandsStateVisit** – a symbol of our enduring commitment to the partnership. **@koninklijkhuis**	10/23/2018	168	50	23
22	Oleg Sentsov's 145 day hunger strike was a damning reflection of the injustice faced by Ukrainian political prisoners held by Russia. I welcome his nomination by @Europarl_EN for this year's Sakharov Prize. If you haven't heard of his struggle	10/12/2018	74	69	19
	Total		20032	6407	4241

Source: https://twitter.com/Jeremy_Hunt (Accessed on 1st Feb 2019)

Jeremy Richard Streynsham Hunt is a British Conservative Party politician serving as Secretary of State for Foreign and Commonwealth Affairs since 2018, and has served as Member of Parliament for South West Surrey since 2005. Jeremy Hunt made 4252 tweets from his twitter account, out of which we found 22 tweets on Foreign policy and Foreign relations. He received 20032 likes for his 22 tweets made on foreign relations and he made 6407 Retweets on the areas of foreign policy related topics. He has received 4241 reply from his followers. We have analyzed his twitter data and we found the following areas/topics which he made tweets, these are listed below:

- Israel support the UK & others in getting the brave White Helmets out of Syria
- Iranian legal system is impervious to the simple fact at the heart of this: an innocent woman is desperate to be reunited with her family
- Syria repeats its horrible use of chemical weapons
- Nazanin and other INNOCENT people wrongly imprisoned in Iran.
- Two Reuters journalists imprisoned for exposing the Rohingya crisis sends a chilling message.
- Russia's reckless behaviour—including in Salisbury—is absolutely vital.
- UK will open new Embassy in Maldives.
- Iran's test firing of a medium range ballistic missile
- UNSC meeting on Burma heard allegations of war crimes and genocide
- Ukrainian political prisoners held by Russia.

From the above tweet topics, it is revealed that Jeremy Hunt visited many places and spoke to the important persons from various countries and discussed the issues and relationshipsof countries.

Table 16: Emmanuel Macron Twitter Data Report

Profile Name: Emmanuel Macron
Total tweets: 8183

Sr. No.	*Contents of tweet*	*Date of Tweet*	*Likes*	*Retweets*	*Reply Received*
1	For his first research center in artificial intelligence outside the USA, Facebook chooses... France! **#LesChosesBougent**	6/2/2015	212	488	39
2	Helmut Schmidt was one of the founders of Europe and the Franco-German couple. Let's relive this ambition and pursue the European dream.	11/10/2015	115	119	19
3	Visit of ARC International in Arques to greet the first co-investment of the Russian and French sovereign funds	6/27/2016	114	61	13
4	At the Hanover Fair, we launch with **@SigmarGabriel** Franco-German cooperation for the industry of the future	4/26/2016	196	151	21
5	In Warsaw, France, Germany and Poland United to support European industry	4/22/2016	317	172	55
6	In Metz with my counterpart Sigmar Gabriel for the Franco-German Council of Ministers	4/7/2016	239	91	40
7	Full solidarity with Berlin and with Germany. France will always stand by your side.	12/19/2016	865	581	29
8	I want Italy and France to work together on this idea of European universities.	9/27/2017	841	253	59
9	Win-win agreement: on STX the operator is European, not Korean as it was several months ago.	9/27/2017	715	243	88
10	Our citizens are waiting for their safety to be guaranteed. Fighting Islamist terrorism is the priority of our foreign policy	8/29/2017	1764	568	278
11	Franco-Swiss friendship is historic. She's tying us up. We are working together in particular on the fight against terrorism and the environment.	7/18/2017	3387	865	346
12	With President Mahmoud Abbas, I have reaffirmed our desire to establish a just and lasting peace between Israel and Palestine.	7/5/2017	4994	1733	369
13	We support the African Union and IOM in helping to return to their countries of origin the African nationals trapped in the camps in Libya.	12/23/2017	1159	286	137

Sr. No.	*Contents of tweet*	*Date of Tweet*	*Likes*	*Retweets*	*Reply Received*
14	France is in favour of two States, Israel and Palestine, living side by side in peace and security	12/10/2017	8086	2316	443
15	Palestine is not alone. We will make sure that it lives in secure and Recognised borders, safely alongside Israel, with Jerusalem as the capital of both states	12/22/2017	10194	4682	996
16	I do not believe that we can build a lasting peace and a political solution in Syria without the Syrians. Syria does not boil down to Bashar al-Assad's regim	19/12/2017	1491	432	175
17	I am proud to be the first french president to visit Ghana. Long live the friendship between France and Ghana	11/30/2017	3912	1562	171
18	LIVE united with Frank-Walter Steinmeier, President of the Federal Republic of Germany, for the centenary of the First World War. Declaration.	11/10/2017	1210	411	121
19	It is not necessary that the actors of the AI are all white males somethings trained in European or American universities. **#AIforhumanity**	3/29/2018	1652	657	610
20	I thank the American people and President @realDonaldTrump for their solidarity after the terrorist attack in Trèbes and Carcassonne. We honour the victims and the hero who gave his life to save others. We stand together with our allies against terrorism.	3/24/2018	5667	1628	436
21	On Salisbury's attack all the Member States of the European Union agree that there is no other plausible explanation than Russia's responsibility. **#EUCO**	3/23/2018	613	206	95
22	Dear **@narendramodi,** Thank you for these three days in India. They have been intense and exciting: we have strengthened our bilateral strategic cooperation, launched the **#ISASummit** and immersed ourselves in Indian culture in Varanasi. We hope to see you soon in France	3/13/2018	4215	1253	120
23	**#IndianYouth,** in a few minutes we will be talking directly. You are not only the future of India but you are also contributing to the	3/10/2018	804	262	39

Sr. No.	Contents of tweet	Date of Tweet	Likes	Retweets	Reply Received
	future of the world. We have a lot to do together, stay tuned: http://www.facebook.com/Emmanu elMacron/videos/2122543144644927/ ...				
24	140 000 Indians came to risk their lives to defend the freedom of France during the First World War. France will never forget the lives lost for our freedom	3/10/2018	1283	403	83
25	When President Trump unilaterally announced the recognition of Jerusalem as the capital of Israel he did not help in the resolution of the conflict. If France were to follow this path, it would lose the role of facilitator, which is the only useful one for the region	3/7/2018	4667	1182	327
26	Announced in May 2017, we launched the Trianon dialogue yesterday. Thanks to the artists, researchers, entrepreneurs... for having agreed to develop the cultural link that unites us with Russia.	2/10/2018	1664	419	189
27	The **#Pyeongchang2018** games will be the Peace Games. Congratulations to South Korea and **@Olympics** for this historic moment. I wish all the best to our **@FranceOlympique** athletes and **@martinfkde**. France is with you	2/9/2018	1735	446	142
28	In the Face of the threat of obscurantism, the only answer to bring is education. Our destinies are inextricably linked and I am committed to this fight for the future of the African continent. **#FundEducation**	2/2/2018	1285	469	139
29	Europe is positive for Italy and an Italy that believes in Europe is positive for Europe.	1/11/2018	1830	583	243
30	With the French community, I am counting on you to make the Franco-Chinese friendship succeed	1/9/2018	1333	324	78
31	The project I am carrying for a strong, sovereign, United Europe that carries its interests and values in the world will make China's natural partner to meet global challenges. Find the entire interview:	1/9/2018	777	238	72
32	The G7 is at a critical juncture for our collective action. The international stakes are considerable, whether it is security, trade,	6/6/2018	3424	827	286

Sr. No.	*Contents of tweet*	*Date of Tweet*	*Likes*	*Retweets*	*Reply Received*
	climate change or the advancement of women. I am pleased with the real convergence between France and Canada.				
33	Ireland has once again made history. This vote will stand as an essential symbol for women's freedom.	5/27/2018	4860	962	194
34	Following my dialogue with Vladimir Putin, there have been significant advances in Iran and Syria.	5/25/2018	624	207	142
35	Here are buried women, men and children who died in Leningrad, so that life in St. Petersburg continued. During the Second World War and the blockade of Leningrad fought all the people, to complete victory. France will never forget the fortitude of the Russian soul.	5/25/2018	580	199	59
36	To avoid an escalation of violence in the Middle East, our common will with Russia: to build a broader framework and complement the nuclear agreement with Iran.	5/24/2018	699	234	80
37	France, Germany and the United Kingdom regret the American decision to leave the Iranian nuclear agreement. The international regime to combat nuclear proliferation is at stake.	5/8/2018	4656	2296	615
38	We will work collectively on a broader framework, covering nuclear activity, the period after 2025, ballistic missiles and stability in the Middle East, especially in Syria, Yemen and Iraq.	5/8/2018	1066	510	152
39	We want to finish the war against ISIS in Syria, and to keep working to build peace in the region within a new inclusive political framework.	4/24/2018	1294	393	185
40	Our thoughts go to the victims, their families and all the Italian people. France is close to Italy in this tragedy and is ready to make all the necessary support. **#Genova#Gênes**	8/14/2018	5139	1400	241
41	Sports can educate and empower people. I am a firm believer in the impact sport can have on each life and the future of a country. It's time to invest in sports in Nigeria!	7/4/2018	2038	672	125

Sr. No.	*Contents of tweet*	*Date of Tweet*	*Likes*	*Retweets*	*Reply Received*
42	Steve Jobs' father was a Syrian refugee. It would seem that nationality has nothing to do with the ability to succeed. If you think that being an Nigerian means you can't succeed then you won't. If you fight and you do succeed you will be a role model!	7/4/2018	21223	8835	1026
43	We just had a very good conversation with President Trump on counter-terrorism, European defense, Iran, Syria, the Gulf region, Libya, and many other issues of common interest for France and the United States.	11/10/2018	1325	401	441
44	On October 17, 1961 was the day of violent repression of Algerian demonstrators. The Republic must look across this recent and still burning past. This is the condition of a peaceful future with Algeria and our countrymen of Algerian descent.	10/17/2018	4717	1783	1020
	Total		118981	41803	10358

Source: https://twitter.com/EmmanuelMacron (Accessed on 3rd January 2019)

Emmanuel Jean-Michel Frédéric Macron is a French politician serving as President of the French Republic since 2017. He made 8183 tweets from his account during the period from June 2015 to December 2018. We have found 44 tweets out of 8183, which are on the topic of foreign policy and security. He received 118981 likes for the tweets he made on foreign policy and security. He made 41803 Retweets on foreign policy, he also received 10358 reply from his followers. This statistics shows that he is the most popular President of France and very active on twitter.

It is revealed from the above tweets that he is active on twitter and answers the information through the social me. We have analysed all the forty four tweets and found the following areas on which he tweets, they are as under:

- First research center in artificial intelligence outside the USA
- Franco-German cooperation for the industry of the future
- Italy and France to work together on this idea of European universities.

- Losting peace and a political solution in Syria
- Franco-Swiss friendship
- Visit to India and Indian culture in Varanasi
- France, Germany and the United Kingdom regret the American decision to leave the Iranian nuclear agreement
- We want to finish the war against ISIS in Syria.

President Macron visited India with Narendra Modi, PM India and talked about the Indian youth in Varanasi. Indian relations with France are good. His tweets are very short.

Table 17: Florence Parly Twitter Data Report

Profile Name: Florence Parly
Total Tweets:1886

Sr. No.	*Contents of tweet*	*Date of Tweet*	*Likes*	*Retweets*	*Reply Received*
1	Terrorism, power strategies, North Korea, cyber: threats are more numerous, more varied, more pernicious **#UED2017**	9/5/2017	39	28	6
2	In Baghdad with **@JY_LeDrian**. Respect to the Iraqis who took over Mosul and attack Tall Afar with the remarkable help of the French forces	8/26/2017	126	80	12
3	Rockfish submarines shipyard in Bombay. A success for our exports, a recognition for our technologies	10/28/2017	96	48	2
4	Inauguration of the factory **@reliancegroup @Dassault_OnAir** in Nagpur: symbol of a mutually beneficial **#Inde** industrial relationship	10/27/2017	239	83	13
5	Arrival in India, 1st stage New Delhi. Two days to strengthen our strategic, operational, industrial and technological cooperation	10/26/2017	130	41	1
6	With **@BrunoLeMaire** and **@robertapinotti** we have made a great new step for the creation of a European naval industrial giant. The alliance between **@navalgroup** and Fincantieri these are jobs, the radiance of France and Italy and a chance for our innovation.	2/1/2018	146	90	10
7	The objective: that our Armed forces learn to know each other and act together. Through exchanges between the staffs and joint exercises, we will create a European strategic	6/25/2018	90	34	6

Sr. No.	*Contents of tweet*	*Date of Tweet*	*Likes*	*Retweets*	*Reply Received*
	culture. We will be ready to anticipate crises and respond quickly and usefully.				
8	The IEI brings together France, Germany, Belgium, Denmark, Spain, Estonia, the Netherlands, Portugal and the United Kingdom. As many militarily capable and politically willing countries for the safety of Europeans	6/25/2018	121	67	9
9	Fruitful exchanges yesterday with my Senegalese counterpart, in the margins of Eurosatory. Sharing of our analyses on the regional situation. Senegal is a leading partner for security in Africa.	6/13/2018	57	25	0
10	Finally, the draft European intervention initiative launched on 26 September at the Sorbonne **@EmmanuelMacron** is still a little more concrete. Strong commitment and decisive step: Germany joins him.	6/19/2018	43	22	2
11	Further co-operation begins around the artillery system of the future. We have also decided to launch the Franco-German military satellite CSO3 on Ariane 6: symbol of the quality of our bilateral cooperation and of France's support to Ariane 6.	6/19/2018	29	10	
12	New stage for Defence Europe and the consolidation of our industry launch of the modernization programme of the Tiger Helicopter "Standard 3" in cooperation with Germany: helicopters adapted to the anticipated evolution of threats To the 2040 horizon.	5/4/2018	266	131	9
13	A few hours before 3:00 in the morning, a maritime force deployed in the Mediterranean and an air raid from France at the beginning of the night fired missiles at strategic objectives of the Syrian clandestine chemical programme. A research centre and production sites have been targeted.	4/13/2018	448	297	85
14	Meeting with my counterpart **@cpyne** in Adelaide. Joint Action against terrorism and cooperation of our defence industries. Australia and France have never been so close to face such great common challenges.	9/24/2018	38	15	2

Sr. No.	Contents of tweet	Date of Tweet	Likes	Retweets	Reply Received
15	In four years of operation, we have trained thousands of Iraqi soldiers, supported the Syrian Democratic forces. Daech was stalked, cornered. And by dint of strikes and gunfire, his caches and terrorists have fallen.	9/19/2018	102	50	7
16	Met yesterday with my Vietnamese counterpart Ngo Xuan Lich. Bilateral cooperation and strong links for the Indo-Pacific region, as was further demonstrated in August by the passage of Operation Pegasus from La **@Armee_de_lair** to Vietnam.	9/18/2018	36	9	1
17	Visit of the Australian submarine shipyards **@navalgroup**. Example of successful and unprecedented cooperation, mutually beneficial for France and Australia.	9/24/2018	28	14	2
18	Operation Shamal, for the past four years, has brought together 1200 military personnel, sailors and airmen, deployed on various bases in Iraq and in partner countries. The mission they lead is in the service of all the French.	9/19/2018	49	21	3
19	Visit of the Australian submarine shipyards @navalgroup. Example of successful and unprecedented cooperation, mutually beneficial for France and Australia.	9/15/2018	331	143	11
20	Back from the government. Europe, combating terrorism, renewing materials, mixing, innovation, improving the living conditions of the military and their families: our forces are counting on us, the French are waiting for us. Work continues, more than ever.	8/22/2018	157	62	7
21	On the sidelines of the summit **@NATO**, informal exchange with my American counterpart Jim Mattis. The transatlantic relationship is essential for collective security. Our bilateral relations are strong, our cooperation effective. Jim can count on my trust and me on his.	7/12/2018	66	23	3
22	An example of a successful joint operation in western Niger: Nigerian and French military (Operation Liza) neutralize about 15 terrorists and recover weapons, ammunition and vehicles. The rising power of the G5 Sahel armies continues.	12/29/2018	482	175	23

Sr. No.	*Contents of tweet*	*Date of Tweet*	*Likes*	*Retweets*	*Reply Received*
23	We have a difference of analysis with the United States. France paid a heavy price because of Daech. The fight against terrorism is a priority of the government. Our analysis: We have a job to finish. **#RTL**	12/21/2018	289	133	33
24	In June, France and Germany decided to develop, together, the combat aircraft of the future. Decisive step today with the agreement to begin the studies of architecture and design and the launch of demonstrators (airplane and engine) by mid-2019. It's moving!	11/20/2018	325	135	19
25	Opening **@SalonEuronaval** this morning. We need a **@MarineNationale** strong, capable of assuming its missions: • deliveries from 2019, • new tankers in partnership with Italy, • launch of studies for the new generation aircraft carrier	10/23/2018	127	61	4
26	A tangible example of successful cooperation: at the request of Burkina Faso, France intervened in the air against members of an armed terrorist group in the north of the country. I welcome in particular the responsiveness of Operation Liza	10/4/2018	158	49	1
	Total		4018	1846	272

Source: https://twitter.com/florence_parly (Accessed on 17th Janurary 2019)

Florence Parly is a French politician, who is serving as Minister of the Armed Forces in the Second Philippe Government, under President Emmanuel Macron. She made 1886 tweets in total, Out of which we found only 26 tweets on foreign policy related topic. For this 26 tweets she received 4018 likes, she Retweets 1846 tweets from her twitter account and received 272 replies from her followers. Being a Minister of the Armed Forces in French Government she actively tweets from her official twitter account which is given above. We have found these tweets from her twitter account for the period of November 2017 to December 2018. While analyzing these tweets we found the following areas related to foreign policy and related topics, they are listed below:

- Respect to the Iraqis who took over Mosul and attack Tall Afar with the remarkable help of the French forces

- Inauguration of the factory of Reliance group and Dassult on Air in Nagpur
- IEI brings together France, Germany, Belgium, Denmark, Spain, Estonia, the Netherlands, Portugal and the United Kingdom.
- Decided to launch the Franco-German military satellite CSO3 on Ariane 6
- France and Germany decided to develop, together, the combat aircraft of the future

It is revealed from the above tweets that she tweets on the relations of France and other countries. She came to India and visited Nagpur (Maharashtra) for the inauguration of a factory of Reliance Group.

Table 18: Russian MOD (SergeyShoygu) Twitter data report

Profile Name: Russian MOD (Sergey Shoygu)
Total tweets: 33K

Sr. No.	*Contents of tweet*	*Date of Tweet*	*Likes*	*Retweets*	*Reply Received*
1	On the statement of NATO representative about the alleged withdrawal of a significant number of Russian troops from the territory of Ukraine	9/24/2014	4	50	4
2	**#Коллегия#Минобороны** will develop cooperation with the armed forces of China and India, and individual countries of the U.-V. Asia and the Arab world	12/19/2014	8	2	2
3	С.**#Шойгу** today military and military-technical cooperation between Russia and China acquires special importance	11/18/2014	4	41	4
4	С.**#Шойгу**: "Strengthening and expanding ties with China is Russia's absolute priority"	11/18/2014	20	80	3
5	The head **#Минобороны** of the **S.#Шойгу** proposed to open a Russian military clinic in Beijing and Chinese-in Moscow.	11/17/2014	10	35	2
6	Russian and Indian servicemen exchanged experience in destroying bandit formations http://function.mil.ru/news_page/country/more.htm?id=11990322@egNews...	10/1/2014	5	25	1
7	Deputy Ministers of Defense of Russia and Greece discussed issues of international military cooperation #Àíòîíîâ #Èñèõîñ in Moscow	3/19/2015	8	49	1

Sr. No.	*Contents of tweet*	*Date of Tweet*	*Likes*	*Retweets*	*Reply Received*
8	**#Антонов:** Despite the difficult period of the Russian-American relations, the contract is **#CHB3** successfully functioning, the problem on it does not arise	3/5/2015	4	15	0
9	It is -**#Антонов#MCIS** expected to address the situation in Afghanistan, the activities of Terroristich. Organisations, projects Betweinnar. Fight Terror	3/5/2015	3	23	1
10	**#Шойгу**: "The cooperation between Russia and Egypt in the military-technical field has a long history and began in 1955."	3/4/2015	8	28	0
11	**#Shoigu#Modi#MoD#India#Russia** The Russian Ministry of Defence is ready to resume training Indian specialists	1/21/2015	32	62	5
12	Chief of the Armed forces of Malaysia Zulkifli **#Зин**: **#АРМИЯ2015** The visit opened my eyes to the scale and possibilities of the Russian mic	6/18/2015	6	45	1
13	**#Армия2015** Pakistani army commander Rachel **#Шариф**: "We believe that Russian tankers are the best in the world"	6/17/2015	7	29	4
14	**#Армия#Шойгу**: Joint efforts of Russia and Kyrgyzstan will create reliable defensive potential of security of our States	6/16/2015	6	19	0
15	**#Армия2015#Шойгу**: Cooperation with Kyrgyzstan is a factor of stability in the Central Asian region	6/16/2015	10	23	0
16	The Chinese specialists of traditional medicine have familiarized the doctor. Composition of the clinic of the Vishnevsky ZWCG with methods, to-e have high level of trust in China	6/9/2015	3	07	2
17	**#Антонов**: The return to Europe of medium- and shorter-range American missiles would have a dramatic negative impact on global security	6/9/2015	4	11	0
18	Russian paratroopers and special forces of the National Guard of Kyrgyzstan oppose conditional terrorists in the Tien-Shan **#ВДВ** Mountains	6/4/2015	6	27	0
19	**#Шойгу**: In the conditions of withdrawal of the international forces from Afghanistan, our aircraft should be ready for any	6/4/2015	3	18	1

Sr. No.	Contents of tweet	Date of Tweet	Likes	Retweets	Reply Received
	development of the situation, even to the most unfavorable				
20	From February 2015 to Time two squads **#ТОФ** of ships perform combat service tasks in the Pacific and Indian Oceans	5/31/2015	11	31	0
21	**#МорскоеВзаимодействие2015** Group of warships of Russia and China has worked anti-piracy actions in the Mediterranean Sea	5/20/2015	19	88	4
22	A detachment of Russian and Chinese warships went from Novorossiysk to the joint teaching in the Mediterranean Sea	5/12/2015	19	63	2
23	**#Шойгу**: We support the words of the President of China Xi Jinping that the Russian and Chinese peoples shoulder to shoulder will protect peace on the planet	5/10/2015	26	121	20
24	**#Росси** said that Argentina appreciates relations with Russia, and noted the intensity of cooperation, including in BRICS	4/22/2015	2	22	0
25	**#MCIS2015#Шойгу**: Russia and Indonesia are associated with long years of cooperation, and relations are built on the principles of mutual respect.	4/15/2015	4	14	0
26	**#MCIS2015#Шойгу**: Intensification of Russian-Korean contacts will serve to strengthen peace and security in Asia	4/15/2015	9	25	2
27	**#Антонов**: We consider it counter-productive to minimize the interaction between the United States and NATO and Russia on Afghanistan under the pretext of the situation in south-east Ukraine	4/11/2015	5	30	0
28	**#Центр2015**: Scouts of Russia & Kazakhstan conducted joint anti-terrorist operation http://on.fb.me/1YmEDHq	9/18/2015	8	29	3
29	#سوريا Information Bulletin of the Centre for Russian reconciliation between the warring parties and monitoring of refugee movements in the Syrian Arab Republic (22 January 2019) https://s.mil.ru/2Wbya6q	1/21/2019	2	02	0
30	**#SYRIA** Supported by Russian aviation, Syrian Democratic Army are conducting offensive on **#Raqqah**, ISIS capital	12/28/2015	20	48	2
31	**#SYRIA#Dronov**: Except for experts from	12/18/2015	16	26	2

Sr. No.	*Contents of tweet*	*Date of Tweet*	*Likes*	*Retweets*	*Reply Received*
	#China and **#UK**, other specialists declined participation in the investigation concerning **#Su24**				
32	**#SYRIA** Near Rashidiya-Ghaubia (**#Hasakah**), column of 15 trucks transporting oil extracted in terrorist-controlled territories was destroyed	12/16/2015	30	47	4
33	**#Rudskoy** For the last several weeks, intensiveness of strikes against **#ISIS** and other terrorist groupings in **#SIRYA** has increased	12/15/2015	16	18	1
34	**#Gerasimov:** Refugees, terrorist attacks in France and onboard rus airliner make it clear: terrorism is to be fought at "distant approaches"	12/14/2015	12	15	0
35	**#SYRIA** Rus MoD comments on statements of US State Department & Department of Defense about oil trafficking in Syria http://on.fb.me/21EXS0v	12/5/2015	48	125	2
36	#SYRIA Last week, Russian aviation destroyed 12 oil transfer stations, 8 oil fields and oil-and-gas complexes, more than 170 oil trucks	12/4/2015	55	111	4
37	**#СИРИЯ** terrorists operating in the area of rescue pilot Su-24m, completely destroyed by the massive fire of VKS RF and systems of the armed forces of Syria	11/26/2015	122	266	21
38	**#СИРИЯ** for two days aircraft of the Russian air group in Syria carried out 85 combat missions to 277 terrorist objects	11/11/2015	37	78	3
39	For assistance in the delivery of luggage departing from the resorts of Egypt Citizens, the Ministry of Defence of the Russian Federation is engaged in military-TRANSP. Aviation	11/7/2015	21	52	4
40	**#Kartapolov**: Russian and US military depts to sign documents on flight safety in the sky of **#Syria** soon. All technical issues are agreed upon	10/16/2015	12	44	3
41	**#SYRIA** Near Bayt-Mnayna (**#Lattakia**) a command centre of one of the **#ISIS** terrorist groups was engaged by pinpoint attack of a **#Su24** bomber	10/5/2015	16	35	0
	Total		661	1898	108

Source: https://twitter.com/mod_russia (Accessed on 1st Feb 2019)

Sergey Kuzhugetovich Shoygu is a Russian politician and General of the Army who has served as Minister of Defense of the Russian Federation and as Chairman of the Council of Ministers of Defense of the CIS since 2012. He made 33K total tweets out of which we found 41 tweets related to topic foreign policy and foreign relations. The period of his tweets is 2014 to 2019. He received 661 likes to his tweets made during the period and he made 1898 retweets on various topics. He received 108 replies from his followers during the period as mentioned in analysis. While analyzing his tweets on foreign policy and related topic we found the following areas on which he tweeted. These areas are listed below:

- Withdrawal of a significant number of Russian troops from the territory of Ukraine
- Develop cooperation with the armed forces of China and India
- Military-technical cooperation between Russia and China
- Proposed to open a Russian military clinic in Beijing and Chinese-in Moscow
- Russia and Indonesia are associated with long years of cooperation, and relations
- Argentina appreciates relations with Russia, and noted the intensity of cooperation, including in BRICS
- Rus MoD comments on statements of US State Department & Department of Defense
- Ministry of Defence of the Russian Federation is engaged in military-TRANSP. Aviation
- Russian and US military depts to sign documents on flight safety in the sky of **#Syria** soon
- **ISIS** terrorist groups was engaged by pinpoint attack of a **#Su24** bomber
- Scouts of Russia and Kazakhstan conducted joint anti-terrorist operation
- Russian aviation, Syrian Democratic Army are conducting offensive on **#Raqqah**, ISIS capital

It is revealed from the above areas that Shoygu has tweeted on various topics which are of interest to Russia and would like to develop relations with other Asian countries.

CHAPTER IX

Conclusion

9.1 Introduction

Since 2004, there has been a widespread growth of the social media. Earlier, Facebook was the top ranked social networking site with around one million users. Slowly, the network began to enlarge and today it has more than around one billion registered users. Through the course of the research it has been proven substantially that social media has an impact and influence on all spheres of life. This includes its impact on foreign policy making in India and across the world. Social media has emerged as the top tool for gathering information and for disseminating information, not just by common citizens but also used by government agents and officials.

The reason why social media has been used so extensively is its power of reach and time. It can spread information at the spur of the moment and among thousands of people at the same time. Traditional forms of media like the television or the newspaper, did not have such a huge impact on normal life like social media does. The Pew Research Center released the Social Media Update of 2014 in January 2015 which stated that around 71 per cent of the Internet users in the US are on Facebook. The Twitter audience rose by 27.7 per cent from 2013 to 2014. India has recorded the highest social networking growth of around 37.4 per cent in 2013. With a rapid expansion of social networking sites, India is expected to be the largest Facebook population country in 2016. Social media unites millions of people across the globe on a single platform.

Apart from unity, the social media is also used by the politicians for the purpose of campaign during election. Likewise, it provides many other advantages. But there are two sides of a coin. These two sides are discussed in detail in this chapter.

9.2 CONCLUSION

9.2.1 The impact of social media on security threats – The social media also possess a serious threats to the national security of a nation. Details of these threats are discussed pointwise in the following paragraphs.

9.2.2 Used by terrorists – Due to the easy availability and widespread use of social media, most of the terrorists use this medium to achieve their goals. Around 90 per cent of the organized terrorism on the Internet takes place through the social media. The terrorist groups spread their messages through the sites like You Tube, Twitter or Facebook and recruit people via them. For example, the terrorist group of the ISIS spreads their messages and activities through the social media.

9.2.3 International users – The other national and international users such as the political parties, NGO's, hackers pose a serious threat using the social media. For example, during the civil turmoil in the Arab Spring Uprising, the various governments were threatened through the social media.

9.2.4 Communal Violence – With the help of social media, people have started attacking each other's religion on this platform by twitter. Sensitive tweets regarding religion are becoming a common phenomenon. Circulation of certain pictures and videos through social media also creates a panic situation among the masses. This is a threat to the internal security of the nation as it disturbs the communal harmony and increase tension of the existing government and public also.

9.2.5 Threat to internal security – With the advent of social media, issues like economics, media and science are open to all. Uploading information related to these fields on the social networking sites can be a threat to the internal security.

9.2.6 Revolution – Some countries in the world feel threatened by the fact that social media can bring the people together and thus, create a revolution. This in turn can cause political instability.

9.3 Social Networking Sites: Examples of Banning

The Social Networking Sites are banned in few counties, either wholly or partially. It is simply a kind of censorship which is taking place around the globe.

North Korea – The networking sites are blocked in this country since the advent of Internet in order to prevent the access to any communication which has not been provided by the government.

Iran – The social networking sites are blocked in Iran since 2009 after the Presidential elections. After the election of Iranian President Hasan Rouhani, the social media has played an important role in his administration's media scheme.

China – China is the most common country known for banning the social media. After the protests by Uighurs (Muslim ethnic minority of China) turned into the deadly riots, the social media started to see its extinction in the country.

Pakistan – It has blocked the You Tube since 2002, when the trailer of a controversial film appeared on the site. The name of the film was "The innocence of Muslims".

Turkey – Twitter was banned in Turkey for two weeks in 2014 and You Tube is banned since March 2014. These sites were banned to decrease the portrayal of government corruption. There were certain evidences related to the corruption of government after the 2014 election.

However, the question is if its impact has been constructive or destructive to any country. Through the course of the research we have seen how social media has been used constructively by two nations to start a dialogue and to strengthen ties, it has been used by security forces to improve security ties and spread information about hazards. It had also been used by the common man to gather strength and raise their voice for and against the government if required. However, apart from these qualities of goodness, social media also has some negative impact on national security. Like leakage of crucial information or state secrets and usage of social media by non-state actors and organizations for recruitment of radicals and spreading terrorism. It has emerged as a threat to internal security in India because of its viral posts which can impact any situation by making a region volatile and sparking tension in the area. We have discussed such examples throughout the course of the research. A small tweet or one WhatsApp forward can entirely inflate a situation and cause a law and order problem. However, we need to note that social media is still a young tool. It is still growing and in its nascent stage and rules for it are still being developed or constructed. We have to still harness the full potential of social media and how it can be used by the government for better good. Examples of the start of this revolution can be the use of social media by the government over the last few years and its effort to reach the common man. Apart from being potential threat tools, Social Media can represent an effective opportunity to preserve national security and/or reach the strategic interests of a state if used properly by civil institutions and, in particular, by security services and/or information security services.

A continuous and deep monitoring of these media can be carried out as a warning tool in case of present and future threats to national security, since the use of Social Media by criminal organizations, terrorist groups, adversary states and other competitors is more and more increasing. For this reason a continuous analysis of Social Media by Intelligence can serve as: early warning: monitoring Social Media in order to recognize the first sign of an hostile or potentially dangerous activity for a state's security (i.e. collecting and analysing messages by opposing movements sent via social network sites for the organization of a violent protest can be useful in order to forestall a rebellion or to mitigate its negative consequences; studying the information shared by crackers in specialized blogs in order to launch an information attack to a critical infrastructure can concur in adopting suitable protection counter-measures; tracking teaching videos for military recruitment, spread via YouTube by an Al-Qaedist group can help find the users who make use of them, understand the attack methods and techniques and devise effective methods to react and counter the terrorist threat; the continuous control of a Facebook profile updates and a careful exam of the photos published on that very profile can allow to trace the movements and the activities of the members of a criminal group and mapping their connections, etc.

It can also act as a strategic warning and horizon scanning aimed at outlining the long-and medium-term trend of threats, at identifying the orientation of the opposing groups and forecasting their choices (i.e. collecting signs of protest from young people through the monitoring of the principal social networking sites can help forecast and maybe nip in the bud a dissent which could change into an organized protest movement or even in a revolutionary group; analyzing the discussions on blogs specialized in international politics and strategic studies (often held by the leading experts or by the representatives of the major think tanks)can be useful to understand the possible long-term evolutions of foreign policy and of the strategic thinking of a state's leadership; studying the discussions of blogs specialized in science and technology can help measure the possible long-term development of scientific and technological expertise in a certain place; mapping the relational networks developed on Social Media by members of subversive groups and analysing their evolution can allow to forecast the possible development of the group itself, etc.

Using Social Media to obtain and analyse data for info-prevision and tactic-strategic warning purposes is of great interest to the US DoD, too, which is developing a specific programme called "Social Media in Strategic Communication" (SMISC) through DARPA, with the aim of monitoring such media so as to obtain a better knowledge of the environment some units deployed abroad work into, and collect useful information to support military missions. Therefore, using Social Media this way can help the commanders of the US deployed locations to better understand the socio-politic, religious, economic and cultural characteristics of the area they work in and detect emerging threats. Even in our country, Broadcast Engineering Consultants India Limited, a Government of India enterprise under the Ministry of Information and Broadcasting has invited bids for controlling the 'Social Media Communication Hub'.

9.4 What Exactly is the 'Social Media Communication Hub'?

It is the creation of a social media monitoring system which can "*...collect Digital media chatter from all Core Social Media Platforms as well as digital platforms like news, blogs and forums....*" It is expected to 'listen and respond' to social media websites such as Twitter, YouTube, Instagram, Facebook, etc. The tool is also expected to have enough infiltration into the internet and social media so that it can analyse the trends which emerge and 'gauge the sentiments among the netizens'. The bid also states, "...*the tool should have the capacity to provide inputs to the Ministry on how to improve the reach of various social media campaigns, how to make a particular topic trending and for the overall general improvement of social media campaigns.*"

Based on whatever has been written on the tender, the Indian government seems to be looking at a technology which can harvest online information available on social media which can help them in pursuing their own interests. Recently, both the Bharatiya Janata Party and the Indian National Congress came under a barrage of criticism for allegedly using the services of Cambridge Analytica, a voter-profiling enterprise which unlawfully harvested the information of over 50 million users in the USA for helping its clients win elections in 2014. What Cambridge Analytica largely engages in is the analysis of voter preferences and reaching out to them through personalised messages to make sure that they are likelier to vote for their clients. If the government is able to harness such valuable data from social media through such a tool, the fear of it misusing it for various purposes, including electoral, is always omnipresent.

The tool is also expected to make some 'predictive analysis' such as:

1. *"How nationalistic feelings could be inculcated in the masses."*

The government has been both praised and criticized from various quarters for being fiercely nationalistic in rhetoric. Many experts point out that the central government's brand of nationalism is very Hindu-centric and that it creates a feeling of alienation amongst people belonging to minority religious communities, especially the Muslims.

2. *"How could the media blitzkrieg of 'India's adversaries' be predicted and replied/neutralized."*

It is not very clear based on the tender who 'India's adversaries' here are. Is it referring to foreign media which may be critical of something the government may not agree with? or Is it a reference to the Indian media? Ever since the current dispensation came to power, many media houses have been labelled as 'anti-national' on social media for having targeted the government at the Centre negatively. or Could it be referring to both?

3. *"How the social media and internet news/discussions could be given a positive slant for India."*
What does it mean by a 'positive slant for India'? It is not particularly very clear. However, based on whatever is written in the tender which has been floated it doesn't just seem to be targeting the social media communication of Indians or the Indian media. It also seems to aim to be attempting to put its fingerprints in the global arena for an image-building exercise.

9.5 KEEPING A CHECK ON HAPPENINGS ABROAD

The 'predictive analysis' of the tool should also be able to be able to gauge the following related to happenings abroad:

1. *"What would be the headlines and breaking news of various channels and newspapers across the globe."*
The bid also states that all this could be done with 'knowledge about their leanings, business deals, investors, their country policies, sentiment of their population, etc'. The examples of media houses given are New York Times, The Economist and The Times.

2. *"What would be the global perception due to such headlines and breaking news."*
Interestingly, The New York Times and The Economist have been extremely critical of the Narendra Modi government. The New York Times editorials have been particularly critical of the government at the Centre. A New York Times editorial in April 2018 titled 'Modi's Long Silence as Women in India Are Attacked', attacked Prime Minister Narendra Modi on his silence on the rape and murder of 8-year-old Bakarwal Muslim girl. The girl was abducted, gang-rape and murdered in the month of January in Kathua, Jammu. Influential members of the Bharatiya Janata Party had come out in support of the accused by demanding their release. After much public outrage and media coverage

in the month of April, Narendra Modi finally said, *"I want to assure the country that no culprit will be spared, complete justice will be done. Our daughters will definitely get justice."*In another editorial by the New York Times on March 23, 2017, titled 'Mr. Modi's Perilous Embrace of Hindu Extremists' it had criticized the elevation of Hindutva hardliner Yogi Adityanath to the chief minister of Uttar Pradesh in the same month. The editorial ended with the line, *"The move is a shocking rebuke to religious minorities, and a sign that cold political calculations ahead of national elections in 2019 have led to Mr. Modi's Bharatiya Janata Party to believe that nothing stands in the way of realizing its long-held dream of transforming a secular republic into the Hindu state."*

There have other editorials criticizing the Narendra Modi government at the Centre in The New York Times as well. In an article in The Economist published on June 24, 2017, titled 'India's prime minister is not as much of a reformer as he seems', it had criticized both 'demonetization' and the Goods and Services Tax (GST), along with the Hindu nationalism that Narendra Modi has been promoting. In another article in The Economist titled 'India's prime minister focuses too much on appearances' it had again been very critical of both demonetization and GST, criticized the BJP's Hindutva agenda of the Uttar Pradesh government, amongst other things. It must also be kept in mind that Narendra Modi has a huge fan following amongst the non-resident Indian community and the people of Indian origin residing in the United State of America, Canada, Australia, United Arab Emirates, etc. Every time he visits a foreign country, Prime Minister Narendra Modi ends up addressing large crowds comprising of people belonging to the Indian diaspora. When he had addressed the Indian community at the Madison Square Garden in New York in September 2014, around 19,000 people had turned up to cheer for him. Narendra Modi has successfully drawn large crowds when he has visited countries like the United Kingdom, Canada, United Arab Emirates, etc. ever since he became India's Prime Minister.

9.6 The Tool Should Be Able to Identify 'Fake News'

The tool is also expected to identify 'fake news', with a particular focus on such conversations on social media and 'specialized' websites. The

Narendra Modi government has also been accused by both opposition and various journalists of having muzzled press freedom ever since it came to power in May 2014. India's current ranking in the World Press Freedom Index is 138. Last week, a sting operation conducted by media website called Cobra post revealed that media managers of organizations such as the Times of India, Hindustan Times, Zee News, India Today, etc. were compromised as they were willing to showcase Hindutva advertorials in the run-up to the 2019 Lok Sabha elections for large sums of money. In April 2018, the Union Ministry of information and broadcasting had announced that the journalists guilty of having broadcasted or written 'fake news' would either lose their accreditation with the Press Information Bureau either permanently or have it suspended temporarily. There was a lot of backlash against this on social media. The very next day the move was withdrawn after orders from the Prime Minister's Office. It is not entirely clear how the 'social media communication hub' will be tracking users' online communication and how it is intended to be utilized by the Government of India. However, based on whatever is written in the tender inviting proposals for the job, it does seem a bit alarming. Prime Minister Narendra Modi said on Wednesday that social media has become a powerful instrument of democracy and it can be used as a "weapon" for good governance. On 8th April, just three days before the start of Lok Sabha elections, the Bharatiya Janata Party's (BJP's) YouTube channel uploaded a video showing youngsters gyrating to a rap song on why Modi deserves the first vote of young Indians. The video, which went viral, talked about key government schemes including Ujjwala Yojana, Digital India and Skill India. What BJP did here was to speak to the target audience in their own language, a clever marketing tactic. Understanding the power of social media platforms, the party created customized and relatable campaigns such as 'Main Bhi Chowkidar', 'My First Vote for Modi' and 'Modi Hai Toh Mumkin Hai' for various social cohorts. Smart personalized content across formats such as short videos, memes and GIFs engaged voters across digital and social media platforms during the elections. The internet population of the country grew by 108 per cent from 250 million in 2014 when the last general elections were held, to 520 million this year making digital platforms an even stronger tool to woo voters with. The usage of social media platforms grew by 155 per cent during this period. The BJP outdid Congress not just in the brute power of media money by spending over Rs 20 crore on digital platforms but also the sheer number of followers it garnered across platforms such as Facebook, Instagram, Twitter and YouTube. Add to that a NaMo app and an army of digital evangelists who individually promoted BJP's content. According to research by digital marketing agency Ad Lift, the BJP has 142 million followers across both Modi and party social media handles, compared with the Congress and Rahul Gandhi's with 23 million digital followers. On Twitter, the BJP trended almost every day with campaigns targeting the youth.

The party used Facebook to create videos which were shareable. Facebook and Google also came in handy to increase interactions with students, corporate India, party workers and other beneficiaries through live videos. WhatsApp was used to not only circulate BJP content but, through lakhs of WhatsApp groups, convert non-BJP votes into those for the BJP. Clever use of influencers (both social media as well as Bollywood stars) over key social media platforms helped influence first-time voters as well as humanize Brand Modi. Videos were the go-to choice for both the BJP and rival Congress. Indians are obsessed with online videos, with average viewings expected to touch 67 minutes per day by 2019-end, according to a report by media agency Zenith. **'Pun kibaat'**, a small format video promoted by the Congress, took apart Modi's various claims in a sarcastic manner.

Adding to the fun quotient were hilarious shareable memes with references to anything which was trending on the internet such as the Game of Thrones or 'How's the Josh' dialogue from the war film Uri. The BJP mostly highlighted the work that its government did. Beginning from an early focus on the neighborhood and the greater developing world over the last decade and more, India's expanding world vision and great power ambitions, emanating from rapid economic growth, instilled a new-found confidence visible in its communication with the global community. The expanded confident outreach has been facilitated by the new media. India's Ministry of External Affairs (MEA) begun to disseminate information through its website launched in 2003. A few years later in 2009,

Shashi Tharoor, the then Minister of State for External Affairs engaged in social networking for communicating directly with the people. This was remarkable given that computers in government offices were still not allowed to access social media. Soon enough, the @Indian Diplomacy Twitter handle was established, followed by a Facebook Page, a YouTube channel, and a BlogSpot page under the same moniker. On 20 October 2010, India's public diplomacy website went live utilizing the full range of Web 2.0 tools thereby formally launching India's digital diplomacy.

The Twitter handle @Indian Diplomacy and its use of the hashtag '#digital diplomacy' for official engagement not only disseminates information on Indian culture for the global audience but is also a global hashtag being used by other foreign governments and international agencies. Two other Twitter handles of the MEA—@MEAIndia and @SushamaSwaraj—apart from assisting distressed Indian citizens abroad—provides an opportunity to the Indian 'citizens to voice how they believe India should present itself to the world'. The then Indian Ambassador to the US, Nirupama Rao used Twitter to communicate support for India's proposal for a 500 MW cross border transmission facility to Pakistan. While the communication attracted criticism from unhappy netizens over India's 'generous' overture towards its estranged neighbor despite the country's inability to overcome domestic electricity supply deficits, Rao tweeted fast to quell such fears.

The incident is an example of senior Indian diplomats utilizing the reach of social media in purposeful foreign policy communication. The Pakistani media responded positively by extensively covering Rao's tweets. The episode personifies the ability of social media to blur borders as mentioned earlier. Despite not being targeted specifically towards a foreign audience, the communication extended its influence to both domestic and external audiences and drew in involved actors while demonstrating diplomatic willingness to 'listen'—fundamental for dialogues 'deserving special status as the starting point for public diplomacy'. The 'listening' character, however, is not integral to all diplomatic communication by India. For instance, Modi's tweets publicizing his bold economic initiatives like demonetization of the Indian currency in 2016 was essentially criticized for being one-way public address with little effort to 'listen' to the difficulties encountered by the Indian people during this state action (Vishnu 2017).

Modi's observation that 'the world of social media has played a key role in democratizing our discourse and giving a platform to millions of people around the world to express their views and showcase their creativity' underscore not just the importance of engaging global and local audiences through social media, but also the need for strategizing such engagement. In a country that has the world's largest young population and where the number of internet users is expected to rise to 720 million by 2020. Indeed, it is hardly surprising that the current aggressive use of social media, for conveying the content and scope of government initiatives to the public, have been without precedence. Such use has been led by Prime Minister Modi himself through tweets reflecting the urge to communicate deep, strong and wide with constituencies:

9.7 Social Media and its Impact on Foreign Relations

Modi's unorthodox engagement tactics through social media platforms has also made international headlines. His use of the Weibo platform before visiting China in 2015, drew widespread attention, evident from his first post on Weibo – 'Hello China! Looking forward to interacting with Chinese friends through Weibo' being heavily forwarded and commented upon by Weibo users. His tweet on the eve of his arrival in Japan also elicited similar enthusiastic response.

These messages could have been part of the push for his Act East policy targeting the region. But they also exposed the other side of social media-enabled direct communication where people are hardly restricted in voicing opinions of leaders, countries and societies. Chinese micro bloggers took the opportunity to draw Modi's attention to the plight of Indian women with one Chinese netizen posting: 'I suggest improving the social status of Indian women and protecting the safety of females! Or we foreign women will not dare travel to India'; the post, while attracting considerable attention underlined challenges that social-media active leaders like Modi can hardly avoid in their attempt to influence perceptions through digital diplomacy. The example underscores an interesting aspect of interaction through social media on image-building: *the risk of pushing particular agendas for specific purposes turning counterproductive*. In this regard, it is not clear to what extent Modi's FB and Twitter posts on his foreign visits and other achievements have actually achieved in terms of better 'perception' of India.

While scholars argue 'Prime Minister Modi's charismatic interaction with world leaders' now represent 'a strategic advantage in the soft power for India in the region', India's absence from *The Soft Power 30*, an index ranking 30 countries in terms of soft power resources, underlines 'India evidently does not yet benefit as much from international awareness, positive associations, or investments in cultural diplomacy as many other countries. Unorthodox engagement tactics by Modi also include 'selfie' diplomacy that has become an integral part of his overseas travels.

Again, much like his FB and Twitter posts, while breaking perception stereotypes and casting the Prime Minister in a charming and engaging light, it is not clear how selfie diplomacy has changed perceptions about India as a nation. It's interesting to note the contrasts between perceptions of Modi and India in this regard: *The Soft Power 30* report marks India's best performing area in the Digital sub-index and highlights the 'Indian Prime Minister Modi's unrivalled skills in digital diplomacy' (*The Soft Power 30* 2018).

The recognition of Modi as a champion of digital diplomacy and India's capacities as a digital nation, is in sharp contrast to its absence from the list of most successful soft power nations in the world. Communication aimed at building of *Brand Modi* and *Brand India* is aimed at the diaspora as one of its major target groups. Modi's Tweets like: 'Our diaspora are our "Rashtradoots". We are immensely proud of their accomplishments and their passion towards India & India's progress' in 2017 underscore the priority. Engaging the diaspora has been a sustained part of Modi's foreign policy communication on the firm belief that 'well-structured diaspora bonds would directly finance key development priorities. And that would give everyone in the diaspora, not just its entrepreneurs and its financiers, the opportunity to translate their long-distance patriotism into tangible economic gain and share in India's growth story, as Modi often encourages them to do'. Initiatives like e-visas and MADAD meaning 'help' for addressing grievances of the overseas Indians online are specific to the diaspora.

In this regard, however, styles of engagement between leaders have shown contrasts. Sushama Swaraj, the foreign Minister, has been visibly dialogue-oriented in engagement: her immediate response to a tweet plea by a Yemeni woman with an 8-month old son married to an Indian in April 2015 is perhaps the best example of digital diplomacy shifting from monologue to dialogue. The *Foreign Policy* magazine acclaimed the Minister 'for fashioning a novel brand of Twitter diplomacy' and included her in the list of 100 Global Thinkers.

Swaraj's social media engagement certainly appears more interactive and distinct from Modi's. This could, however, be due to the nature of her portfolio given that the foreign ministry has to focus on addressing grievances as part of its responsibilities, which several other Ministries and Ministers, including the Prime Minister need not.

In conclusion our findings have been very clear, with over 2 billion users on Facebook, 328 million on Twitter and many other platforms, the influence of social media cannot be denied. Social media is in fact used by the public to put across their views to the government nowadays and the government also listens to them through the media. The study of social media and its uses at various levels is invaluable for political activism. It can help diffuse ideas and information easily across the globe. In our survey, we found that the tool which is

mostly used on social media to influence foreign policy is Twitter and Facebook, wherein the Ministry of External Affairs has also increased its activity by 400 per cent.

The PM's visit to foreign nations is covered extensively on these mediums as they are the only source of factual and correct information about the meetings between the world leaders. The spokespersons account is the constant source of news and updates for the people of the country. Social media, hence, does have the power to influence policy decisions and sway the government opinion. However, through our survey we have found that the influence is contingent on certain conditions. As there are various challenges on foreign policy reporting like lack of understanding of subject by the reporter, disclosure of information by the ministry, etc.

Through our survey we found that 29 per cent users use social media for their personal use while 28 per cent use it as students. YouTube was found to be the most used with 34 per cent saying yes to our survey and then came in Facebook with 31 per cent users. Also, around 34 per cent of our respondents used social media to obtain knowledge and information, which is a big win for national security of our country.

Among others, 23 per cent used for personal work, 17 per cent for upkeep of information and knowledge and 15 per cent for personal study. In fact through our survey, we found that 11 per cent or 112 respondents used social media because they were interested in foreign policy news. Through our survey, it also became clear that at least 82 respondents or 16.97 per cent users used social media to express their views on foreign policy. In fact, 22 respondents visited the official MEA website daily, 52 users visited the site monthly and 137 people visited the website occasionally to get information about foreign policies and its updates.

Another important conclusion which was drawn after our survey was that at least 55 per cent or 266 respondents felt that social media incidents can change or affect policies of the government. In fact 68 per cent users said they have witnessed slight changes in policies of the government after a social media incident and 3 per cent said they witnessed complete change in the policy. The respondents even gave examples to support their claim which has been mentioned in our findings. This goes on to show how much impact social media has on people and how people perceive social media as a game changer in policy making. In our survey, 379 respondents or 78 per cent people said that social media is very important for foreign policy making. At least 59 per cent said that social media also has positive impact on national security of the country.

We can draw a conclusion that people in India also think that social media is playing a greater role in policy making like in the P5 or world's top five countries. In our survey, 294 respondents or 61 per cent people said that P5 countries use social media for their governments benefit and even in India our respondents agreed that the government uses social media for policy making. 45 per cent of our respondents said that social media influences foreign policy directly. To gauge the interest of the respondents on social media and foreign policy, we concluded that 25 per cent people used social media daily to update themselves only about foreign policies on social media while 43 per cent updated themselves occasionally on social media if they wanted to know about foreign policy.

We conclude from the results of our research and survey that people use social media as a tool which has an immense impact on policy making. People believe that social media is a powerful tool which can influence foreign policies and also make the government change its policies.

9.8 RECOMMENDATIONS

In Indian situation, we do not have fully control over the use of social media applications by the people of India because our country is democratic country. Few recommendations are made here based on the information collected from the stakeholders. The details of the recommendations are discussed in detail in the conclusion to avoid duplications.

1. A continuous and deep monitoring of these social media applications can be carried out as a warning tool in case of present and future threats to national security, since these tools are used by criminal organizations, terrorist groups and adversary states and other competitors is more and more in use and increasing rigorously.
2. Continuous analysis of Social Media information by Intelligence can serve as early warning for state and central government authorities. Hence it is recommended to develop such mechanism to analyse each information which is upload on social media.
3. It is recommended that **Social Media Hub** may be created to each state in India with filtaration of all messages of all social media technological tools, such as WhatsApp, YouTube, Twitter , Instagram etc. The mechanism should be developed and monitored by independent agency. And this agency should made report to State government to their respective state if anything happened wrong related to the security aspect of the state and particularly country, it should be immediately reported to Central Government to take immediate action.

4. It is also recommended to the Central Government of India to develop a tool and mechanism to identify fake news which appears in social media applications and tools and other media. Majority of the fake videos are uploaded by public or unknown persons who has created fake account on YouTube which is most powerful and preferred social media tools by public.
5. By using social media to obtain data and analyse information for info-prevision and tactic-strategic warning purposes is a great help and interest to the US DoD to develop a specific programme called "Social Media in Strategic Communication (SMISC) through DARPA with the aim of monitoring such media to obtain better knowledge of the situation and environment, some units deployed abroad to work into and collect information to support missions of the Military. On the basis of this Indian government also establish such programme "India SMISC" (Indian Social Media Strategic Communication).
6. It is suggested that mechanism should be develop to keep track and check on happenings abroad. This will help to our intelligence agencies to keep track on such incidents happens abroad and which are related to our country's security.
7. It is also recommended that a separate agency is to be established to collect information and public opinions on India's foreign policy from social media and provide such information to Policy makers of the Indian government which helps to frame foreign policy of India.

APPENDIX I

Questionnaires

Personal Information

Name : ______________________________

Designation : ______________________________

Qualifications : ______________________________

Working experience : ______________________________

Email ID : ______________________________

Contact No. : ______________________________

1. Do you use social media networking? Yes or No
If yes, at what levels?

a) personal
b) student
c) research-scholar
d) teacher
e) media personnel
f) political purpose
g) government official
h) in general

2. Do you use any of the following social media tools?
(Twitter, Facebook, My Space, Ning, Blog, LinkedIn, Flickr, Youtube, Slideshare, Meebo, Snapchat, etc.)

If yes, please specify

3. For what purpose are you using the above social media tools ?
   a) personal
   b) to obtain knowledge and information in various subject areas
   c) to upkeep the information and knowledge
   d) personal study and research
   e) personal interest in India's Foreign Policy

4. Do you use social media tools for contributing your views regarding various nationwide problems or policy making of the government? Yes or No

   If yes, please specify the areas in which you contribute.

5. Have you expressed your views on India's Foreign Policy through social media tools? Yes or No

   If yes, please clarify.

6. Do you visit the website of The Ministry of External Affairs, Govt. of India, to get recent updates on India's Foreign Policy? Yes or No

   If yes, how frequently do you visit the website? Daily/ weekly/ monthly/ occasionally/never

   ____
   ____
   ____
   ____

7. Do you think that the various incidents, that happen in a country, play a decisive role in framing the Foreign Policy of the country?

   Yes or No

   If yes, could you please explain any one of the incidents / events etc., where the govt. has decided the Foreign Policy.

   ____
   ____
   ____
   ____

8. Do you think that as and when there is a change in the Central Government, there is an inevitable change in the Foreign Policy?

   a) slight changes as per situation
   b) completely changes in certain cases
   c) completely revised
   d) never changes
   e) any other: please specify

   ____
   ____
   ____
   ____

9. Do you think that the use of social media tools could influence and affect India's National Security? Yes or No

   If yes, please express your views.

   ____

10. Do you think that social media has been influenced by or has an impact on the India's National Security and India's Foreign Policy. Yes or No
If yes, please give details.

11. Do you think that the present government is more active on social media as compared to the previous government? Yes or No
If yes, please specify the areas in which the present government is active.

12. Do you think that powerful nations like the U.S., UK, China, Russia, France, etc, are active on social media to influence the Foreign Policies? Yes or No

13. In spite of China playing an important role in International power politics, do you think that it is not actively involved on social media ? Yes or No
If yes, please support your answer.

14. "Do you agree, that strategic think tanks influence Foreign Policies through social media?"
Agree or Disagree
If agree, please give your views on the above statement.

15. Does social media reflect meaningful political competition over India's Foreign Policy? If so, what relationship can social media reveal, and what are the limitations of social media as data for the use of research scholars?

16. Do you think that social media has an impact on the Foreign Policy?
Yes or No
If you think so, please give details.

17. What is the criteria that leads editors to include items concerning war, peace or any other Foreign Policy events in the news or any media? Do journalists follow rules in making such decisions or do they act spontaneously?

18. Do you think religion, minorities, class, caste, poverty are some of the factors that affect the Foreign Policy of India? Yes or No
If yes, please give details.

19. What role do the internal security challenges in Kashmir, the North East or insurgencies like the Naxalites play in framing India's Foreign Policy? What role does social media play in it?

20. Can scholars of International relations and conflict use social media data to illuminate questions of Foreign Policy and in particular does the structure on social media reflect off-line behavior?

21. How frequently do you use social media to understand India's Foreign Policy?
    a) daily
    b) weekly
    c) monthly
    d) occasionally

22. How can social media be related with the India's National Security issues? Give your views / opinions.

23. Are you aware of Indo-US strategic partnership in the Nuclear deal ? Yes or No
Which social media tools are most effective for this strategic partnership ? Please select from the below mentioned choices / options:
a) through electronic media
b) print media
c) news channels
d) social media
e) published literature

24. Are you aware of Indo-China border dispute? Yes or No
According to you, can social media raise this issue to Policy Makers, so as to have an influence on India's Foreign Policy?

25. How were you aware of India-Pakistan conflict during Kargil War/ Parliament Attack/Mumbai Attack and other similar issues? Was it through social media? If yes, please select from below mentioned options:

a) through electronic media
b) print media
c) news channels
d) social media tools
e) published literature

____

____

____

____

Bibliography

1. Abraham, Rhea (2011), *Media and National Security*, KW Publication Pvt. Ltd, New Delhi.
2. Adan, A.M. (2017), Influence of the media on foreign policy of a state: Kenya and Britain, United States International University. Thesis Report, Degree of Master of Arts (International Relations) United States International Univerisity-Africa (2017).
3. Adan, A. M. (2017), *Influence of the Media on Foreign Policy of a State: Kenya and Britain*, United States International University.
4. Aday, S. (2017), *The US Media, Foreign Policy, and Public Support for War*, The Oxford Handbook of Political Communication.
5. Aday, S. (2017), *The US Media, Foreign Policy, and Public Support for War*, The Oxford Handbook of Political Communication.
6. Allmer, Thomas, "Critical Theory and Social Media, Between Emancipation and Commodification," Taylor & Francis: Print Publication, April, 2015; Online Publication 2015.
7. Areg Galstyan, S.M. (2017), *Inside Russia's New Foreign Policy Master Plan*, National Interest.org.
8. Barnett, S. (2016), "The tragic downfall of the British media," Foreign Policy.com, July 8, 2016, Blog, https://foreignpolicy.com/2016/07/08/the-tragic-downfall-of-british-media- tabloids-brexit
9. Barnett, S. (2016), "The tragic downfall of the British media," Foreign Policy.com.
10. Barton, William P. (1950), Indian Foreign Policy, *The Australian Quarterly*, Vol. 22, No. 4 (Dec., 1950), pp. 25-34 Published by Australian Institute of Policy and Science Stable URL: http://www.jstor.org/stable/20633300.
11. Barton, William P. (1950), Indian Foreign Policy, *The Australian Quarterly*, Vol. 22, No. 4 (Dec., 1950), pp. 25-34 Published by Australian

Institute of Policy and Science Stable URL: http://www.jstor.org/stable/20633300.

12. Baru, Sanjaya (2009), The Influence of Business and Media on Indian Foreign Policy, *India Review*, Vol. 8, No. 3, July–September, 2009, pp. 266–285.
13. Baru, Sanjaya (2009), The Influence of Business and Media on Indian Foreign Policy, *India Review*, Vol. 8, No. 3, July–September, 2009, pp. 266–285.
14. Belkin, P. (2011), France: Factors Shaping Foreign Policy, and Issues in US-French Relations. *Congressional Research Service.*
15. Bindra, Sukhwant S. (2004), Domestic milieu of India and foreign policy making process: a theoretical perspective, *The Indian Journal of Political Science*, Vol. LXV, No. 2, April-June, 2004.
16. Bindra, Sukhwant S. (2004), Domestic milieu of India and foreign policy making process: a theoretical perspective, *The Indian Journal of Political Science*, Vol. LXV, No. 2, April-June, 2004.
17. Chanan, Naveh (2002), Role of the media in foreign policy decision making: a theoretical framework, *Conflict and Communication online*, Vol. 1, No. 2, 2002, pp. 2-13.
18. Chanan, Naveh (2002), Role of the media in foreign policy decision making: a theoretical framework, *Conflict and Communication online*, Vol. 1, No. 2, 2002, pp. 2-13.
19. Chatterjee, Manas and Jacques Fontanel Ed., *War, peace and Security*, Emerald Group Publishing Limited, UK, 2008.
20. Chatterjee, Manas and Jacques Fontanel Ed., *War, peace and Security*, Emerald Group Publishing Limited, UK, 2008.
21. Chatterjee, Manjiri Miller and Kate Sullivan De Estrada (2017), Pragmatism in Indian foreign policy: how ideas constrain Modi, *International Affairs* 93: 1 (2017) 27–49, published by Oxford University Press on behalf of The Royal Institute of International Affairs.
22. Chatterjee, Manjiri Miller and Kate Sullivan De Estrada (2017), Pragmatism in Indian foreign policy: how ideas constrain Modi, *International Affairs* 93: 1 (2017), 27–49, published by Oxford University Press on behalf of The Royal Institute of International Affairs.
23. Chuanjie, Z. (2011, January), Media, Public Opinion, and China's Foreign Policy, *Carnegie- Tsinghua Center for Global Policy.*
24. Coban, F. (2016), The Role of Media in International relations, *Journal of International Relations.*
25. Coban, F. (2016), The Role of Media in International relations, *Journal of International Relations.*

26. Coombs, Timonthy W., Jesper Falkeimer, Mats Heide, Philip Young, Strategic Communication, Social Media and Denmocracy, The challenge of the digital naturals, Taylor & Francis: Print Publication, August 2015; Online Publication 2015.
27. Country Overview, The World Bank. http://www.worldban.org/en/country/india/overview (accessed on 30th December 2018)
28. Cross, Michael, Social Media Security,1st Edition, Leveraging Social Networking while Mitigating Risk. ISBN:9781597499873: Imprint: Syngress: published 15th November 2013, p. 346.
29. Cui Zhang, Charles and William Meadows (2012), International Coverage, Foreign Policy, and National Image: Exploring the Complexities of Media Coverage, Public Opinion, and Presidential Agenda. International Journal of Communication 6 (2012), 76–95 1932–8036/20120076
30. Cui Zhang, Charles and William Meadows (2012), International Coverage, Foreign Policy, and National Image: Exploring the Complexities of Media Coverage, Public Opinion, and Presidential Agenda, *International Journal of Communication* 6 (2012), 76–95 1932–8036/20120076
31. Dahibhate N.B. and Patil, S.K. Library and Information services using social media tools: need of the future, *Asia Pacific Journal of Library and Information Science*, Vol. 3, No. 2 (Jul–Dec 2013)
32. Dahibhate N.B. and Patil, S.K., Library and Information services using social media tools: need of the future, *Asia Pacific Journal of Library and Information Science*, Vol. 3, No. 2 (Jul–Dec 2013)
33. Danylyuk, O. (2018), *Total Control: Anatomy of Russian Media Influence*, International Policy Digest.
34. Dixit, J.N., Jawaharharlal Nehru: Architect of India's Foreign Policy, in Nehru Revisited, Mumbai: Nehru Centre, 2003, pp. 58-60.
35. Dixit, J.N. (2001), India's Foreign Policy and It's Neighbours: Gyan Publishing House, New Delhi, p. 21, DOI: 10.1080/17517575.2016.1245872 36. DOI: 10.1080/17517575.2016.1245872
37. Elena Labzina, M.D. (2017), *State-controlled Media and Foreign Policy*, Washington: Washington State University.
38. Fuchs, Christian (2012), "The Political Economy of Privacy on Facebook," *Television and New Media* 13(2): 139–59.
39. Fuchs, Christian (2012), "The Political Economy of Privacy on Facebook," *Television and New Media* 13(2): 139–59.
40. Grant, R. (2004), The Democratisation of Diplomacy: Negotiating with the Internet, *SSRN Electronic Journal*.

41. Griffiths, J. (2018), *Trump is right that China uses its media to influence foreign opinion, but so does Washington*, Retrieved May 21, 2019, from CNN: https://edition.cnn.com/2018/09/29/politics/china-media-influence-intl/index.html
42. Gunguli, Sumit & Manleet S. Pardeshi, "Exploring Sixty Years of india's Foreign Policy", http://www.tandfonline.com/loi/find20, accessed on 19th December, 2018
43. Hallin, D. (1986), The uncensored war: the media and Vietnam, The Open University
44. Hallin, D. (1986), The uncensored war: the media and Vietnam, The Open University.
45. Herman, E., & Chomsky, N. (1988). *Manufacturing Consent.*
46. Herman, E., & Chomsky, N. (1988). Manufacturing Consent. https://en.wikipedia.org/wiki/Russian_interference_in_the_2016_United_States_elections
47. Jayakumar, Shashi, State, Society and National Security, Challenges and Opportunities in the 21st Century; SRajaratnam School of International Studies, NTU, Singapore, June 2016,:p. 296
48. Jazeera, A. (2018), *France: Macron's new media strategy. Al Jazeera.*
49. Johnson, Thomas, A. Power, National Security, and Transformational Global Events Challenges Confronting, America, China, and Iran, Taylor & Francis Group, LLC, 2012.
50. Kantar China Social Media Impact Report 2017, https://cn- en.kantar.com/media/social/2017/kantar-china-social-media-impact-report-2017/ (accessed on 20/01/2019).
51. Kantar China Social Media Impact Report 2017 https://cn- en.kantar.com/media/social/2017/kantar-china-social-media-impact-report-2017/ (accessed on 20/01/2019).
52. Kapur, Ashok (1971), Nuclear Weapons and Indian Foreign Policy: A Perspective, *The World Today*, Vol. 27, No. 9 (Sep. 1971), pp. 379-389 Published by Royal Institute of International Affairs Stable, URL: http://www.jstor.org/stable/40394547 (accessed: 05-01-2016, 20:12 UTC)
53. Kapur, Ashok (1971), Nuclear Weapons and Indian Foreign Policy: A Perspective, *The World Today*, Vol. 27, No. 9 (Sep. 1971), pp. 379-389 Published by Royal Institute of International Affairs Stable URL: http://www.jstor.org/stable/40394547 (accessed: 05-01-2016, 20:12 UTC)
54. Kapur, Devesh (2009), Public opinion and Indian Foreign policy India review, *India Review*, Vol. 8, No. 3, July-September, 2009, pp. 1–27
55. Kapur, Devesh (2009), Public opinion and Indian Foreign policy India review, *India Review*, Vol. 8, No. 3, July-September, 2009, pp. 1–27

56. Katoch C. Dhruv, Shaping of India's Security Discourse, The Impact of Regional Conflicts, 28th December, 2016
57. Kumar, Atul, An Historical Perspective on Indian Foreign Policy, World Affairs, Spring 2010, Vol. 14, www.India.Journals.com, accessed on 23rd December,2018
58. Loader, B.D., and Dan Mercea (2011), "Networking Democracy? Social Media Innovations and
59. Loader, B. D., and Dan Mercea (2011), "Networking Democracy? Social Media Innovations and
60. Macshane, D. (2017), Brexit's impact on Britain's foreign policy, *Carnegie Europe*, Blog, July 28, 2017, https://carnegieeurope.eu/strategiceurope/72665.
61. Macshane, D. (2017), Brexit's impact on Britain's foreign policy, *Carnegie Europe.*
62. *Marxists on-line* (1982), Retrieved May 21, 2019, from Encyclopedia of Anti-Revisionism On-Line: https://www.marxists.org/history/erol/ncm-7/lrs-china-foreign.htm
63. Matlack, C., & Williams, R. (2018), *France to Probe Possible Influence on Yellow Vests*, Bloomberg.
64. Ministry of External Affairs, INDIA: Bilateral Treaties and Agreements, Vol. 7, http://www.mea.gov.in/Portal?legal/Treaties Doc/RU7181557.pdf, (accessed on 21st December, 2018).
65. Mukherjee, Rohan and David M. Malone (2011), Indian foreign policy and contemporary security challenges, *International Affairs (Royal Institute of International Affairs* 1944-), Vol. 87, No. 1 (January 2011), pp. 87-104, http://www.jstor.org/stable/20869612 (accessed: 11-04-2017 08:59 UTC).
66. Mukherjee, Rohan and David M. Malone (2011), Indian foreign policy and contemporary security challenges, International Affairs (*Royal Institute of International Affairs* 1944-), Vol. 87, No. 1 (January 2011), pp. 87-104, http://www.jstor.org/stable/20869612 (accessed: 11-04- 2017 08:59 UTC).
67. Nurmi, Maria (2012), Social media in Public diplomacy: Survey on the social media communication of the Finnish missions abroad, Master Thesis, Organisational Communication & Public Relations Department of Communication University of Jyväskylä.
68. Nurmi, Maria (2012), Social media in Public diplomacy: Survey on the social media communication of the Finnish missions abroad, Master Thesis, Organizational Communication & Public Relations Department of Communication University of Jyväskylä.

69. Pandalai, Shruti, The 'Social Media' Challenge to National Security: Impact and Opportunities, A Conceptual Overview, Monograph No. 55, 2016.
70. Pande, Aprana (2017), *From Chanakya to Modi,Evoluatio of India's Foreign Policy*, Harper Collins Publishers, pp. 25-26 (accessed on 21st December, 2018).
71. Pande, Aprana (2017), *From Chanakya to Modi,Evoluatio of India's Foreign Policy*, Harper Collins Publishers, p. 14. (accessed on 21st December, 2018).
72. Participatory Politics: *Information, Communication and Society* 14(6): 757–69.
73. Participatory Politics: *Information, Communication and Society* 14(6): 757–69.
74. Penni, Janice (2017), The future of online social networks (OSN): A measurement analysis using social media tools and application, *Telematics and Informatics* 34 (2017) 498–517.
75. Penni, Janice (2017), The future of online social networks (OSN): A measurement analysis using social media tools and application, *Telematics and Informatics* 34 (2017) 498–517.
76. Pew Research Center, "Social Networking Popular Across Globe", December 12, 2012, Retrieved October 6, 2016 (http://www.pewglobal.org/2012/12/12/social-networking- popular-across-globe/).
77. Pew Research Center. "Social Networking Popular Across Globe", December 12, 2012, Retrieved October 6, 2016 (http://www.pewglobal.org/2012/12/12/social-networking- popular-across-globe/).
78. Ravinder (2014), Analysis of the Basic Factors of Indian Foreign Policy, *International Research Journal of Commerce Arts and Science*, Vol. 5, Issue 12, 2014, pp. 142-152.
79. Ravinder (2014), Analysis of the Basic Factors of Indian Foreign Policy, *International Research Journal of Commerce Arts and Science*, Vol. 5, Issue 12, 2014, pp. 142-152.
80. Rubenzer, Trevor (2017), Social Media and Foreign Policy, *World Politics Online*, Aug, 2017, DOI: 10.1093/acrefore/9780190228637.013.485.
81. Rubenzer, Trevor (2017), Social Media and Foreign Policy, *World Politics Online*, Aug, 2017, DOI: 10.1093/acrefore/9780190228637.013.485.
82. Schmidt, C. (2018), *How France beat back information manipulation (and how other democracies might do the same)*. NiemanLab.
83. Schulz, Kerstin (2013), Foreign Policy Involvement Matters: Towards

an Analytical Framework Examining the Role of the Media in the Making of Foreign Policy, *Global Media Journal* German Edition ISSN 2196-4807, Vol. 3, No.1, Spring/Summer 2013.

84. Schulz, Kerstin (2013), Foreign Policy Involvement Matters: Towards an Analytical Framework Examining the Role of the Media in the Making of Foreign Policy, *Global Media Journal*, German Edition ISSN 2196-4807, Vol. 3, No.1, Spring/Summer 2013.
85. Seib, P. (2011), *The Al Jazeera Effect*, University of Southern California.
86. Seib, P. (2011), *The Al Jazeera Effect*, University of Southern California.
87. Shafi, Abdulhamid, Muhammad, Privacy and National Security Challenges in Online Social Networks, LAMBERT Publication: Paperback: Import, 24th January 2013.
88. Shah, A. (2012), Media in the United States, *Global Issues*.
89. Shah, A. (2012), Media in the United States, *Global Issues*.
90. staffer, C. (2018), *The UN Security Council*, Council on Foreign Relations.
91. Statista (2019), The Statista portal, https://www.statista.com/statistics/507405/uk-active-social- media-and-mobile-social-media-users/ (accessed on 19/01/2019).
92. Statista (2019), The Statista portal, https://www.statista.com/statistics/507405/uk-active-social-media-and-mobile-social-media-users/ (accessed on 19/01/2019).
93. *The Guardian*, https://www.theguardian.com/society/2018/apr/09/social-media-has- poisoned-us-young-brits-on-why-they-are-unhappy (accessed on 19/01/2019).
94. *The Guardian*, https://www.theguardian.com/society/2018/apr/09/social-media-has-poisoned-us- young-brits-on-why-they-are-unhappy (accessed on 19/01/2019).
95. Tully, Stephen (2014), Social Media in the Conflict Between Law and Democracy Chapter, In the book *"Law and Democracy,"* ANU Press, 2014.
96. Tully, Stephen (2014), Social Media in the Conflict Between Law and Democracy Chapter, In the book *"Law and Democracy"*, ANU Press, 2014.
97. Ummu, Slma Bava, India's Role in the Emerging World Order FES Briefing Paper 4, March 2007, p. 4, (accessed on 24th December, 2018),
98. Vera Zakem, P.S. (2018), *Media's Role in Russia Policy and Decision Making*, CNA.
99. Vindaya Senadheera, Matthew Warren & Shona Leitch (2017), Social media as an information system: improving the technological agility, *Enterprise Information Systems*, 11:4, 512-533,

100. Vindaya Senadheera, Matthew Warren & Shona Leitch (2017), Social media as an information system: improving the technological agility, *Enterprise Information Systems*, 11:4, 512-533,
101. Westcott, N. (2008), Digital Diplomacy: The Impact of the Internet on International Relations, *SSRN Electronic Journal*.
102. *Wikipedia* (n.d.). Retrieved May 21, 2019, from Russian interference in the 2016 United States elections, https://en.wikipedia.org/wiki/Russian_interference_in_the_2016_United_States_elections
103. Wikipedia (n.d.), Retrieved May 21, 2019, from Russian interference in the 2016 United States elections
104. Williams, P. (2004), Who's Making UK Foreign Policy? *International Affairs (Royal Institute of International Affairs 1944-)*, https://onlinelibrary.wiley.com/doi/epdf/10.1111/j.1468-2346.2004.00425.x
105. Williams, P. (2004), Who's Making UK Foreign Policy?, *International Affairs (Royal Institute of International Affairs 1944-)*.
106. Wynton, El., Social Media in Japan: An Investigation of the Impact Social Media Has on Cyber-Security and Politics in Japan, Electronic Thesis, Publisher: University of Arizona.
107. Wynton, El., Social Media in Japan: An Investigation of the Impact Social Media Has on Cyber-Security and Politics in Japan, Electronic Thesis, Publisher: University of Arizona.
108. Zavattaro, Staci, Thomas Bryer. Social Media For Government: Theory and Practice, Taylor & Francis: Print Publication, March 2016, Online Publication, March 2016.
109. Khare, V. (2019), Terrorism & Counterterrorism, New Delhi: Pentagon Press LLP, ISBN: 9789386618719.
110. Khare, V.S. (2013), Strategic and Security Thoughts of Dr. Babasaheb Ambedkar, Germany: Scholar's Press, ISBN: 3639705416/9783639705416.
111. Khare, V.S. (2005), Dr. Babasaheb Ambedkar and India's National Security, New Delhi: Kilaso Books , ISBN: 8179080285/9788179080283.

Index

#digital diplomacy, 278
@aBalkhi-Taliban, 6
@almanarnews-Hezbollah, 6
@Alqassambirgade-Hamas, 6
@alsomood-Taliban, 6
@HSMPress-al-Shabaab, 6
@MatteoRenzi, 126
@MEAIndia, 278
@MYC_Press-AlShabaab, 6
@narendramodi, 228-31
@ShamiWitness, 26
@SushamaSwaraj, 278

Anvil Media, 20
Arab Spring Movement, 15
Arnold Wolfers, 21
Association of South-East Asian Nations (ASEAN), 57
Axel Schultze, 20

Barton, William P., 39
Baru, Sanjaya, 46
Baum, Matthew A, 43
Blogs, 33
Bottle PR, 20
Buffer, 226

*Mohan, C Raja , 55
Cabinet and Cabinet Committees, 66
Capilanou, 20
Chanan, Naveh, 38
Charles Maier, 21
Chatterjee, Manjiri Miller, 42
China, 27-28, 194, 270
Chinese Foreign Policy, 75
 and Social Media, 74-89
  Challenges, 80
   International Reporting, 80
   Market Pressure, 81
  Decision-making Process, 78
  Chinese Media Abroad Perception, 80
   Weight and Reporting, 80
   Worldwide Reputation, 80
  Financial News Frozen, 87
  First iCloud Arrest, 87
  Global Supremacy, 77
  Huawei and Foreign Governments, 81
  Internet in China, 81
  Media Control by Chinese Communists, 86
  Public Opinion, 79
  Soft Power Influence Globally, 83
  Stockholm Hotel Syndrome, 82
  Technological Advancement in Data Technology, 88
 Asia, 76
 Latin America, 77
 Mideast, 76
 Socialist Foreign Policy, 75
Constructional Changes, 55

Content Communities, 32
Cui Zhang, Charles, 40
Cyber Bullying, 20

Dahibhate N.B., 39
Dark Side, 20
Dav Willis, 13
David Amerland, 7
David M. Malone, 39
Directory of Open Access Journals (DOAJ), 37
Emmanuel Macron Twitter Data Report, 254-58
European Union (EU), 64-65, 94

Facebook, 33
Fake News, 20
Flickr, 34
Florence Parly Twitter Data Report, 259-62
Folksonomies or Tagging, 33
Foreign Policy, Actors, 64
  Collective security organizations, 65
  Economic organizations, 64
  Ethno-cultural organizations, 64
  INGOs, 64
  Media, 65
  Non-state actors, 64
  States actors, 64
France, 27, 194
  Foreign Policy and Social Media, 89-110
    Anti-Semitism, 98
    Emmanuel Macron, 100
    Facebook, French Government, 106-7
    Elections, 2017, 102
    Prepared, 103
    Responded, 103-4
    French Broadcasting, 99
    Global Perspective, 93
    History, 90
    Media Development, Global South, 100
    Media's Role in this?, 104-5
    Multilateralism, 95
    Multipolarity, 97
    Pre-war years, 91
    Religion and State, 98
    Shape French Foreign Policy, Factors, 92
    Use of Force, 96
    Why did Macron Gate not Work?, 102
    Yellow Vests Protests, 107-8

G2, 60
Gandhi, Indira, 53-54
Gandhi, Rajiv, 54
Gavin Williamson Twitter Data Report, 246-48
George Madlikosi, 20
Google+, 34

Harold Brown, 21
Harold Lasswell, 21
Hu Yaobang, 75

Idealism to Realism, 53
India
  Foreign Policy Decision Making , 63-73
    Institutions Involved, 65
    Primary Stage, 51
    Procedures of Making, 72
    Role of Cabinet, 67
    Role of Cabinet Committees, 68
    Role of Prime Minister, 69
India's Foreign Policy, 51
India-China Border Disputes, 165-67
Indian media activities, 2
Indo-Pakistan Relations
  Post Mumbai Attack, 167-71
Inflammatory Lines, 20
Instagram, 34
Iran, 270
Iraq War, 140-41
Islamic State of Iraq Syria (ISIS), 6, 44

Jeremy Hunt Twitter Data Report, 249-52
Joint Intelligence Commerce and Industry, 70

Kapur, Ashok, 40
Kapur, Devesh, 42
Kate Sullivan De Estrada, 42
Keeping Check Happenings Abroad, 274
Klear, 226
Klout, 226

Lazworld, 19
LinkedIn, 34

Malcolm X, 1
ManageFlitter, 226
Micro-blogging, 33
MikePompeo Twitter Data Report, 240-44
Ministry of Defense, 70
Ministry of External Affairs (MEA), 22-23, 66
Ministry of External Affairs Website, 182
Mukherjee, Rohan, 39

Narendra Modi, Indian Prime Minister, 5, 15, 22, 27, 42, 49, 58
Narendra Modi's Twitter Data Report, 228-31
National Defence Collage of India, 21
National Security Advisory Board, 70
National Security Council, 70
NDA government, 58
Nehru, Pandit Jawaharlal, 50-53, 56
Nirmala Sitaraman Twitter Data report, 232-33
Non-Alignment Movement (NAM), 73
North Korea, 270
Nurmi, Maria, 45
Online Collaborative Projects, 33

P.V. Narshimha Rao, 57
P5, Importance, 158-63
    Veto Power, 159
    India, 160
    India, Media, 162
Pakistan, 270
Palestine Liberation Organisation (PLO), 76
Paradigm Shift, 58
Parliament, 71
    Role on Foreign Policy Making, 71
Patil, S.K., 39
Penni, Janice, 39
Philip B K, 43
Pinterest, 34
Prabhakaran Paleri, 21
Pragmatism, 42
Pressure Groups and Media, 71
Prime Minister's Office (PMO), 63, 69, 72
Prof. Joseph Framkel, 21
Prof. Tailor, 20

Raksha Mantri Twitter Data Report, 234-35
Reddit, 34
Rubenzer, Trevor, 43
Russia, 27, 194
    Foreign Policy and Social Media, 143-58
        Analyzing Media, 151
        Anatomy of Media Influence, 151
        and State-owned Media, 147
        Media and Authoritarian Regimes, 145
        Media Effects and Political Behavior, 145
        State-owned Media, 146
Russian MOD (SergeyShoygu) Twitter Data Report, 263-66
Russian State Media, 108-9

Schulz, Kerstin, 38
Senadheera, Vindaya, 37
Sharing inappropriate content, 20
Tharoor, Shashi, 278
Snapchat, 34
Social Media, 2, 7
    Traditional Media, 8

Characteristics, 11
Communal Violence, 269
Communication Hub, 272
Global Politics Impact, 171-73
History, 9
Impact Foreign Relations, 279
Impact on Security Threats, 269
Importance of, 17-18
International Users, 269
Networking Use, 176
Revolution, 269
Role, 13
Positive, 13
Negative, 15
Technical Tools, 31
Terms, 20
Threat to Internal Security, 269
Tools Purpose Using, 179
Tools Use, 177
Used by Terrorists, 269
What is?, 9
Social Media and Social Networking
Difference Between, 8
Social Networking Sites, 32
Banning, 270
Strategic Policy Group, 70
Subterranean Nuclear Explosions Project (SNEP), 54
Sukhwabt, Bindra, 38
Sushama Swaraj Twitter Data Report, 236-38
Sushma Swaraj, former Indian Foreign Minister, 5, 239, 281

Tea Party Movement, 15
The Soft Power 30, 280
Theresa May Twitter Data Report, 245
Tool Able to Identify Fake News, 275
Trolling, 20
Tully, Stephen, 41
Turkey, 270
tvb.org, 20
Twitter, 4, 6, 27, 33
Analytics, 225
Tools, 225
Twitter Data
Searching Methodology, 226
Data, What is?, 225

UK, 27, 193
@Foreign Office, 126
Foreign Policy and Social Media, 124-43
BBC Report on Muslim Village in Vitez, 140
British Intervention Bosnia, 140
Examples Media Influence, 135
Importance of Media, 134
Media in Chechnya, 141
Using Media in Diplomacy, 135
Foreign Policy, History, 127
Anglo-Japanese Alliance, 128
Britain and Migrant Policy, 132
Britain's Boer War and Media, 129
Britan's Foreign Policy and Brexit impact, 129
Foreign Policy of Sir Edward Grey, 128
Policy of Isolation, 127
Middle East Policy, 135-36
Prime Minister @Number10gov
UK's Global Defense of Media Freedom, 136-39
Unintended Consequences, 20
US, 27, 193
and Social Media, 110-24
and Cold War, 114
and Vietnam War, 116
and War on Terror, 115
Advertising, Primary Income Source Encourages Dumbing Down, 113
Al Jazeera Effect, 121
Chomsky/Herman Propaganda Model, 113
CNN Effect, 114
Cultural Bias, 121
Government Disseminating Prepackaged, even Fake News, 120

Media Power is Political Power, 112
Political Pressure, 112
Presidential Elections, 2016, 118
Press Freedom, 111
Reliance on Official Sources, 114
Size & Concentrated Ownership, 113
Social Media and Foreign Policy, 117
Trump and Social Media, 118

Vimeo, 34

Walter Lippmann, 21
Wikipedia, 19
William Meadows, 40
Wynton, El, 44

YouTube, 6, 34